D1520291

BLUE AND WHITE: *Chinese Porcelain and Its Impact on the Western World*

Catalogue of an exhibition at
The David and Alfred Smart Gallery,
The University of Chicago,
October 3 – December 1, 1985

By John Carswell
with contributions by
Edward A. Maser and
Jean McClure Mudge

BLUE AND WHITE
Chinese Porcelain and Its Impact on the Western World

ELMHURST COLLEGE LIBRARY

OCT 1987

The exhibition is supported in part by a grant from the National Endowment for the Arts.

The exhibition and accompanying symposium are partially supported by a grant from the Illinois Arts Council, a state agency, and the National Endowment for the Arts.

The catalogue is published with the assistance of the J. Paul Getty Trust.

The Smart Gallery also acknowledges a generous grant toward the catalogue from the National Palace Museum, Republic of China.

Title page: Figure 1. *Manuscript painting* in an album. Samarkand *or* Tabriz. Fifteenth century. 25 x 48 cms. Topkapu Saray Library, Istanbul. H.2153.

Library of Congress Catalogue Card Number 85-072386
International Standard Book Number ISBN 0-935573-00-3
Copyright © 1985, The University of Chicago, The David and Alfred Smart Gallery. All rights reserved.

Designed by Harvey Retzloff
Composition by Continental Composition, Inc.
Printed in the United States of America
by Congress Printing Company

CONTENTS

LENDERS TO THE EXHIBITION

The Art Institute of Chicago, Chicago
Ashmolean Museum, Oxford, England
Asian Art Museum of San Francisco, The Avery Brundage Collection, San Francisco, California
Benaki Museum, Athens, Greece
The British Museum, London, England
Buffalo Society of National Sciences, Buffalo Museum of Science, Buffalo, New York
The Cleveland Museum of Art, Cleveland, Ohio
The Colonial Williamsburg Foundation, Williamsburg, Virginia
The Dayton Art Institute, Dayton, Ohio
Field Museum of Natural History, Chicago
Freer Gallery of Art Study Collection (Smithsonian Institution), Washington, D.C.
Indianapolis Museum of Art, Indianapolis, Indiana
The Metropolitan Museum of Art, New York
Museum of Fine Arts, Boston, Massachusetts
National Museum, Damascus, Syria
The Nelson-Atkins Museum of Art, Kansas City, Missouri
The Oriental Institute Museum, The University of Chicago, Chicago
The University of Michigan Museum of Art, Ann Arbor, Michigan
Collection of Mr. J. Chase Gilmore
Collection of Ivor Noël Hume, Williamsburg, Virginia
John Philip Kassebaum Collection
The Madina Collection, New York
Collection of Mr. and Mrs. Robert McCormick Adams, Washington, D.C.
Collection of Alexandre and Helen Philon
Private Collection, London, England
Private Collection, New York
Private Collection, United Kingdom
Anonymous Lender

FOREWORD

Any exhibition involving loans from many different museums and collections is dependent for its success on the generosity and goodwill of the individuals concerned, and this exhibition is no exception. The David and Alfred Smart Gallery would like to express its sincere thanks to all who have contributed their services, not only in organizational terms but also in helping through their advice to expand and refine the original concept of the exhibition.

The theme of the exhibition was conceived a decade ago, when the writer was invited by the Comité du Musée Nicola Sursock in Beirut to organize an exhibition entitled *Porcelaine de Chine et ses aspects Islamiques dans les Collections Libanaises.* Based on blue-and-white porcelain from Syria, the exhibition was to explore the influence of Chinese porcelain on Islamic ceramics. For reasons of which we are all too well aware of today, the exhibition was never realised; but it is appropriate that I should acknowledge the initial encouragement I received from the Secretary, Maître Camille Aboussouan; and from my friend, M. Henri Pharaon, the study of whose unparalleled collection of blue-and-white was largely responsible for my own interest in this subject. I should further mention Dr. Robert Gulbenkian, whose timely assistance was responsible for the documentation of much important material which would otherwise have been lost.

In Chicago, the present exhibition is the result of an invitation from Edward A. Maser, then Director of the Smart Gallery, to put together an exhibition on a similar theme. My thanks are also due to Reinhold Heller, who as Acting Director was responsible for the implementation of the original invitation. The funding of the exhibition has been made possible in part by grants from The National Endowment for the Arts, a Federal Agency; The Illinois Arts Council; and a special grant from The J. Paul Getty Foundation towards the cost of the catalogue. I should also record my appreciation here of the support for the project from The University of Chicago, and in particular that of the Deputy Provost, Ralph W. Nicholas, and the Chairman of the newly-created Governing Board of the Smart Gallery, Sidney Davidson.

The Smart Gallery has been fortunate in securing loans for the exhibition from collections both in the United States and abroad, and we must thank the numerous individuals who have helped in the organization of what is the most complex undertaking the Gallery has so far attempted. In the United States, The Metropolitan Museum of Art in New York has made a major contribution to the exhibition with loans from three different departments. We are specially grateful to Stuart Cary Welch, Special Consultant in Charge of the Islamic Department, and to his Curatorial staff, Marie Lukens Sweitochowski, Marilyn Jenkins, and Carolyn Kane; to Olga Raggio, Chairman of the Department of European Sculpture and Decorative Arts, and Curators Jessie McNab and Clare Le Corbeiller; and to Suzanne G. Valenstein, Curator in the Department of Far Eastern

Art. We are also indebted to Herbert Moskowitz for coordinating the various loans, and to staff members Marceline McKee and Mary Doherty.

Another large section of the exhibition has been drawn from the collections of The Art Institute of Chicago, and for this our thanks are due to James Wood, Director, and Kathleen Lee, Assistant Director; both are already closely associated with the Smart Gallery as members of the Committee on Visual Arts. In the Oriental Art Department, we are most grateful to Jack Sewell, Curator of Oriental and Classical Art, and Yutaka Mino, Curator of Chinese and Japanese Art, ably assisted by Janice Mann and Craig McBride. We have also had every assistance from Lynn Springer Roberts, Curator of European Decorative Arts, and her Assistant, Rita McCarthy, as well as Mary Pawlus, who we must thank for a number of carefully-researched catalogue entries. We were further helped by Wallace D. Bradway and Mary Solt, of the Registrar's Office; and Howard Kraywinkel and Maebetty Langdon in the Photography Department.

For two important loans from the Field Museum of Natural History we are indebted to Bennet Bronson, and his assistant Carolyn Moore, and the Registrar, Terry Novak. For a loan from the Oriental Institute I must thank the Director, Janet H. Johnson; and it is a pleasure to acknowledge the help of my old staff in arranging this, Barbara Hall, Anita Ghaemi, John Larsson, Eileen Caves, Raymond Tindel and Jean Grant.

Further afield, our thanks go to The Indianapolis Museum of Art, to its Director, Robert A. Yassin; to James Robinson, Curator; and to Vanessa Wicker Burkhart, Registrar; Catherine Ricciardelli Davis, Assistant Registrar; and Janet Feemster. The Director of The Cleveland Museum of Art, Evan Turner, enthusiastically endorsed our requests for loans; we specially thank Michael Cunningham, Ann Lurie, Henry H. Hawley, and Patrick de Winter in their Curatorial capacities; Elinor Pearlstein; Delbert Gutridge, Registrar; Carolyn Thum, Assistant Registrar, and Paula De Christofaro. At the University of Michigan in Ann Arbor we are grateful to Evan M. Mauer, Director of the University Museum of Art; and his Curator, Marshall Wu; and Carole C. McNamara, Registrar; and also to Karl Hutterer and Henry Wright of the Department of Anthropology for showing us an important collection of comparative material. In Boston, we thank the Director of the Museum of Fine Arts, Jan Fontein, and his Curator, James C. Y. Watt, as well as Linda Thomas, Registrar; Alison Hatcher, Assistant Registrar, and Sandra Mongeon. At The Dayton Art Institute the Director, Bruce H. Evans; Curator, Clarence W. Kelley; and Registrar, Dominique H. Vasseur, hold the record for the fastest and most efficiently choreographed loan of all.

Thomas Lawton, Director of the Feer Gallery of Art, Smithsonian Institution, kindly allowed material in the Study Collection to be examined and borrowed; and we thank Eleanor Radcliffe for making the necessary arrangements; also at the Smithsonian we are grateful to Peggy Loar, Anne Gosset, Mary Jane Clark and Fred Williams. For some most unusual material in the exhibition we are indebted to the Director of the Buffalo Museum of Science, Ernst E. Both; his Curator Richard Michael Gramley; and the Registrar, Betty Robins, who arranged its shipment. At Colonial Williamsburg, Ivor Noël Hume not only kindly agreed to a personal loan but also arranged for us to borrow material from the Foundation, through the good offices of Graham Hood, Curator, and Margie Gill, Registrar. In San Francisco we are most grateful to the Director of the Asian Art Museum, René-Yvon Lefèbre d'Argencé; the Acting Director, Clarence Shangraw; the Registrar, Jack Foss, and his assistant, Barbara Geib, for the loan of an important piece. Our thanks also go to Mark Wilson, Director of The Nelson-Atkins Museum of Art in Kansas City; to his Curatorial staff Wai-Kam Ho, and Catherine Lippert; and Ann Erbacher, Registrar. At the Flint Museum of Art, we thank Christopher R. Young for a loan from the Kassebaum Collection.

Outside of the United States we are specially indebted to Dr. Sabahattin Türkoğlu, Director of the Topkapu Saray Museum, for permission to photograph a famous fifteenth-century manuscript; in the same context we are most appreciative of the help of Professor Nurhan Atasoy and Dr. Filiz Cagman, and the photographer Reha Günay, in Istanbul, and my colleagues in the Center for Middle Eastern Studies in Chicago, John Woods, Richard Chambers and Bruce Craig.

We are grateful to Laurence Smith, Keeper, and Jessica Rawson and Michael Rogers of the Department of Oriental Antiquities at The British Museum; and Annette Lefort, Executive Officer who coordinated all the English loans; James C. Harle, Keeper, and James Allan, Oliver Impey, and Mary Tregear of the Department of Eastern Art, at the Ashmolean Museum, Oxford; Angelos Delivorrias, Director, and Helen Philon, Curator of Islamic Art, at the Benaki Museum, Athens; and Afif Bahnassi, Director of the National Museum in Damascus. We owe special thanks to H. E. Rafiq Jouejaiti, Syrian Ambassador to the United States, for negotiating the Syrian loan; and to H. E. Clovis Maksoud, Ambassador of the Arab League to the United Nations, for his pertinent advice. We are also appreciative of Dr. Nagaraja Rao's efforts in Delhi, as Director-General of the Archaeological Survey of India, to secure a loan from India.

We thank a number of private lenders to the exhibition, including John Philip Kassebaum; Maan Madina; Alexandre and Helen Philon; J. Chase Gilmore; and collectors in London, the United Kingdom, New York, and Winnetka, Illinois, who wish to remain anonymous. For valuable advice in the planning of the exhibition, we are most grateful to Esin Atil, Ross Edman and Harrie Vanderstappen. I would particularly like to thank those who assisted me with translations of Arabic, Persian and Chinese texts, James Chang, Fred Donner, Heshmet Mouayyad, and Michael Rogers; I am also most grateful to Amy McNair, who checked the spelling of Chinese according to the *pinyin* system. Four students in the Department of Art contributed greatly to the catalogue and deserve our special thanks; John Baum, Adrienne Kochman, Amy Rule, and Laura Satersmoen. I should also thank Jean McClure Mudge and Edward A. Maser, not only for their valuable contributions but for their cooperation when subjected to a very tight schedule.

Our debt to the designer of the catalogue, Harvey Retzloff, is obvious, and he has our heartfelt thanks. All the drawings are my own and the maps were drawn by Catherine Lindsey. The catalogue entries were written by myself, except for those marked M.P. (Mary Pawlus) and J.M.M. (Jean McClure Mudge).

On a personal note, I must thank my wife Peggy, who has lived with the progress of the exhibition and catalogue for many months, and who has given her cheerful and unfailing support.

Finally, it is a pleasure to thank my staff for their hard work and unflagging efforts; Vivian Heller, Administrative Assistant; Richard Born, Curator; Mary E. Braun, Registrar; Karen Bornstein, Director of Public Relations; Jean Hall, Secretary; and Rudy Bernal and Muneer Bahauddeen, Preparators. As anyone who has ever worked in a museum will know, these are the people who really count; long may it be recognized.

John Carswell, *Director*

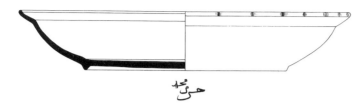

INTRODUCTION

The influence of Chinese blue-and-white porcelain on the pottery of the Near East and Europe is obvious, but less evident are the reasons why it should have had such a powerful effect on such widely diverse cultures. It could be argued that it was simply the technical perfection of the porcelain body that made such a strong impression, but this does not explain why blue-and-white continued to be so popular over so long a period of time and such a wide geographical area. Somehow, the porcelain became linked in the eye of the beholder with its blue-and-white decoration, and it was a synthesis of the two which exercised its universal attraction.

What appealed about blue-and-white was its essential quality, a combination of superior ware and confidently assured decoration. In the Islamic world enthusiasm for blue-and-white so permeated the culture that *any* blue-and-white, of whatever quality, appeared to evoke an automatically positive response. In Europe, exposed to blue-and-white at a relatively late stage of its technical and aesthetic development, what was by then a fairly standardized, mass-produced product had a catalytic effect on western taste. In both the Near East and Europe this fascination with blue-and-white continued throughout the eighteenth and nineteenth centuries and is still with us today.

A primary aim of the exhibition is to present the Chinese blue-and-white side by side with its imitations, and the catalogue is intended to serve both as a detailed record and also as an extension of this concept. Cross-cultural comparisons are the building blocks from which much of art history is constructed; but these comparisons are usually confined to illustrations in scholarly treatises, a sort of a *musée imaginaire*.

Here the originals and the copies have been brought into close conjunction with each other, as indeed they must have been in the past. Nowadays, due to the geographic and chronological departmentalization of most museums, such comparisons can only be made by visiting several different departments. This was forcibly brought home assembling the exhibition, when it was often necessary to deal with three or more departments within a single institution.

It is hoped that the juxtaposition of the Chinese blue-and-white with its derivatives will show not only the essential technical differences, but also the different aesthetic responses to the prototypes. This is not necessarily to the detriment of the copies. Frustration is the mother in invention, and can generate both technical innovation and new styles with a life of their own. At the same time, the Chinese potters themselves were not insensitive to influence, and both the shapes and the decoration of blue-and-white were affected by the market for which they were intended.

It is hardly possible to do justice to such a complex subject in an exhibition restricted to a hundred or so examples, and the limitations of both the exhibition

Figure 2. *Dish*. China, Jingdezhen, Yuan dynasty. First half of fourteenth century. Porcelain, with underglaze blue decoration; Arabic/Persian mark on unglazed base. Height 7.9 cm. Diameter 45.4 cm. Collection of H. E. Henri Pharaon, Beirut. From Syria.

and the catalogue are obvious. A comprehensive bibliography of all the areas touched by the material would alone fill the catalogue, to the exclusion of all else. For this reason, the choice of material displayed has been severely selective, and makes no claim to be anything like a comprehensive survey.

Finally, a word about the time span of the exhibition. While concerned with the antecedents of blue-and-white, it is confined to Chinese porcelain only of the Yuan and Ming dynasties, and to its Near Eastern, European and Hispanic copies up until the end of the seventeenth century. When the world finally discovered the secret of true porcelain — a secret, incidentally, which had been a Chinese monopoly for over a thousand years — the history of ceramics took another turn, and the European porcelain industry was born. This is another story, and while the continuing impact of Chinese porcelain in the eighteenth century and later is equally worthy of research, it lies outside the scope of the present work.

Blue-and-White Porcelain in China

John Carswell

THE ETYMOLOGY OF PORCELAIN

The word "porcelain" (of which the *Oxford English Dictionary* lists no less than twenty-one variants) is first used to describe Chinese pottery by the Venetian traveler Marco Polo, in the late thirteenth century. Marco Polo's account of his travels was not an autograph, but written down by one Rustichello of Pisa, who shared a dungeon with him when Polo was imprisoned in Genoa in 1298. Rustichello, a professional composer of romances, set down Polo's account in the dialect of Languedoc, a mixture of Italian and French. Although the original manuscript has not survived, the oldest known copy of the early fourteenth century is in the same Italianate-French. Thus the first record of Marco Polo's use of the word is *porcelaine*.[1]

The word actually used by Marco Polo would have been the Italian, *porcellana*. Moreover, he used the same term to describe two quite different commodities which he encountered in China. First, when traveling through the province of Yunnan, he used *porcellana* for the cowry-shells which served there as currency. Secondly, he described as *porcellana* the fine pottery which he saw being manufactured at Tingiu, near the southern port of Zaytun.[2]

The etymology of "porcelain" is a curious one, and Marco Polo's usage of the same word for two different things provides a clue to its origin. Porcelain derives from the Italian *porcellana*, which was first used in Europe as a term for the cowry-shell, *Cypraea moneta*. *Porcellana* is an adjectival derivative of the Latin *porcella* ("sow"), the feminine of *porcellus* ("little pig"), a diminutive of *porcus* ("pig"). The cowry-shell, with its humped back and snout-like protuberance, does indeed resemble a piglet. Some etymologists have drawn attention to the vulva-like slit on the underside of the shell and drawn a grosser conclusion about the origin of the word.[3]

As for the shell itself, "cowry" derives from the Hindi, and Urdu, *kauri*, and ultimately from the Sanskrit, *kaparda*, *kapardika*. The Arabic for cowry shells is *wa'dah*, and the Chinese, *bei*.[4] Cowries were widely used as currency in India, Africa and the Far East, as well as in China. The source of the cowry shells is the Maldive Islands, in the middle of the Indian Ocean. As early as 851 A.D., an Arab merchant mentions them in a list of Maldivian products.[5] Almost five hundred years later, when the Arab traveler Ibn Battuta visited the Maldives, he described the method by which they were gathered and cleaned. He also noted their use as currency in the islands, their export to Bengal and their use as ballast on ships sailing to the Yemen. When he first arrived in Male, the capital island, he was presented with 100,000 cowries by the *vizir*, to cover his expenses.[6]

The use of the word *porcellana* in Europe to describe cowry shells predates Marco Polo, and in the maritime code of Barcelona circa 1250 A.D. *porcelanas*, along with cotton, wool, alum and elephant's teeth are among the list of prod-

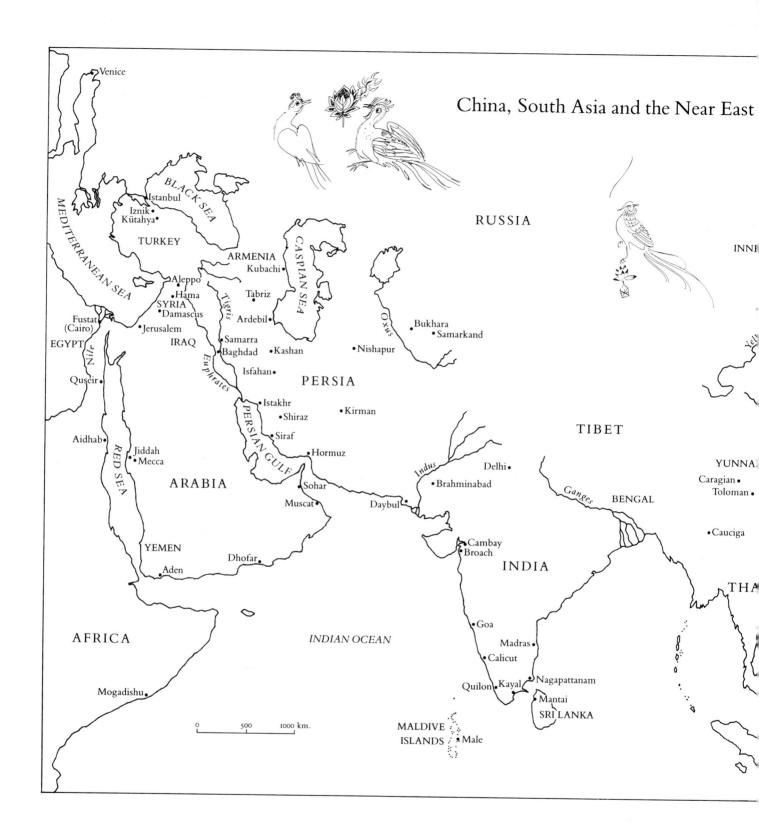

China, South Asia and the Near East

Venice

MEDITERRANEAN SEA

BLACK SEA

Istanbul
Iznik
Kütahya
TURKEY

ARMENIA
Kubachi

CASPIAN SEA

RUSSIA

INNE

Aleppo
Hama
SYRIA
Damascus
Jerusalem

Tabriz
Ardebil

Fustat
(Cairo)
EGYPT

Nile

IRAQ

Tigris

Samarra
Baghdad
Isfahan

Kashan

Oxus

Bukhara
Samarkand

Nishapur

Quseir

Euphrates

Istakhr
Shiraz
Siraf

PERSIA

Kirman

TIBET

Aidhab

RED SEA

Jiddah
Mecca

PERSIAN GULF

Hormuz

Sohar

ARABIA

Muscat

Daybul

Indus

Delhi
Brahminabad

Ganges

BENGAL

YUNNA
Caragian
Toloman

YEMEN

Aden

Dhofar

Cambay
Broach

INDIA

Cauciga

AFRICA

INDIAN OCEAN

Goa

Madras

Calicut

THA

Quilon
Kayal

Nagapattanam
Mantai
SRI LANKA

Mogadishu

0   500   1000 km.

MALDIVE
ISLANDS

Male

14

LIAONING
JAPAN
NGOLIA
Beijing (Peking)
(Dadu)
KOREA
SIÑAN
Cizhou
Nanjing
Shanghai
Hangzhou
CHINA
Ningbo
Yangtze
Jingdezhen
Changsha
Jizhou
Fuzhou
Quanzhou (Zaytun)
TAIWAN
Tongan
Swatow
uangzhou (Canton)
VIETNAM
ND
Manila
PHILIPPINES
BORNEO
Malacca
Singapore
MATRA

ucts imported from Alexandria.[7] So, when Marco Polo encountered cowries in China, he knew the right word for them. He says that when he was in the province of Caragian [Yunnan], of which the capital was Iaci:

> They have money in such a way as I shall tell you, for they spend white cowries (*porcelaine*) for money, those which are found in the sea and which are also worn on the neck for ornament and put on the necks of dogs, & of which they make vessels; and the eighty cowries are worth one *saggio* of silver which are of the value of two of our Venetian groats of Venese, which is twenty-four pounds. Any you may know that the eight *saggi* of fine silver are worth one *saggio* of fine gold.[8]

Riding onwards ten days further, and still in the same province, he says:

> Gold-dust is found in great profusion in this province, that is one finds it in the large rivers and again it is found there in lakes; and also in the mountains gold from veins larger than dust. They have so much gold that I tell you they gave one *saggio* of gold for six of silver. And in this province also they spend the cowries of which I have told you above for money. And again I tell you that these cowries are not found in the province, but they come carried there by merchants from Indie.[9]

Cowries have been found on late Neolithic sites in China, and their imitation in mussel-shell, bone and stone in the Shang dynasty suggests that they were already being used as currency by the second millenium B.C. Later imitations of cowries, in the middle of the first millenium B.C., were of bronze, and strung together through a small hole at one end.[10]

Except as ornament the use of cowries died out in China after the first century A.D. They are next encountered in Chinese texts of the Mongol period, where cowries are mentioned as common currency in Yunnan, corroborating what Marco Polo had said. It is recorded that Qibilai's administrator, Sayyid Ajjal, experienced difficulties trying to introduce paper money in Yunnan to replace the cowry currency, and finally gave up the attempt.[11] The use of cowries continued in the province well into the Ming dynasty.

Marco Polo's other references to cowries occur on his voyage home. Describing the province of Toloman (of uncertain location, but probably contiguous with Yunnan) he says:

> For their money is gold, and the money which they spend in small sums is of cowries from Indie in such a way as I have told you above. And likewise all these provinces spoken of above, that is Bangala [Bengal] and Cauciga [Tonking] and Amu [also Tonking] spend gold and cowries.[12]

Further on, after leaving Java, he describes the province of Lohac on the mainland (probably Thailand), and says:

> And from this kingdom go all the cowries which are spent in all the other provinces of the world as I have told you before.[13]

The cowries in fact came from the Maldives, and their use in Thailand continued into the nineteenth century. The Chinese traveler Ma Huan notes their use in Thailand for currency in the early fifteenth century,[14] and this is confirmed in later sixteenth and seventeenth-century texts. Salaries were still paid in cowries as late as the 1840s; and an even later development towards the close of the nineteenth century was the use of porcelain coinage:

> In the Shan states or Siam [Thailand] about ten years ago [c. 1894]...[the porcelain coins] were of white China, with a blue figure, and about the size of a Keating's cough lozenge, but thicker.[15]

With its hard white lustrous surface, and the fact that porcelain breaks with a shell-like fracture, it is easy to see why Marco Polo used the same word both for cowries and for the pottery he saw being made at Tingiu, later on in his travels in China. His description is sufficiently detailed to be worth quoting in its entirety; after describing the port of Çaiton (Zaytun/Quanzhou) he says:

> And again I tell you the most beautiful vessels and plates of porcelain, large and small, that one could describe are made in great quantity in this aforesaid province [Fugiu/Fujian] in a city which is called Tingiu, more beautiful than can be found in any other city. And on all sides they are much valued, for none of them are made in another place but in this city, and from there they are carried to many places throughout the world. And there is plenty there and a great sale, so great that for one Venetian groat you would actually have three bowls so beautiful that none would know how to devise them better. And these bowls are made in this way, as he was told, of this kind of earth; namely, that those of the city gather as from a mine mud and rotten earth and make great mounds of it, and leave them thus in the wind, in the rain, and in the sun for thirty and forty years that they do not move the mounds. And then in this space of time the said earth being so long time in those mounds is so worked up that the bowls made of it have the color of azure, and they are very shining and beautiful beyond measure. And you must know that when a man gathers that earth he gathers for his sons or grandsons. It is clear that owing to the long time that it must lie quiet for its working up he does not hope to gain profit from it nor put it into use, but the son who will survive him will reap the fruit of it.[16]

Previous commentators on Marco Polo's text, in the search for the pottery-manufacturing site he refers to, have tried to equate "Tingiu" either with Jingdezhen, or with Dehua north of Quanzhou, or with Longquan just over the border in Zhejiang, the premise being that it must be one of the centers known to have been operating during his time.[17] Recent research in China, however, shows that the answer is actually much simpler, and that Marco Polo meant what he said. Three kiln sites have been excavated at Tongan close to Quanzhou; these contained both Song and Yuan material, green wares and *qingbai* of a type known to have been exported at least as far west as Sri Lanka, and in quantity to Japan;[18] Tongan is thus a clear candidate for Tingiu. At the same time, Quanzhou has been shown to have been a pottery center; ten kilns have been found in the area of the city, including a kiln outside the eastern gate producing *qingbai* ware.[19]

Marco Polo's remark that the bowls were "the color of azure" would fit well as a description of *qingbai*, with its bluish glaze; indeed, the term often used as a modern alternative for *qingbai* is *yingqing*, meaning "shadow blue." As for the length of time he maintains that the raw material was left in the open air, we have no means of knowing whether this was true or not. Certainly, it was necessary to pulverize and wash the basic material before use, and it is not impossible that exposure to the elements may have helped in the process of refinement. Nor is it unreasonable to suppose that a stockpile of clay would pass from one generation of potters to the next; it would, after all, represent part of the capital investment of any family engaged in the trade.

The story that the clay was kept for many years was repeated by various writers, and crept into Dr. Johnson's Dictionary.[20] In an ingenious etymology, he says, "*pourcelaine*, Fr., said to be derived from *pour cent années* because it was believed by Europeans that the materials of *porcelain* ware were matured under ground one hundred years." His description of the material is very neat: "China, china-ware: fine dishes of a middle nature between earth and glass and therefore semipellucid."

It is an odd coincidence that two of the greatest travelers of the medieval world, Marco Polo and Ibn Battuta, should both have made detailed and independent observations about pottery manufacture in China, at the time immediately preceding the introduction of blue-and-white porcelain. As seen above, Marco Polo accurately identified Tongan and Quanzhou as pottery-making centers during the early Yuan dynasty. He also noted that the raw material was mined and refined by exposure to the elements for a number of years.

Ibn Battuta, who was born in Tangiers and who died in Fez, traveled the length of Asia from the Mediterranean to China, visiting the Near East, Iran and India as well as the Maldives; in fact his itinerary included almost all the countries with which we are specially concerned for the history and export of Chinese porcelain. His term for porcelain, unlike Marco Polo's, is generic rather than specific, in the sense that he does not use any special word for it. The phrase he uses, *al-fakhkhar as-sini*, means no more than "Chinese pottery," and *sini* was used in Arabic in exactly the same way as we use "china" today.[21]

However, there was no doubt that he appreciated its special qualities; as he says, "it is the most marvellous of kinds of pottery." Nor is his first reference to it in China itself, for when he was traveling in Syria he mentions it in the course of an anecdote about an incident he witnessed in Damascus. In the street, a slave-boy was in deep distress because he had dropped and smashed his master's Chinese pottery dish (*sahfatan min al-fakhkhar as-sini*); a small crowd gathered and someone advised the boy to gather up the fragments and take them to the *awqaf*, or religious foundation, which would reimburse him for the accident. This he did, and with the money the slave-boy was able to buy a new Chinese dish. The implication of this is that Chinese ware was readily available in the *suq*, or market.[22]

When Ibn Battuta reached China, he described Chinese pottery on three different occasions. In light of the recent analyses of Chinese wares discussed below, it is worth examining the Arabic text to find out exactly what he said.

The first text deals exclusively with "Chinese pottery":

The mention of Chinese pottery (*al-fakhkhar as-sini*). As for Chinese pottery none of it is made except in the city of Zaitun [Quanzhou] and Sin Kalan [Canton/Guangzhou]. And it is of the earth of the mountains there in which the fire ignites like charcoal; we will describe this later. And they add to it stones which they have there and they apply the fire to it three days then pour water on it so that the whole returns to earth. Then they ferment it [i.e. the earth] and the best of it is that which is fermented a whole month but no more than that; and the lesser [quality] is that which is fermented ten days and it has a price there equivalent to pottery in our country or [even] cheaper. And it is carried to India and to the other climes so that it even reaches our country in the Maghreb. And it is the most marvellous of kinds of pottery.[23]

He correctly identifies both Quanzhou and Guangzhou as pottery manufacturing centers. He also tells us that the clay comes from the mountains, and that it is admixed with stones, presumably his way of describing *kaolin* and *petuntse*.[24] What is more curious is his reference to firing the raw material and fermenting the resulting material, for greater or lesser periods of time. His distinction between wares of higher and lesser quality is accurate, and his remark that it is exported to India and even as far as Morocco is provocative. It is certainly true that Chinese wares of the period reached India and the Near East; their presence in Morocco and the Maghreb has yet to be verified, but not to be discounted out of hand. North Africa was in close contact with the Near East both through trans-

ذكر الفخار الصيني

وأمّا الفخار الصيني فلا يُصنعُ منه إلاّ بمدينة الزيتون وبصين كلان ، وهو من تراب جبال هنالك تَقِدُ فيه النار كالفحم ، وسنذكرُ ذلك ، ويضيفون إليه حجارة عندهم ، ويوقدون النار عليها ثلاثة أيّام ، ثمّ يصبّون عليها الماء فيعودُ الجميع تراباً ، ثمّ يخمّرونه ، فالجيّدُ منه ما خُمّر شهراً كاملاً ، ولا يزادُ على ذلك ، والدون ما خُمّر عشرة أيّام ؛ وهو هنالك بقيمة الفخّار ببلادنا أو أرخص ثمناً ، ويُحمل إلى الهند وسائر الأقاليم حتّى يصل إلى بلادنا بالمغرب ، وهو أبدع أنواع الفخّار .

Saharan trade, and by the movement of pilgrims performing the *Hajj*, journeying to Egypt, the Red Sea and Mecca.

His second mention of Chinese pottery is peripheral to a description of an artificial fuel in China:

> The mention of the earth which they burn in place of charcoal. All of the people of China and Khita [Kathay, northern China] their charcoal is an earth which they have and it is thickened[?] like dried mud (*tafal*)[?] among us, and its color is the color of dried mud. And the elephant brings loads of it, and they cut it into pieces the size of pieces of charcoal among us and they light fire in it and it ignites like charcoal and it is stronger in heat than the fire of charcoal. And when it has become ashes they knead it with water and dry it and they bake it a second time, and they continue to do that to it till it disappears. And from this earth they manufacture the vessels of Chinese pottery. And they add to it other stones as we have mentioned.[25]

ذكر التراب الذي يوقدونه مكان الفحم

وجميع أهل الصين والخطا إنّما فحمهم تراب عندهم منعقد كالطَّفَل عندنا ، ولونه لون الطفل ، تأتي الفيلة بالأحمال منه ، فيقطعونه قطعاً على قدر قطع الفحم عندنا ، ويشعلون النار فيه فيَتّقِد كالفحم ، وهو أشدّ حرارة من نار الفحم ، وإذا صار رماداً عجنوه بالماء ويبَّسوه وطبخوا به ثانية ، ولا يزالون يفعلون به كذلك إلى أن يتلاشى . ومن هذا التراب يصنعون أواني الفخّار الصيني ويضيفون إليه حجارة سواه كما ذكرناه .

This appears to have been some kind of natural combustible material. How it could have also been used for pottery is not clear, unless it was used like limestone, in the production of glaze-ash.[26]

His final description is of the production and marketing of pottery, towards the end of his travels in China; he says:

> And we traveled on this river twenty-seven days and every day a little before midday we let anchor in a village where we bought what we wanted and made our midday prayer. Then we descend in the evening in another village and so until we reach the city of Sin Kalan [Canton/Guangzhou] which is the city of Sin as-Sin. And in it is made the pottery [*al-fakhkhar*, variant *al-fakhkhar as-sini*] and also in Zaitun [Quanzhou] and there the river Ab-i Hayat [Persian; lit. "the father of life"] pours out into the sea and they call it the place of the joining of the two seas. And it is among the largest of the cities and among the most beautiful of them for markets and among the largest of its markets is the pottery market [*suq al-fakhkhar*, variant *suq al-fakhkharin*, "the potters' market"] and from it [i.e. the pottery] is carried to the other countries of China and to India and to Yemen.[27]

وسافرنا في هذا النهر سبعةً وعشرين يوماً ، وفي كلّ يوم نرسو عند الزوال بقرية نشتري بها ما نحتاج إليه ، ونصلّي الظهر ، ثمّ ننزل بالعشي إلى أخرى ، وهكذا إلى أن وَصَلنا إلى مدينة صين كَلان ، وهي مدينة صين الصين ، وبها يُصنَع الفخّار ، وبالزيتون أيضاً ، وهنالك يصبّ نهر آب حياة في البحر ويسمّونه مجمع البحرين ، وهي من أكبر المدن وأحسنها أسواقاً . ومن أعظم أسواقها سوق الفخّار ومنها يحمل إلى سائر بلاد الصين وإلى الهند واليمن .

In this passage he again identifies Guangzhou and Quanzhou with the manufacture of pottery, and makes special reference to the pottery market in Quanzhou, which would be in character with the port's leading role in the export of pottery. He also refers to the export of pottery to other parts of China, and to India and the Yemen. As for China, Ibn Battuta's visit was just about the time of the departure of the ship wrecked off the Sinan coast of China. Recently excavated, this vessel is believed to have sailed from the port of Ningbo in the province of Zhejiang in 1323 A.D.; it carried a cargo of pottery from all over China, indicating the movement of pottery within the country.[28] As for India, recent finds of Chinese pottery at Kayal near Cape Comorin, Nagapattanam on the Coromandel coast and in Sri Lanka, corroborate such a trade existed in Ibn Battuta's time.[29] And as for Yemen, the country has not so far yielded much evidence of Chinese export ware, but its key role in Red Sea and Indian commerce is well documented, and it is highly likely that future archaeological evidence will be forthcoming. Essentially, Ibn Battuta's references are important as indicative of the countries he considered as playing a leading role in the export market.

THE PORCELAIN BODY

True porcelain is defined as having a hard white translucent body and producing a ringing note when struck. The traditional belief, based on the observations of the French Jesuit, Père d'Entrecolles, who visited Jingdezhen in the early eight-

And they [the Chinese] have excellent clay (ghadar) from which are made cups in the fineness of glass in which the light of water can be seen even though it is of clay.
—The Merchant Sulaymen, 851 A.D.[30]

eenth century, is that porcelain is composed of two basic materials, *kaolin* and *petuntse*.[31] *Kaolin* is white china-clay, so named after the locality, Gaoling ("high ridge"), near Jingdezhen from which it comes. *Petuntse* consists of pulverized and refined porcelain-stone. Both derive from granite, and when fired at high temperature, c. 1,280°F., the two materials fuse to form a hard, vitrified body.

Until as recently as five years ago, this *kaolin/petuntse* recipe for porcelain was cited in all standard works on Chinese ceramics. But since then research has shown that the composition of early Chinese porcelain is nothing like as uniform as had been previously assumed. In 1982, at an international conference on ceramic technology held in Shanghai, it was revealed that Ding ware, a white-bodied high-fired ware from north China of very complex structure, was composed almost entirely of a silted clay with the probable addition of dolomite, and contained no porcelain-stone at all. By contrast the early white wares from major southern kilns including Jingdezhen were shown to have porcelain-stone as their primary ingredient, and some of them contained no *kaolin*.[32]

Much further work remains to be done on the analysis of the porcelain body. Previous reliance on d'Entrecolles' description of eighteenth-century practice has led to the false conclusion that what he saw was a survival of earlier methods. The situation has been further confused by the assumption that the compositions of Chinese and European porcelain are analogous. This ignores the basic difference in the nature of the respective raw materials.

In England, the major source of china-clay, or *kaolin*, is in Cornwall. Here the *kaolin* is in the form of a fine white powder deriving from decomposed granite outcrops. In the eighteenth century and later the clay was washed out, originally by diverting the local streams across the rock. The resulting solution was pumped up by water-driven pumps and settled in a series of tanks, to remove the unwanted mica and quartz particles. The slurry was then dried in kiln-sheds and cut up and packed in wooded casks for transportation to the potteries. The porcelain-stone was mined in the same area as the *kaolin*.[33]

In China, the *kaolin* was mined rather than washed out of the rock, and at Gaoling north-east of Jingdezhen there are large underground deposits. The mica and quartz, comprising over seventy per cent of the total volume, were washed out on the spot. The porcelain-stone was also mined, one source being at Sanbaopeng fourteen kilometers to the south. The porcelain-stone was ground to a powder in the vicinity using water-powered trip-hammers and refined by washing several times. After it had dried hard it was cut into *petuntse* (literally, "little white bricks") for transportation to the potteries. An additional component was glaze-stone, mined at Yaoli sixty kilometers to the north-east, and processed in a similar manner to the porcelain-stone. The glaze for the porcelain was prepared from a mixture of glaze-stone and lime-ash, the latter manufactured by firing together limestone and bracken. All these materials are still available in the area today and are used for the modern industry at Jingdezhen.[34]

The abundance of these raw materials was doubtless the primary reason for the growth of Jingdezhen as a major center for porcelain production. It is not known exactly when porcelain was first made there, but it was already well established as a pottery-manufacturing center by the tenth century, and by the eleventh it was producing *qingbai* ware.

Qingbai (also known as *yingqing*) is the descendant of the high-fired stoneware   5, 12
of the Tang dynasty, and the ivory-toned Ding ware. It is the precursor of all later porcelain; its main component is a kaolinised porcelain-stone and its glaze produced from the same material with the addition of glaze-ash, or lime. Not as

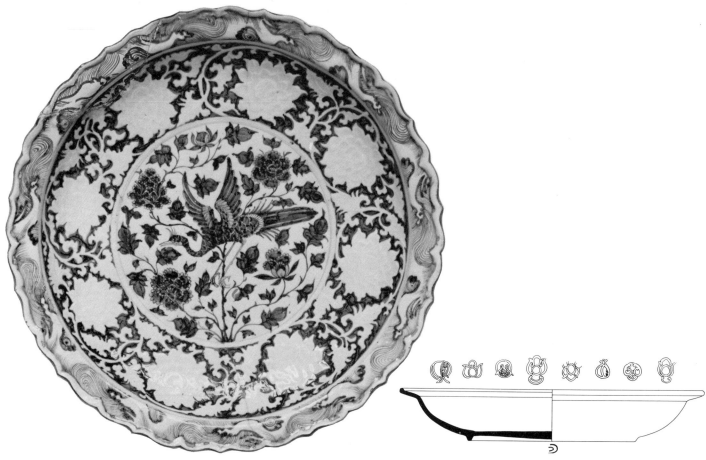

Figure 3. *Dish*. China, Jingdezhen, Yuan dynasty. First half of fourteenth century. Porcelain, with underglaze blue decoration; eight molded flowers in cavetto, each with a different center; double horseshoe mark on unglazed base. Height 6.8 cm. Diameter 41.1 cm. Private Collection, United Kingdom. From Syria.

highly fired as the porcelain which succeeded it, it is characterized by its translucent body and clear glaze with a marked bluish tinge. *Qingbai* pieces are generally small in scale, and typical of them are small bowls with foliate rims, decorated with graceful carved and combed designs, the bluish glaze pooling in 5 the incised lines and giving them a gentle emphasis.[35] Although primarily a Southern Song product, *qingbai* continued to be produced into the fourteenth century, and was widely exported, notably to south-east Asia but also as far afield as Sri Lanka and the Near East.[36]

6, 7   A distinctive white ware of quite different character is called *shufu*; its name derives from the characters *shu* and *fu* molded on the interior of bowls of this kind of ware. The characters have been variously interpreted as referring to a court office, "privy council," and *shufu* has been traditionally associated with the rulers of the Yuan dynasty. This did not, however, prevent its wide circulation all over south-east Asia, where it was popularly used for little molded export pieces. *Shufu* ware is generally more robust and less finely pared down than *qingbai*, and its distinctive glaze is opaque, with a dull eggshell finish. The composition of the body requires it to be fired at a higher temperature than the relatively low-fired *qingbai*. Again, *shufu* is limited to relatively small-scale pieces, including bowls with molded or slipped decoration, some with angular profile, stem-cups and three-footed censers. It appears to have been produced concurrently with *qingbai* in the late thirteenth and fourteenth centuries.[37]

Finally, underglaze-painted porcelain makes its appearance during the late Yuan dynasty, some time shortly after 1325 A.D. The body is of white porcelain, and the glaze of *qingbai* type, lustrous and transparent. The underglaze decora-11e tion is in cobalt blue and more rarely, copper-red. Perhaps the single most strik-

Recent analysis by Nigel Wood of all three types of white ware, *qingbai*, *shufu* and underglaze-decorated ware, has confirmed the suggestion first made by Addis that the body of the underglaze-decorated porcelain differs from the other two. In 1978, using the results of previous analyses of the porcelain body, Wood maintained that *qingbai* ware was made from a kaolinised porcelain-stone, composed of quartz, mica, albite (sodium feldspar) and kaolinite, with no additional *kaolin*, or china-clay. In 1984 he amplified his conclusions and also drew attention to the use of lime, in the form of glaze-ash, for the preparation of the glaze.[38]

Even more recent research by Tite, Freestone and Bimson has taken Wood's analysis a stage further.[39] They have demonstrated that two methods of manufacture were used concurrently in the Yuan dynasty. In the first method, body and glaze both consisted of kaolinised porcelain-stone, with glaze-ash added for the glaze. In the second, the body was composed of porcelain-stone with little trace of kaolinite and mixed with *kaolin* clay; glaze-ash was again added to the glaze.

Both methods were used to make *qingbai*. But for *shufu* and underglaze-decorated porcelain, only the second method was used. They speculated that the shift to the use of additional *kaolin* may well have been connected with the solution of the technical problems of making much larger vessels. Not only would the additional *kaolin* give greater plasticity in forming the vessels, but would also allow greater control of the actual proportions of the body ingredients. Whatever the reason may have been, it is clear that the introduction of a radically new type of underglaze-decorated Chinese porcelain corresponded with a technical change in the body material of equally far-reaching consequence.

CONSTRUCTION

The addition of *kaolin* to the body material to enhance its plasticity allowed forms to be constructed on a far greater scale, so that the underglaze-decorated wares of the Yuan dynasty often assumed monumental proportions. Firing techniques at Jingdezhen by that time were apparently sufficiently sophisticated to be able to tackle the problems posed by the larger pieces.

The large dishes, often with bracketed, raised rims and molded decoration in the cavetto, were made in molds (Figures 2, 3). Close inspection of a number of examples reveals the impression of a fine, muslin-like cloth on the center of the dish, to reduce the adhesive effects of the clay when removed from the mold.[40] The base was carved out of the body, the dish being turned upside down on a slow wheel, leaving a short, angular foot-ring.[41] The bottom and inside of the foot-ring were left unglazed, and often fired an orange-red color due to the oxidization of the ferruginous clay.

The bowls, both large and small, were thrown on the wheel and finished with either an inverted or everted rim. Again, the base and foot-ring were carved from a solid mass of clay; some of the bowls are inordinately heavy, and measurement shows that the base is two centimeters or more thick, the potter evidently unaware how much more could have been pared away without weakening the structure of the bowl. Large bowls with an inverted rim, concave on the outside, appear to have been based on Mamluk metal prototypes. The influence of Near Eastern metalwork becomes even more pronounced in the Ming dynasty.

The large vases, of *meiping*, double-gourd or rectangular form, as well as unique pieces such as the David vases, appear to have been built up from several sections luted together. Additional features such as ornamental handles were separately molded and then applied to the vessel with a thin slip as an adhesive. The large *guan*, or wine jars, were also wheel made, and often further embellished with panels cut away from the body and filled with an appliqué of molded floral ornament, with beaded frames.

Smaller wares include stem-cups made of two separate elements luted together. The cups were often molded with an impressed design on the interior. Again, section drawings show that the stem-cups have thicker bases than was structurally necessary. Spouted bowls, their form of metallic origin, often with a suspension loop beneath the spout, were simply constructed from bowls turned on the wheel, to which the carved spout and loop were added.

Ewers were basically constructed from the bottle-vase form of the *yuhuchun ping* type, to which was added the handle and curving spout, with a reinforcing bridge joining the spout to the neck.[42] Part of a *yuhuchun ping* vase in the Freer Gallery shows that on this form the foot-ring was not carved from the body, but consisted of a separate ring luted on to the base. A visible join on the vase, both inside and out, shows how the body was made in two separate pieces.[43]

DESTRUCTION

As a famous archaeologist once remarked, pottery is easy to break but hard to destroy. Chinese blue-and-white is no exception to the rule, and in the Islamic world seems to have been considered valuable enough to keep even when broken. Much of the blue-and-white found in Syria in recent years had been riveted and an early sherd from Fustat in the present exhibition (12a) had a hole drilled in it for just such a purpose. So had a number of pieces of blue-and-white found in the garden of a Tughlaq palace in Delhi, dating to the period before its destruction in 1398 A.D.[44]

The technique of repair, still practiced in the *suq* in Aleppo to this day, consists of drilling pairs of holes on either side of the break with a bow-drill. Then the ends of a heated, U-shaped brass rivet are tapped into place, and when the rivet cools and contracts, draws the pieces tightly together again.

THE COBALT BLUE

Controlling the decoration of white porcelain in underglaze cobalt blue and preventing it from diffusing in the glaze was the great achievement of the Chinese potters at Jingdezhen. Surprisingly, the cobalt blue itself was initially of Near Eastern origin; for at least a century earlier than its use in China, it had been used less successfully by the Persian potters at Kashan. In the wares produced in Persia, the blue tended to flux with the glaze and produced a smeared effect; the Persian solution was to define the diffused areas of blue with a more stable black outline, a device which they continued to use until the eighteenth century.

Thanks to a treatise on pottery by a Persian craftsman, Abu'l Qasim, written in A.H. 700/1301 A.D. there is available specific information on the preparation of raw cobalt immediately prior to its introduction into China about 1325 A.D. In his list of raw materials he states:

> §8. The sixth is the stone *lajvard*, which the craftsmen call *Sulaimani*. Its source is the village of Qamsar in the mountains round Kashan, and the people there claim it was discovered by the prophet Sulaiman. It is like white silver shining in a sheath of hard black stone. From it comes *lajvard* color, like that of *lajvard*-coloured glaze . . . .[45]

A more recent account described how the ore was prepared, by mixing it with potash, borax, *shireh* (grape treacle) and pounded quartz, and then heating it in a

The fine materials make it weak,
Porcelain, by being pure is apt to break.
—Dryden.

22

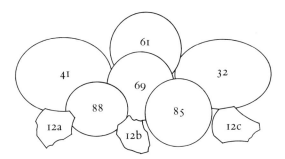

Figure 4. *A Group of Blue-and-White.*
12a,b,c. Chinese porcelain, fourteenth century.
32. Chinese porcelain, fifteenth/sixteenth century.
41. Vietnamese, fifteenth/sixteenth century.
61. Chinese porcelain, seventeenth century.
69. Syrian pottery, fifteenth century.
85. Persian pottery, seventeenth century.
88. Japanese porcelain, seventeenth century.

furnace. The resulting compound was used for decorating pottery by grinding it up again with an equal quantity of quartz, and gum as a fixative. In the fourteenth century it was presumably exported to China in the form of smalt.

Various scholars have linked the introduction of cobalt blue in China to the existence of Persian merchant communities on the China coast and in the larger cities, affluent enough to order porcelain from Jingdezhen and to introduce the new color to the potters. That the market for early blue-and-white was stimulated by Arab/Persian patronage has been argued from the fact that many of the shapes, large dishes and capacious bowls, are more suitable for the eating habits of the Islamic world rather than Chinese cuisine. Indeed, later Persian miniatures are full of scenes of feasting and celebration with massive platters and bowls of blue-and-white piled high with food.

Further testimony to Islamic patronage is provided by the existence of at least two pieces of fourteenth-century blue-and-white with Arabic/Persian inscriptions under the glaze:[46]

In both cases it is clear that the Chinese potter was unfamiliar with the script. More pieces have been noted where the unglazed base of fourteenth-century ware has been inscribed in ink with Arabic/Persian characters, probably merchants' marks or owners' names (Figures 2, 3).[47] The ink appears to be indelible, and it is not clear whether they were inscribed before or after firing. The practice of writing on the unglazed base was also a Chinese one; a Longquan celadon dish, for instance, found in Syria, had a cyclical date in Chinese characters on the base equivalent to 1381 A.D.[48] As for the Moslem population in China, numerous texts refer to the size and importance of the Moslem communities; in the fourteenth century, Ibn Battuta records that most cities had a mosque and a Moslem quarter. He also mentions meeting in Zaitun (Quanzhou) a Persian merchant Sharif ad-Din of Tabriz, whom he had previously encountered in India.[49]

Apart from any special preparation of the imported cobalt, the porous surface of the unfired porcelain body would have instantly absorbed and fixed the pigment. From the earliest stage the artists used varying tones of blue, ranging from a faint wash to a rich, dark blue where the pigment was so thickly applied that it tended to fire with blackish spots in those areas. The application of the cobalt blue decoration allowed for no second thoughts, and the accuracy and mastery with which these early wares were painted are nothing short of amazing. One must also remember that when the blue was applied it was gray-black in color, and it was not until after the vessel was glazed and fired that the vibrant blue appeared.

The blue on Chinese porcelain is far from uniform, and along with other diagnostic criteria, can often provide a clue to the dating of a piece. Technical analysis of Chinese blue-and-white has shown that during the fourteenth century, imported cobalt was invariably used. But by the fifteenth century, the Chinese began to mine their own cobalt and mix it with the imported ore, producing a softer and less striking color.[50] In the sixteenth and seventeenth centuries, the Chinese cobalt was generally used alone, although analysis has shown that occasionally there was an admixture of imported ore. In the Jiajing period (1522–1566 A.D.) the blue was of an almost violet intensity. By the end of the seventeenth century and the reign of Kangxi, an immaculate, hard cobalt blue became the norm, of faintly repellent character when contrasted with the warmth of some of the earlier blue-and-white. Indeed, in the eighteenth century there appears to have developed a sort of reverence for the use of the blue on earlier pieces, and the blue was accented with consciously applied darker dots, in imitation of the accidental speckling on fifteenth-century wares. It is interesting to note that the same phenomenon occurs on mid-sixteenth century Turkish pottery, inspired by Chinese prototypes. In the fourteenth-century wares, the blue color was affected by the presence of iron in the pigment; subsequent refinement of the ore produced a blue with less obvious impurities. The blue was also dependant on the control of the firing and could vary greatly on two pieces which are otherwise identical, and also on various areas of the same piece exposed to a greater or lesser degree to the heat source in the kiln.[51]

12c

Finally, some mention should be made of the use of cobalt blue underglaze decoration in China in the Tang dynasty, long before its use in fourteenth-century porcelain. Lead-glazed earthenware was stained with green, ocher/brown and cobalt blue, in the technique known as *sancai* ("three colors"). Cobalt blue made its appearance as early as 664 A.D., on the fragment of a lid from a dated tomb.[52] A sherd of a bowl decorated in *sancai* with splashes of blue was recently found at Mantai, in Sri Lanka, and can be paralleled with a bowl found in the tomb of the Princess Yongtai in Shaanxi, who died in 706 A.D.[53] Like the other pigments, the blue used on Tang earthenware was difficult to control and used either within the confines of a deeply incised outline, or simply allowed to flood all over the piece, making a virtue out of its undisciplined spontaneity.

3

Where did the cobalt come from in the Tang dynasty? Here again, scientific analysis has shown that it was imported from Persia,[54] providing yet another example of the numerous contacts between central Asia and western Iran under the Tang and the delight in all sorts of foreign exotica. There is no link, however, between its use in the Tang period and its reintroduction in the late Yuan; by the early eighth century A.D., its use in China appears to have died out.

NOTES

1. A. C. Moule and Paul Pelliot, *Marco Polo, The Description of the World*, I–II, London, 1938, for a complete and literal translation of the manuscript known as 'F,' in the Bibliothèque Nationale, Paris, Ms. Fr. 1116., considered to be the best of all extant manuscripts, and written in Italianate French in the first half of the fourteenth century. Moule and Pelliot's translation includes additions and insertions from other manuscripts, particularly the Italian, 'R', and the Latin version, 'Z'. The original text of 'Z', discovered by Sir Percival David in Toledo in 1932, is printed in full in Volume II. The relative importance of the variant texts is fully discussed by the translators in their Introduction.

For an invaluable discussion of the text, see Pelliot's further work, *Notes on Marco Polo*, I–III, Paris, 1959–1973. For 'porcelain,' pp. 805–812; 'cowries,' pp. 531–562; 'Tingiu,' pp. 853–856.

2. For *porcellana*, cowry-shells, in Yunnan, Moule and Pelliot, *op. cit.*, pp. 277–8; for *porcellana*, pottery, at Tingiu, p. 352.

3. Pelliot, *op. cit.*, pp. 805–7.

4. *Ibid.*, p. 532.

5. *Voyage du marchand arabe Sulayman en Inde et en Chine, rédigé en 851, suivi de remarques par Abu Zayd Hasan*, Translated by G. Ferrand, Paris, 1922, pp. 31, 33, 50.

6. *Voyages d'Ibn Batoutah*, I–IV, Translated by C. Defrémery and B. Sanguinetti, Paris, 1858, IV, pp. 121–2, 139.

7. Pelliot, *op. cit.*, p. 807. H. Yule and A. Burnell, *Hobson–Jobson*, London, 1903, pp. 725–6.

8. Moule and Pelliot, *op. cit.*, I, p. 277.

9. *Ibid.*, p. 278.

10. See the cowries and imitations in the exhibition, nos. 1, 2; also Pelliot, *op. cit.*, pp. 533–4.

11. *Ibid.*, pp. 545–6.

12. Moule and Pelliot, *op. cit.*, p. 298. Pelliot, *op. cit.*, pp. 857–8, for location of Toloman.

13. Moule and Pelliot, *op. cit.*, p. 370.

14. Ma Huan, *Ying-yai sheng-lan. 'The Overall Survey of the Ocean's Shores'* [1433], Translated and edited by J. V. G. Mills, Cambridge, 1970, p. 107.

15. Pelliot, *op. cit.*, pp. 555–6.

16. Moule and Pelliot, *op. cit.*, p. 352.

17. Pelliot, *op. cit.*, pp. 853–5.

18. P. Hughes-Stanton and R. Kerr, *Kiln Sites of Ancient China*, The Oriental Ceramic Society, London, 1982, pp. 26–7. *Exhibition of Ceramic Finds from Ancient Kilns in China*, Hong Kong, 1981, pp. 52–3. John Carswell, "Chinese Ceramics from Allaippidy in Sri Lanka," *A Ceramic Legacy of Asia's Maritime Trade*, Southeast

Asian Ceramic Society, West Malaysian Chapter, Kuala Lumpur, 1985, pp. 31–49, particularly Figure 87.

19. Hughes-Stanton and Kerr, *op. cit.*, pp. 32–4; *Exhibition of Ceramic Finds from Ancient Kilns in China*, p. 57.

20. Samuel Johnson, *Dictionary of the English Language*, 1819 (Philadelphia edition), 'porcelain.'

21. Ibn Battuta, *Rihlat Ibn Battuta*, Dar Sadir and Dar Bayrut, Beirut, 1963. I am indebted to Professor Fred Donner for his generous assistance in determining the literal meaning of the original text.

22. John Carswell, "A Fourteenth Century Chinese Porcelain Dish from Damascus," *American University of Beirut Festival Book, (Festschrift), 1866–1966*, Beirut 1967, pp. 39–58.

23. Ibn Battuta, *op. cit.*, pp. 627–8.

24. See below, p. 19.

25. Ibn Battuta, *op. cit.*, p. 630.

26. See below, p. 19.

27. Ibn Battuta, *op. cit.*, p. 634.

28. National Museum of Korea, *Exhibition of Cultural Relics Found off Sinan Coast*, Seoul, Korea, 1977.

29. John Carswell, "Sri Lanka and China," *Festschrift for James Rutnam*, Colombo, 1985, (in press).

30. M. Reinaud, *Relations des voyages faits par les Arabes et Persans, dans l'Inde et à la Chine dans le IX siècle de l'ére Chrétien*, Paris, 1845, I. p. 34, Arabic text, pp. 35–6.

31. Père d'Entrecolles (B. Lyon, 1664 – D. Beijing 1741) described the manufacture of porcelain in two letters, written from Jaochou on September 1, 1712 , and from Jingdezhen on January 25, 1722; translated by Robert Tichane, *Ching-te-chen: views of a porcelain city*, New York State Institute for Glaze Research, New York, 1983, pp. 49–128, with a brief biographical note.

32. Jessica Rawson, "A Gift for Ceramics," *Times Literary Supplement*, London, June 24, 1983.

33. *Wheel Martin Museum: Guide to the China-Clay Museum with Historical Notes*, St. Austell, Cornwall; 5th. ed., 1983.

34. John Addis, "Porcelain-Stone and Kaolin; Late Yuan Developments at Hutian," *Transactions of the Oriental Ceramic Society*, 45, 1980–81, pp. 54–6; also "The Evolution of Techniques at Jingdezhen with particular reference to the Yuan Dynasty," *Jingdezhen Wares, The Yuan Evolution*, Oriental Ceramic Society, Hong Kong, 1984, pp. 11–19.

35. Philip Wen-Chee Mao, "Qingbai Wares," *Jingdezhen Wares, The Yuan Evolution*, pp. 32–8.

36. John Carswell, "Chinese ceramics from Allaippidy in Sri Lanka," *A Ceramic Legacy of Asia's Maritime Trade*, Southeast Asian Ceramic Society, West Malaysian Chapter, Kuala Lumpur, 1985, pp. 31–49.

37. Duncan Macintosh, "Shufu Wares: Their Origins, Development and Decline," *Bulletin of the Oriental Ceramic Society of Hong Kong*, 4, 1978–80, pp. 39–43; also "Shufu Wares," *Jingdezhen Wares, The Yuan Evolution*, pp. 39–43.

38. Nigel Wood, "Chinese porcelain," *Pottery Quarterly*, 12.47, pp. 101–128; – Oriental *Glazes*, London, 1978; – "Some implications of recent analyses of Song yingqing ware from Jingdezhen," and "Body-lime glazes and qingbai porcelain," *Proceedings of International Conference on Ancient Chinese Pottery and Porcelain*, Shanghai, 1982, (in press).

39. M. Tite, I. Freestone and M. Bimson, "A technological study of Chinese porcelain of the Yuan dynasty," *Archeometry*, 26.2, 1984, pp. 139–154.

40. For an illustration of this, E. Smart, "Fourteenth-century Chinese porcelain from a Tughlaq Palace in Delhi," *Transactions of the Oriental Ceramic Society*, 1975–77, 41, p. 201, Plates 72, 78(b). A fourteenth-century dish in the Larsson Collection, London, demonstrates precisely the same features.

41. *Ibid.*, Plate 73(a), (b), show the concentric and radial chatter-marks of the knife on the base.

42. For an elaborate plain white qingbai ewer, and an example decorated in copper-red, both with reinforcing bridges, see M. Medley, *Yüan Porcelain and Stoneware*, London, 1974, Plates 10, 50b.

43. (11d) in the present exhibition; published by John Pope, "Two Chinese porcelains from the Umezawa Collection," *Far Eastern Ceramic Bulletin*, June 1959, pp. 17–18, Plate IV, Figures 8–10.

44. Smart, *op. cit.*, p. 200, Plates 78, 81, 84, 87.

45. James W. Allan, "Abu'l Qasim's Treatise on Ceramics," *Iran*, XI, 1973, pp. 111–120.

46. One is a dish in the Fogg Museum at Harvard; the inscription (a) is reversed on a blue ground, in the cavetto just below the rim; John Ayers, "Some Chinese wares of the Yuan period," *Transactions of the Oriental Ceramic Society*, 29, 1954–55, p. 83, Figure 37. The second dish is in the Ardebil collection; the underglaze blue inscription (b) is underneath the rim; John Pope, *Chinese Porcelains from the Ardebil Shrine*, Washington 1956, pp. 55–56, 67, Plate 20. See Carswell, "A Fourteenth-Century Chinese Porcelain Dish from Damascus," *American University of Beirut Festival Book, (Festschrift), 1866–1966*, Beirut, 1967, pp. 39–58., for a discussion of the translations of the inscriptions.

47. For instance, (12b) in the exhibition. Pope, *Chinese Porcelains from the Ardebil Shrine*, Plate 30, has published an early fifteenth century dish with a long Chinese text on the base, also written in ink, and probably inscribed before firing.

48. Collection of M. Georges Antaki, Aleppo (unpublished).

49. *Voyages d'Ibn Batoutah*, translated by Defrèmery and Sanguinetti, IV, p. 270.

50. Sir Harry Garner, "The Use of Imported and Native Cobalt in Chinese Blue and White," *Oriental Art*, New Series, II.2, London, 1956, pp. 48–50.

51. *Ibid.*, p. 50. For an example of a piece fired different shades of blue, see (12c) in the exhibition.

52. W. Watson, *Tang and Liao Ceramics*, New York, 1984, p. 50.

53. W. Watson, *The Genius of China*, London, 1973, pp. 136–7, 141, No. 282.

54. Garner, *op. cit.*

Blue-and-White in China, Asia and the Islamic World

John Carswell

The exact date at which porcelain decorated in underglaze blue began to be manufactured has long been debated; some scholars have maintained that it was a Song innovation, and others that it was a late Yuan development. The majority opinion at the moment inclines towards the latter proposition, and more precisely to the second quarter of the fourteenth century.

The David vases of 1351 A.D. (Figure 5) provide the first chronological fixed point; such is the mastery and sophistication of their decoration, there must have been a reasonably long period of experimentation leading up to their production. Although it has been suggested that the tentative use of cobalt blue took place in the early fourteenth century, the full flowering of the new technique appears to have occurred some time after 1325 A.D. Apparent corroboration of this is to be found in the cargo of a ship wrecked off the coast of southern Korea in 1323 A.D.[1] This precise date is provided by a series of wooden tags recovered from the shipwreck, attached to bronze coins and herbal products, one of which is inscribed with the equivalent of June 1st of the third year of Zhizhi, that is 1323 A.D.[2] Of the eighteen thousand or more pieces of Chinese pottery so far recovered from the ship, representing just about every type of ware, there was not a single sherd of blue-and-white. Both *qingbai* and *shufu* wares were found in quantity, often of types known to have been also decorated in blue-and-white. The implication of this is that the ship went down just before the introduction of blue-and-white, for the vessel carried only the white wares of the Jingdezhen kilns.

The David vases, according to an inscription on one of them, were presented to a Daoist temple in Yushan district some hundred and twenty kilometers south-east of Jingdezhen.[3] The shape of these massive vases betrays their bronze origin, with moldings of metallic form. They are decorated in underglaze cobalt blue with consummate skill, and as they are the first dated examples of blue-and-white, it is worth noting the various motifs which were current at the time of their manufacture (Figure 5).

On the neck is a wreath of chrysanthemum, some with cross-hatched centers, on a thin stem; the leaves are of two types, either knobby or short and spiky. The trumpet-shaped neck is divided in two by a horizontal convex molding. Above, there is a ring of vertical plantain leaves; here, on one of the vases, is the six-column dedicatory inscription. Elephant-head handles spring from just above the molding and curl down to join the lower half of the neck, which is painted with a pair of male and female phoenixes, *feng huang,* swooping up and down against a background of clouds. The wide convex molding at the junction of the neck and the body is decorated with lotuses on a stem bearing pointed, lobed leaves with pairs of spikes on either side.

The bodies of the vases are painted with four-clawed dragons, advancing to the left on one and to the right on the other. From the heel of each claw spring sinuous clusters. In the background there are stylized clouds, cloud-scrolls and flames, and below the dragons are two tiers of breaking serpentine waves, separated by another convex molding. There is a peony wreath on the upper foot, with the flowers shown both in full and in profile, and the stem bearing fleshy five-pointed leaves and peony buds. Below there is a ring of lotus-panels filled with Daoist auspicious emblems.

From this list one can note that by 1351 A.D., the repertoire already included the chrysanthemum, lotus and peony, each with clearly-differentiated leaves, including the spiked, lobed leaf accompanying the lotus, for which no precedent exists in the natural world. The use of this distinctive leaf in blue-and-white decoration appears to be confined exclusively to the fourteenth century (Figures 2, 3). The serpentine-wave motif also appears fully developed on the David vases. One omission from the fourteenth-century repertoire is the use of contrasting panels of blue-on-white, and white reserved on a blue ground; the David vases are confined to blue-on-white. The cross-hatched centers of the chrysanthemum are a Yuan feature which also occurs on molded celadon of the same period.

What could have been the antecedents of the David vases? It has been suggested that the earliest blue-and-white included the numerous little molded vessels sketchily painted in cobalt blue, found in quantity in south-east Asia. The shapes are duplicated both in plain *qingbai* and *shufu* ware, and in others decorated with ferruginous brown spots, a number of which were found on the Sinan wreck. But the most convincing argument for the early date of this sketchily-painted blue-and-white comes from the tomb of Ren Renfa, near Shanghai. Ren Renfa died in 1327 A.D., and his tomb contained a tripod incense-burner and a carinated bowl of *shufu* type white ware;[4] almost identical plain pieces were found on the Sinan wreck,[5] and the carinated bowl type loosely painted in cobalt blue is known in south-east Asia.[6]

Finally, a sherd from Fustat in the exhibition (Figure 4)(12a) may be one of the earliest surviving examples of blue-and-white. This is the base of a bowl with a *qingbai* glaze, molded on the inside with tiers of radiating chrysanthemum petals. The type is also known in *shufu* and there is a good example in the exhibition from the Cleveland Museum; another is in the Ashmolean; the molded design ultimately derives from a silver prototype. What lends special interest to the Fustat fragment is the fact that the molded design at the center of the bowl is overpainted with a spray of underglaze blue chrysanthemum, in the same early style noted above. The centers of the flowers are cross-hatched, and on the outside of the bowl is a ring of serpentine waves, motifs common to the David vases. Here we have an example of an existing type of molded porcelain decorated in the new blue.

A variety of techniques was practiced at Jingdezhen in the late thirteenth/early fourteenth centuries, particularly in *qingbai*; these included carving, molding and the application of sprigged decoration to the various forms.[7] Remarkable among these are vessels with cut-out panels filled with applied floral decoration and pearl-beaded borders. The most famous example is the Fonthill vase, transformed with European silver-gilt mounts into a ewer some time towards the end of the fourteenth century, and certainly one of the first pieces of Chinese porcelain known to have reached the western world.[8] It was first recorded in a French drawing in the early eighteenth century, complete with the mounts. It subsequently entered the collection of the eccentric William Beckford, and was listed among the contents of the sale of Fonthill Abbey in 1822. It later lost its mounts and reverted to a vase, finally to reappear in the collection of the

Figure 5. *Two vases.* China, Jingdezhen, Yuan dynasty. 1351 A.D. Porcelain with underglaze blue decoration. Height 63.6 cm. The Percival David Foundation of Chinese Art, University of London. B613, B614.

National Gallery in Dublin. This type of beaded and applied decoration was also extensively used for the manufacture of *qingbai* figures, such as the large Bodhisattva in The Nelson-Atkins Museum of Art, dated 1298/9 A.D.[9] Making and firing these large figures, often in excess of fifty centimeters high, represents a considerable technical achievement.

This skill in constructing large-scale porcelain objects was not lost when underglaze decoration began. It is no surprise that when underglaze blue decoration appears it should be in association with the various techniques of molding and applied decoration. A large jar in the David Foundation in London exemplifies this amalgam of techniques, with cut-out panels, pearl-beaded and applied decoration, and painted both in cobalt blue and copper red.[10] Besides such large jars there are a number of dishes with molded floral designs in the cavetto, and sometimes on the rim, combined with blue-and-white decoration (Figure 3). Other early massive forms include *meiping* vases; large bowls with either inverted or everted rims, and sometimes with a pedestal foot; enormous double-gourd shaped vases; and large flasks of rectangular section and round necks, with two pairs of loop handles on the sloping shoulders.

The scale of these early pieces and the fact that so many of them have survived in collections in India, Persia and Turkey and elsewhere in the Near East, have led to the speculation that this early blue-and-white, like the little jarlets and other forms so common in south-east Asia, was primarily an export ware. There are a number of economic reasons to support such a theory, including the fact that under the Mongol supremacy the Near and Far East became a single political entity, which was conducive to long-distance international trade. The ceramic trade was largely sea-borne, continuing the maritime tradition established in the Tang dynasty and flourishing in the Song. It has already been noted that Moslem, and specially the Persian, merchants resident in the various Chinese ports were in a key position to commission the early blue-and-white and to arrange for its export. It has also been argued that the massive scale of the ware reflects Moslem rather than Chinese taste.

But this was not the entire story. An increasing number of large pieces are coming to light in China itself, such as the spectacular vase from the tomb of Mu Ying, dated 1369 A.D.[11] Many of the vases of this type are painted with scenes from various Yuan dramas, which would have been singularly inappropriate for a Moslem market.[12] Although it has been suggested that the all-over patterning and compartmentalization of the designs of fourteenth-century blue-and-white, particularly the bracketed dishes, reflect a Near Eastern predilection, this is hardly true of the individual design motifs. The phoenix and the dragon, carp and ducks, peacocks and deer, cicadas and fantastic *qilins,* combined with cloud-scrolls and breaking waves, chrysanthemum, lotus and peony, are redolent of Chinese taste. Quite apart from the explicitly Buddhist or Daoist emblems in the designs, the symbolism of the flora and fauna would have been quite lost on Moslem patrons. In fact, it is surprising that, if the Moslem community was so deeply involved in the ceramic trade, there was not *more* Islamic influence.

It is true that most of the smaller wares — again leaving aside the special case of south-east Asian export wares — seem to have been confined to the home market. In this category is an interesting group of blue-and-white sherds collected by John Pope in Beijing in 1945–6, of which four are in the exhibition, and more are in the study collection of the Freer Gallery in Washington. The Yuan capital, Dadu, was at present-day Beijing, and these sherds are evidence of the market for blue-and-white in that city. There are the remains of two stem-cups

11

11c painted in the simple, early floral style; parts of a vase with a deer and a figure of
11d the kind decorated with Yuan dramatic scenes; and another vase with lotus and
spiked, lobed leaves and an unusual disc base.[13]

The evolution of blue-and-white in China during the successive periods of
the Ming dynasty is a complex subject and still the topic of intensive study; not
only do the shapes and technical characteristics change in the post-Yuan period,
but also the philosophy of the decoration. Economic considerations were
paramount, and what happened at Jingdezhen was largely conditioned by the
amount and kind of patronage that the potters received. However individual and
versatile some of the craftsmen may have been, they were not artist-potters producing work for their own sake, but functioning craftsmen with the ultimate
client in mind. Unlike some of the craftsmen of the Islamic world, their works
were never signed; the only identification was the reign-mark of the emperor
during whose rule the porcelain was produced.

18, 19,
20 The custom of marking pottery with the emperor's *nianhao*, or reign-mark,
became established in the Xuande period (1426–1435 A.D.), abandoned during
the Interregnum and re-introduced during the period of Chenghua (1465–1487
A.D.), with a continuous succession of reign-marks up till the end of the Ming
dynasty, and later. For the Yuan and early Ming dynasty before Xuande, other
criteria have to be used for dating, such as style, decoration and the occasional
fortuitous fixed point, like the David vases, pieces from a dated tomb, a shipwreck or from a secure archaeological context. Theoretically from Xuande onwards, the reign-marks should provide all the information needed for the
classification of later Ming porcelain. Unfortunately it is not so simple; the
reigns themselves were of longer or shorter duration, and the rhythm of dynastic
and political change was not necessarily mirrored in the products of the kilns. A
real complication arises through the Chinese reverence for the past; later pieces of
blue-and-white were often marked with the reigns of periods particularly admired by Chinese connoisseurs. For instance, a piece with a Xuande mark could
either be of the period, or of the sixteenth century, or later. Seventeenth-century
bowls with Chenghua marks are common.

In considering the development of blue-and-white during the later Ming dynasty, the main issue is not so much the finer points of stylistic change, as the
patterns of economic expansion, when the blue-and-white flooded out of China
and affected the pottery of other regions. When did the major exports of blue-
and-white take place? The initial wave was during the Yuan and early Ming dynasties, and much of the porcelain was destined for India. More went on to
Egypt, and to Syria; because of the difficulties of navigating up the Red Sea, it
would have been landed on the coast and sent either up the Nile to Fustat, or up
the *Hajj* pilgrimage route through Arabia to Syria. Fourteenth-century blue-
and-white sherds have been found at Hormuz, and porcelain would have been
shipped to the Gulf for Persia and Iraq. More found its way to the coast of East
Africa. When it reached Turkey is an open question; the Topkapu Saray inventories show that Chinese porcelain was relatively scarce in the late fifteenth century, and the bulk of the collection, including the fourteenth-century wares, may
have arrived as booty from the Ottoman conquest of Syria and Egypt in the early sixteenth century.

What happened in the fifteenth century is more difficult to determine, for although fifteenth-century blue-and-white abounds in the Topkapu and Ardebil
Collections, it is apparently rare in India, and among the eight hundred pieces of
11a, b the Yuan and Ming dynasties catalogued from Syria, there are only three of the

Figure 6. *Dish*. China, Jingdezhen, Ming dynasty. Early fifteenth century. Porcelain, with underglaze blue decoration; detail of the center, with the "Three Friends"—pine, prunus and bamboo. Height 6 cm. Diameter 34 cm. Collection of H.E. Henri Pharaon, Beirut. From Syria.

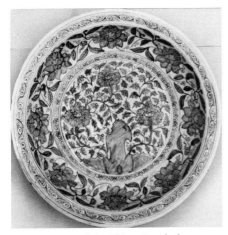

Figure 7. *Large dish*. China, Jingdezhen, Ming dynasty. Fifteenth/sixteenth century. Porcelain, with underglaze blue decoration. Height 8.8 cm. Diameter 52.2 cm. Collection of H.E. Henri Pharaon, Beirut. From Syria.

Figure 8. *Bowl*. China, Jingdezhen, Ming dynasty. Zhengde mark and period (1506–1521 A.D.). Porcelain, with underglaze blue decoration; Persian and Arabic inscriptions. Diameter c. 28 cm. The Freer Gallery of Art, Smithsonian Institution. FGA. 53.75.

first half of the fifteenth century (Figure 6). In India, much of the porcelain would have been transhipped at such ports as Calicut for countries further west. In Syria, the lack of fifteenth-century porcelain can be explained by the collapse of the economy, as a result of the devastation of the towns and villages by Timur, in his invasion of 1400–1401. Further reasons were a decline in population, and pestilence, and for most of the fifteenth century in the post-Timurid period, the economy of Egypt and Syria was relatively stagnant. This must have had an immediate effect on the quantity of imports, including porcelain. It was not until the end of the century that a second great wave of Chinese blue-and-white hit the Near East (Figure 7). Oddly enough many of these were often decorated with designs, such as the lotus-spray, in a debased fourteenth-century style. Both in Syria and in Egypt, in the absence of large quantities of Chinese porcelain in the fifteenth century, great efforts were made to fabricate local blue-and-white. To this period belong numbers of hexagonal blue-and-white tiles, in both Syria and Egypt, of obviously Chinese inspiration, but also attempting to Islamicize the designs, notably in the tendency to symmetry, and the introduction of abstract geometric patterns. Small-scale building in the Mamluk empire was the order of the day, rather than the construction of major monuments, and it was in such smaller foundations, like the Tawrizi tomb and mosque in Damascus, that the tiles were placed.

Paradoxically, in the first quarter of the fifteenth century, the Chinese sent a series of maritime expeditions to the West, in the most concentrated attempt ever undertaken to establish contact with south Asia, India and the Near East.[14] Why the emperor Yongle (1403–1424 A.D.) dispatched these naval expeditions under the command of the Moslem eunuch, Zheng He, is not clear; but the scale was extraordinary. Six expeditions took place during Yongle's reign, and a seventh under Xuande. The first expedition, in 1405–7, consisted of three hundred and seventeen ships and twenty-seven thousand eight hundred and seventy men, and visited Java, Semudera, Lambri, Ceylon and Calicut. Subsequent expeditions visited many parts of south Asia; the fourth reached as far as Hormuz; the fifth, sixth and seventh to Aden and East Africa. The expeditions were chronicled by Ma Huan, who was appointed official translator to Zheng He; he himself actually got as far as Mecca ("the Land of the Heavenly Square" [the Ka'ba]) on the seventh expedition. Ma Huan lists all the products that were traded on these missions, and among them is "blue porcelain," which he specifically states was popular in Vietnam, Java, Ceylon and Dhofar, and which was among the products taken to Mecca.[15] Nothing, however, came of these expeditions in the way of establishing permanent commercial relationships between China and the West.

In the sixteenth century, under the reign of Zhengde (1506–1521 A.D.), the powerful control exercised by the Moslem eunuchs directly affected the porcelain industry, for there is the evidence of a number of pieces of blue-and-white with Arabic or Persian inscriptions, and often with the six-character Zhengde mark (Figure 8).[16] This porcelain must have been primarily for home consumption, for the use of Moslems in China; this is confirmed by the sherd in the exhibition found in Beijing and by the forms of many of the pieces, which are Chinese, such as hat-stands, pen-rests, plaques and tripod incense-burners. The incense-burners are an interesting case in point; based on Chinese bronze forms, their reproduction in porcelain seems bizarre. It is difficult to imagine what purpose they served in a Chinese Moslem household, unless simply decorative.[17]

While the potters at Jingdezhen were filling the orders of their Moslem patrons, towards the end of Zhengde's reign clients of a more alien kind arrived on

25

32, 33

34

66–70

71

37, 38

36

the scene. The Portuguese established their first direct contact with China in 1517, when Manuel I sent an embassy to Beijing. A small group of porcelain decorated with the armillary sphere and the royal arms of Manuel I is believed to date from the period of this initial contact with China, and heralds the beginning of the trade of blue-and-white to Europe, the expansion of which was largely due to the Portuguese (Figure 9).[18] Two bowls in the Topguku Saray Collection in Istanbul with Arabic inscriptions and Zhengde marks have been considered as examples of blue-and-white made specifically for the Near East, rather than for Chinese Moslems. With their long Quranic inscriptions they are unlike most of the same group of Arabic/Persian inscribed pieces; they could, of course, have been purchased in China and brought back to Turkey, and it has been suggested that they may have belonged to the Turkish merchant 'Ali Akbar, who stayed three years in China in the early sixteenth century.[19]

What was the impact of Chinese blue-and-white in the Near East? Certainly by the end of the fourteenth century, Syrian imitations were being made of Chinese ware, and probably Egyptian and Persian as well. By the second quarter of the fifteenth century, tiles and ceramics decorated in the blue-and-white style were common. In Turkey, the tiles in the Murad II mosque at Edirne, capital of the Ottoman Turks before the conquest of Istanbul in 1453, of fine white ware and carefully painted in shades of cobalt blue, are a combination of Chinese and Islamic motifs.[20] The Chinese elements are based on both fourteenth and fifteenth-century porcelain which presupposes that the potters had access to a number of actual pieces of blue-and-white. These tiles are the bridge between the earlier Turkish "Miletus" ware (also showing signs of Chinese influence in their design) and the beginning of the pottery industry at Iznik.

When the potteries at Iznik started producing a fine white ware decorated in underglaze blue is a matter for conjecture; but certainly by the beginning of the sixteenth century the potteries were well established (Figure 10). The early Iznik wares are formal in design, owing much to contemporary manuscript illumination, and possessing shapes of metallic origin; by the beginning of the sixteenth century the designs become freer and more painterly, and turquoise is added to the cobalt blue along with olive green. By the end of the second quarter of the sixteenth century, the palette is extended to include manganese purple, gray, and sage green. And in the second half of the century, with the addition of a brilliant relief red and viridian green, the fully-fledged Iznik court style emerges. Throughout, the influence of Chinese blue-and-white is constant; but it is a more thoughtful response than that of either Syria or Egypt. The blue-and-white often provides the inspiration for Iznik polychrome designs, but the style evolves in a manner which is purely Turkish, and with an authority of its own.[21]

In Persia, with the sixteenth century "Kubachi" wares, the debt to China is more direct. In the seventeenth century, the "Kubachi" polychrome wares, while still deriving from the Chinese, become looser and include more specifically Persian motifs, often with figural subjects. On the other hand, seventeenth-century Persian ware of the Kirman type, with its composite white body, cobalt blue and clear glaze, often takes a Chinese blue-and-white design as a direct point of reference, transforming the details with sometimes ludicrous results (Figure 11). The Persian contribution in the finest pieces is the combination of Chinese subjects drawn in the Persian manner, with contrasting, lightly-incised plain white panels. The Persian pottery shows that seventeenth-century Chinese ware was reaching Persia in quantity. Persian copies showing a familiarity with the Transitional style, with landscapes painted in graded washes, were even exported to the

13a
64

72, 73

65
76

77, 78

79–85

79

Figure 9. *Flask*. China, Jingdezhen, Ming dynasty. 1552 A.D. Porcelain, with underglaze blue decoration; inscribed in Portuguese. The Walters Art Gallery, Baltimore.

Figure 11. *Dish*. Persia. Seventeenth century. Pottery with underglaze blue decoration. Diameter 30.2 cm. Courtesy, Museum of Fine Arts, Boston. Gift of Mr. and Mrs. George W. Wales, 95.431.

32

Figure 10. (*Catalogue no. 72*).
Bowl. Turkey, Iznik, Ottoman
dynasty. Early sixteenth century.
Pottery, underglaze blue
decoration. Height 13.1 cm.
Diameter 25.2 cm. The
Metropolitan Museum of Art.
Rogers Fund, 1932, 32.34.

East. A group of dishes in this style has been recorded from the Maldive Islands.[22] Dutch records mention that Persian pottery was shipped to Galle in Ceylon in 1652, and to Batavia in 1654.[23]

Although Chinese blue-and-white continued to be exported to the Near East in the sixteenth and seventeenth centuries, it appears to have had less effect than it did in Persia. In Egypt, the production of glazed ware was in sharp decline, and the demand for pottery met by Chinese, European or Turkish imports, or unglazed earthenware. In Syria, sixteenth-century tiles and pottery owed their inspiration more to Iznik ware than to Chinese blue-and-white; by the beginning of the seventeenth century, the Syrian industry was limited to producing poor-quality tiles. In Jerusalem, the major sixteenth-century enterprise was the manufacture of tiles, *in situ,* for the restoration of the Dome of the Rock. Again, the influence of blue-and-white was slight, the designs being basically a combination of Persian and Turkish elements. Nor did the Jerusalem work lead to the establishment of a local industry; instead, after completing the commission the potters moved off to Syria.

In Turkey, the Iznik potters were more responsive to early fifteenth-century blue-and-white than to contemporary Chinese imports, and subsequently worked from designs produced by the *nakkashane,* or Ottoman court designers. By the mid-seventeenth century, the potteries were in decline, due to lack of official patronage, producing feeble versions of earlier Iznik patterns, rather than responding to the novelty of Wanli and Transitional blue-and-white. That such seventeenth-century porcelain reached the Near East is certain, for much of it has been recorded in Syria. But the bulk of the *kraakporselein* would have bypassed the Mediterranean altogether, shipped in Portuguese *carracks* round the Cape of Good Hope and destined to make its impact on Europe instead.

NOTES

1. National Museum of Korea, *Special Exhibition of Cultural Relics Found off Sinan Coast,* Seoul, Korea, 1977; John Ayers, "The Discovery of a Yüan ship at Sinan, South-West Korea," *Oriental Art,* New Series, XXIV.1, London, 1978, pp. 79–85; Kim Ki-Woong, "The Shinan Shipwreck," *Museum,* XXXV.1, Paris, 1983, pp. 35–36; Donald Keith, "Shinan-gun," *INA Newsletter,* 6.3, College Station, Texas, 1979, pp. 2, 4; Youn Moo-Byong, "Recovery of Seabed Relics at Sinan and Its Results from the Viewpoint of Underwater Archaeology," tr. by Shigetaka Kaneko, *The Sunken Treasures off the Sinan Coast,* The Chunichi Shimbun, Tokyo, 1983, pp. 81–83.

2. Chung Yang Mo, "The Kinds of Ceramic Articles Discovered in Sinan and problems about them," *The Sunken Treasures off the Sinan Coast,* pp. 84–87.

3. The David vases have been published innumerable times; for excellent photographs of the vases including the inscription, and a translation and select bibliography, see, "The Ceramic Art of China," *Transactions of the Oriental Ceramic Society,* 1969–71, London, 1972, no. 138, pp. 101–102, Plates 94, 95.

4. Sir John Addis, *Chinese Ceramics from Datable Tombs and Some Other Dated Material: A Handbook,* London, 1978, p. 39, no. 27.

5. *The Sunken Treasures off the Sinan Coast,* p. 70, no. 58.

6. William Sorsby Ltd., London, *South-East Asian and Early Chinese Export Ceramics,* (sale catalogue), 1974, p. 23, no. 23; Leandro Locsin and Cecilia Locsin, *Oriental Ceramics Discovered in the Philippines,* Vermont, 1967, p. 100, no. 81.

7. John Ayers, "Some Chinese Wares of the Yüan period," *Transactions of the Oriental Ceramic Society,* 29, 1945–55, London, 1957, pp. 69–90.

8. Arthur Lane, "The Gagnières-Fonthill Vase: a Chinese porcelain of about 1300," *Burlington Magazine,* 103, 1961, pp. 124–132.

9. Laurence Sickman, "A Ch'ing-pai Porcelain Figure Bearing a Date," *Archives of the Chinese Art Society of America,* XV, 1961.

10. "The Ceramic Art of China," *Transactions of the Oriental Ceramic Society,* no. 134, Color Plate C.

11. Addis, *op. cit.,* pp. 48–55, no. 30. See also a *meiping* vase, in R. Y. L. d'Argencé, *Treasures from the Shanghai Museum,* Shanghai Museum and the Asian Art Museum of San Francisco, San Francisco, 1983, p. 163, no. 91, Color Plate XXIX; W. Watson, *The Genius of China,* Royal Academy, London, 1973, nos. 364, 365, 369, 370.

12. Kikutaro Saito, "The Yuan Blue-and-White and the Yuan Drama in the Middle of the 14th Century, Part I," *Kobijutsu,* 18, Tokyo, 1967, pp. 25–41; Kikutaro Saito, "The Yuan Blue-and-White…, Part II," *Kobijutsu,* 19, Tokyo, 1967, pp. 52–74.

13. The smaller fourteenth-century wares also reached the Near East; for instance, nos. (12a, b, c), in the exhibition, from Fustat; and

more sherds from the same site in the Freer Gallery Study Collection.

14. Ma Huan, *Ying-yai sheng-lan, 'The Overall Survey of the Ocean's Shores'* [1433], Translated and edited by J. V. G. Mills, Cambridge, 1970.

15. *Ibid.,* pp. 85, 97, 129, 153.

16. Sir Harry Garner, "Blue-and-White of the Middle Ming Period," *Transactions of the Oriental Ceramic Society,* 1951–53, London, 1954, pp. 61–72, Plates 17–19; Sir Harry Garner, *Oriental Blue and White,* London, 1954, pp. 28–30, Plates 43–45; John Pope, *Chinese Porcelains from the Ardebil Shrine,* Freer Gallery of Art, Smithsonian Institution, Washington, D.C., 1956, pp. 121–123, Plates 75–77.

17. The Arabs were responsible for supplying incense, a product of South Arabia; Ma Huan, *op. cit.,* pp. 152–153, states that the Chinese expedition bartered porcelain and other commodities for frankincense and myrrh at Dhofar.

18. Clare Le Corbeiller, *China Trade Porcelain: Patterns of Exchange,* The Metropolitan Museum of Art, New York, 1974, pp. 12–16.

19. Soame Jenyns, "The Chinese porcelains in the Topkapu Saray, Istanbul," *Transactions of the Oriental Ceramic Society,* 1964–66, London, 1967, pp. 48–49, Plate 37a, b.

20. John Carswell, "Six Tiles," *Islamic Art in The Metropolitan Museum of Art,* Edited by R. Ettinghausen, The Metropolitan Museum of Art, New York, 1972, pp. 99–124.

21. John Pope, "Chinese Influence on Iznik Pottery, a re-examination of an old problem," *Islamic Art in the Metropolitan Museum of Art,* pp. 125–139; Walter Denny, "Blue-and-White Islamic Pottery on Chinese Themes," *Boston Museum Bulletin,* LXXI, 368, Museum of Fine Arts, Boston, 1974, pp. 79–97.

22. John Carswell, "China and Islam in the Maldive Islands," *Transactions of the Oriental Ceramic Society,* 1975–77, London, 1977.

23. J. Volker, *Porcelain and the Dutch East India Company as Recorded in the Dagh-Registers of Batavia Castle, those of Hirada and Deshima and other Contemporary Papers, 1602–1682,* Rijksmuseum voor Volkenkunde, Leiden, 1954.

The European Imitators and Their Wares

Edward A. Maser

The admiration felt for these mysterious productions of the magical East, however they may have come to the West, prompted not only imitation of their forms and decoration, but even more, research into their composition with manufacture in mind.[1] This was prompted as much by commercial considerations as anything else — the cost of imported Eastern ware was in proportion with their rarity — but something else tantalized the minds and energies of Renaissance princes — the magical properties attributed to these vessels. They had, for instance, long been supposed to crackle and break if they came into contact with poison. While this may seem a very practical idea for a prince from the age of Machiavelli, it was probably as much this association with the magical, with the idea that all things in the physical world had some connection with the supernatural world — with the world of astrology and alchemy in short — which prompted princes to collect the few pieces to come their way and, in one documented instance, to try to make them.

ITALY

The influence of Chinese blue-and-white on the ceramics of Europe came more by way of the wares of the Islamic Near East and North Africa than by any amount of Chinese products, which came in only relatively isolated examples until the fifteenth century. From Egypt and by way of the Iberian peninsula, tin-glazed earthenware instead was the actual bearer of Far and Near Eastern decorative motifs. Because it arrived in Italy by way of the island of Majorca, it was called *majolica* and its manufacture began to flourish on the Italian peninsula from the beginning of the century. By 1500 it was being produced in a host of centers like Florence, Faenza, Venice and Urbino, but by the beginning of the seventeenth century the greatest days of Italian *majolica* were over, although its influence on the rest of Europe remained.

The forms and decoration of the Italian wares derived from and were refinements on those from the Hispanic centers. Since *majolica* is tin-glazed earthenware, the basic glaze provided a white surface on which the colored decoration was then applied (cobalt blue, iron red, copper green, antimony yellow and manganese purple), after which a clear glaze was applied. Italian productions worthy of note were the blue-and-white "oak-leaf" jar of fifteenth-century Florence (a decorative motif of Gothic origin) or the pharmacy jar, the *albarello*, decorated with palmette or peacock feather patterns of Near Eastern origin. It had become the fashion to paint them with fanciful designs and bright colors as decorations for pharmacies, which were, at the time, meeting places and informal social centers. In Venice, by nature of its commercial importance in the trade with the East, influences from China appeared very early, not only in blue-and-white but in a mode of decoration of sketchily painted vines and flowers called

Figure 12. (*Catalogue no. 51*). *Still Life*. 1663. Willem Kalf (1619–1693). Oil on canvas. 60.4 x 50.2 cm. The Cleveland Museum of Art. Purchase, Leonard C. Hanna Jr. Bequest, 62.292.

alla porcellana, derived ultimately from Iznik pottery and Ming blue-and-white porcelain. Fashions in decoration spread quickly along the Italian peninsula, so that all these motifs can be found among the many other *majolica* centers. In spite of humble materials, the potters and painters of *majolica* often produced superb works of art treasured and admired even in their own day — chiefly for their decoration — and are still today regarded as one of the finest achievements of the Renaissance in Italy.

The best known attempt to produce porcelain in imitation of the Chinese[2] is provided by Francesco I de' Medici, Grand Duke of Tuscany (reigned 1574–87) in his court workshops in Florence (Figure 13).[3] He was apparently not content simply to acquire pieces of Oriental porcelain as various members of his family had done before him, but actually sought the means to reproduce it. In this he was different from all the noble collectors about whom some record exists, like, for instance, the Duke of Normandy who in 1363 was known to possess examples of Oriental wares, or the Duc de Berry in 1416, or Charles VII of France in 1447. Records (and only records, for no pieces of porcelain can be specifically associated with any of these examples) show that in 1461, the Sultan of Egypt sent Doge Pasquale Malipiero of Venice twenty pieces of porcelain as a gift and that Lorenzo de' Medici, *il Magnifico*, received a similar gift from Egypt in 1487.[4] But it is not until the latter part of the sixteenth century that we find actual pieces still in the remains of princely collections, the oldest documented ones those from the Kunstkammer of Archduke Ferdinand of Tyrol, now in the Viennese art collections today displayed at Schloss Ambras outside of Innsbruck from which they had originally come.[5] Through this inherited collection and his own assiduous collecting activity, Oriental porcelain in considerable quantities was found in the vast art and curiosity collections of Emperor Rudolph II in Prague,[6] whose inventories reveal many examples of *Indische Porzellan* ("porcelain from the Indies"), all of it Chinese or Near Eastern imitations.[7]

We know today, in spite of the legends and negative judgments during the past, that the emperor, one of the most fascinating figures in the history of art, was not accumulating a meaningless mass of material, artistic or otherwise, but seemed actually to be attempting to collect systematically an encyclopedic survey of all aspects of the natural world (including its monstrosities, its *lusi naturae*) but also all productions of human society, and its artifacts, or as this category was called its *artificialia* (the products of man's intellect and invention), as opposed to *naturalia* (the works of Nature).[8] Something as fine and beautiful as Oriental porcelain, with its translucent resonant body and its exotic decoration, so different from the earthenware of the West, would naturally find its place among the wonders of such a grandiose overview of God and man's creativity.

Related by marriage to the house of Hapsburg, Francesco de' Medici, the introspective, highly cultivated heir to the Grand Duchy of Tuscany created by his father, Cosimo I, who was, like his cousin, Rudolf, also greatly interested in the variety and the fascinating, not to say magical, properties of the world's wonders.[9] Like his Tuscan countrymen, his interest apparently went more toward artifice, toward embellishing and improving on Nature, and in trying to understand its creations by attempting to imitate them through research into their components and then combining them. Toward this end he greatly expanded the court workshops which his father had established until he was forced to move them from Palazzo Vecchio to the Casino di San Marco away from the center of Florence. Here in the famous *Fonderia*, he, himself, enjoyed working with the lapidaries, metal workers, distillers of perfume and other essences, and

Figure 13. *Portrait of Grand Duke Francesco de' Medici.* 1586. Pastorini. Italy, Florence, Medici factory. Soft-paste porcelain. Museo Nationale, Florence.

— relevant to this discussion — the potters and chemists who sought to match this mysterious material from the distant and legendary kingdoms of the East, half glass, half earthenware, unlike any material known to all the experts of the West.

The practical aspects of this search have been discussed in every publication dealing with the origins of porcelain making in the West. Francesco's interest in its production, dealt with by local scholars, has been as well, so that the various attempts at reproducing the material, some of the craftsmen involved, the fact that their search only succeeded through the help of a Levantine who had "traveled in the Indies," do increase our knowledge greatly but do not explain the Prince's interest in it.[10] It is, however, known that all means of converting the materials of Nature into artifacts did interest him. His collection of objects — vessels, chalices, etc. — made of rare and exotic materials displayed in the cupboards of his private studio, the *Studiolo*, in the old palace, itself a wonder-work of painting and sculpture organized in a complex iconographic program, is though well-known not yet fully explained, and perhaps never will be.[11] That the *Fonderia* finally did produce what the age thought was true porcelain, not the counterfeits made probably of opaque milk glass which Venice produced, *porcellana contrefatta*,[12] may have been prompted by considerations that have their roots in the primordial scientific concerns of the day, in alchemy.

This pseudo-science, today looked at with a certain respect, for within it and through it developed the modern science of chemistry among others, was largely based on the belief that the raw materials of Nature could, given the right process, be changed one into the other. The most glamorous and desirable of such a conversion was, of course, the transmutation of base metal into gold (and, indeed, the eventual discovery of the method of making true Oriental porcelain was actually made by a "gold-maker" in Dresden, Johann Friedrich Böttger). This idea was based on the Aristotelian theory of the four elements: earth, air, fire and water, and the *prima materia*, a sort of fifth element, out of which they all are made and which they all contain. It seemed to have a definite relation to and might even have been porcelain, this magical substance out of the East. How much more lofty was such an aim as this, than mere commercial gain as being the motivating factor in this search. Made as it was out of and by means of all the "elements" this substance led the searchers somewhat away from the facts (today we know that it was the specific materials as much as the process which determined the manufacture of true porcelain) toward ever more esoteric distillations, sublimations and combinations. Innate Florentine common sense, however, prompted the prince to use ceramic experts and by 1582, success was achieved (Figure 14) apparently through the fortuitous use of clay from Vicenza which contained a certain proportion of kaolin.

What Francesco de' Medici and his co-workers achieved was not the porcelain of China, but what is today called "soft-paste" or *pâte tendre* porcelain, something half-way between earthenware and true porcelain.[13] Yet it was a triumph, for their intrinsic beauty alone would justify such a term. With their often homely sixteenth-century Italian shapes (Figure 15), like the typical Italian oil and vinegar bottles with their opposed openings, called by the witty Florentines *la suocera*, "the mother-in-law," (the fact that oil and vinegar do not mix represented by the opposed mouths of the joined bottles, being like mothers who rarely see eye-to-eye with those who marry their children) joined to the simple blue decoration usually as often Persian or Turkish as it is Far Eastern, and even sometimes based on Italian Renaissance ornament popular in Florence at the 92

Figure 14. *Plate*. Italy, Florence, Medici factory. c. 1580. Soft-paste porcelain. The Cleveland Museum of Art, John L. Severance Fund, 49.489.

Figure 15. *Oil and vinegar flask with silver mounts (suocera)*. Italy, Florence, Medici factory. Soft-paste porcelain. Österreichisches Museum für Angewandte Kunst, Vienna.

time, the productions of the Medici workshops are today properly revered as the first successful attempt of which we have evidence to produce the prized porcelains of the East. The output of the Florentine manufactury was small — only about sixty pieces, almost all in public collections today, are known — so their influence on subsequent developments in Europe was equally small. Yet as evidence of the primacy of Florence in the search for the means for making true porcelain, these few bottles, ewers, plates and bowls represent a landmark in the history of ceramics. As has been pointed out, and not solely with regard to Duke Francesco's activity, it is a fallacy to assume that mistaken or unsuccessful enterprises are necessarily bad for they can often be the beginning of the path to the discovery of truth.[14] Just as alchemy can be said to have led to chemistry, so did Medici porcelain point the way toward not only true porcelain but to such more esteemed modern accomplishments as the science of mineralogy and its related fields.

It is interesting that all the Medici ware was decorated in cobalt blue on white, the one known exception in polychrome has been strongly doubted by scholars of the subject.[15] The long tradition of polychromed Italian *majolica*, one of the great achievements of Italian art during the fifteenth and sixteenth centuries, might have suggested to the ceramists of the *Fonderia* that other colors be used. Yet only sometimes was manganese purple used for outlines, otherwise all was in blue-and-white.

HOLLAND

While all this was going on in Florence, where after the death of Francesco de' Medici in 1587 the production of Medici porcelain struggled on fitfully for another thirty-odd years, at first in Florence and then, apparently, in Pisa, the supply of genuine porcelain from the East was steadily increasing. It had been first the Portuguese who brought more and more shiploads of Chinese wares to the ports of the Mediterranean and the Atlantic. During the early decades of the seventeenth century it was the maritime and mercantile activity, soon to become paramount upon the seas, of the new Dutch republic which took over the trade. The ever-increasing supply did not, however, necessarily lower the price of these arduously imported wares, so great was the appetite of the wealthy and powerful of Europe for the blue-and-white productions of the East (Figure 12). This taste, which soon became a fashion, not to say a mania, steadily increasing as the seventeenth century progressed, also worked to the advantage of the local ceramics industries of Europe as well, in the case of Holland at mid-century, for the tiny town of Delft near Rotterdam.[16] Here, because the local brewing industry was declining, there were suitable quarters already available for the many potters who now settled there, and who often took the names of the former breweries, and their attached taverns, such as "The Three Bells," "At the Sign of the Greek A," or "The Golden Flowerpot" for their own undertakings. They found a large and eager market for those of their products which imitated the popular blue-and-white decoration of the expensive imports, in spite of the ever increasing supply from the East. Blue-and-white wares were produced at Delft and elsewhere (Haarlem, Dordrecht, etc.) from about the second quarter of the seventeenth century on, to such an extent that almost any earthenware decorated with blue-and-white produced in Holland (and later elsewhere in northern Europe and in England) was called "delftware," a misleading term still in use today.

Imitating the blue-and-white decoration of the Wanli period (1573–1619 A.D.) and of the following "Transitional" period between the end of the Ming dynasty

97, 98

Figure 16. *Wig-stand*. Holland, Delft. Late seventeenth century. Delftware. Mark: SVE [Samuel van Eenhorn]. The Victoria and Albert Museum, London.

and the accession of Kangxi, Dutch potters produced such fine, thin earthenware 96, 97 which had been given, over the white tin-glaze and the blue decoration, a clear lead-glaze known as *Kwaart* that they did often bear a close resemblance to the Chinese originals. Indeed, the Dutch referred to these productions as *porselein* or *porcelein*. In their minds it was solely the physical appearance and not the composition of their wares which justified this nomenclature. At first almost slavishly copying the well-known Chinese types, they gradually, as the century progressed, introduced Dutch figure subjects and landscapes, and typically Baroque European forms and ornament (Figure 16). So famous and so widespread did the Dutch delftware become that it, in its turn, was widely imitated in all other ceramics factories in Europe.

Figure 17. *Dish*. Germany, probably Frankfurt. Seventeenth century. Tin-glazed earthenware. The Metropolitan Museum of Art, Bequest of Mrs. Mary Mandeville Johnston, 1914, 14.102.380.

GERMANY

Most notable among the other factories were those established in such port cities as Hamburg, but even more in Central Germany along the Main river at Frankfurt and the nearby town of Hanau.[17] Frankfurt, an Imperial free city renowned for its various handicrafts, and even more for its fairs which were famous throughout Europe, had its first fine earthenware factory in 1666 and began by imitating the productions of Delft, or at least used the same Chinese models as did the Dutch (Figure 17). By virtue of the quality of its wares, its location and its 100, 101 commercial connections, Frankfurt productions became immensely popular, 102, 103 even in Holland, flourishing during the latter half of the seventeenth century and the early eighteenth. Like the potters at Delft, the Frankfurt manufactories added an additional lead-glaze which gave a brilliant surface to their wares which resembled the Chinese models. Here too such fine wares were referred to as *porzellan* and, as a matter of fact, the largest and most famous factory in Frankfurt was known as the *Porzellanhof*, although as in Delft, true porcelain was never produced there.

FRANCE

Figure 18. *Ewer*. French, Nevers. 1650–1680. Faience. The Victoria and Albert Museum, London.

With a long medieval tradition of pottery-making behind it, France and its many potteries scattered throughout the country and its constant contact with Italy was open to all the artistic influences emanating from it. The majority of its productions during the fifteenth and sixteenth centuries derive from there, although in such creations as the "Henri Deux" ware of Sainte Porchaire and the work of Bernard Palissy first done nearby and then in Paris, France made distinctive contributions of its own.[18] But the rising tide of imports from the East, through the 93, 95 Portuguese and the Dutch, soon made itself felt, first in the imitation of Eastern prototypes at potteries at Nevers, notably the use of *blu persan* in the so-called Persian decoration of its wares with birds and flowers usually painted in opaque white on a deep blue background, and secondly by the establishment of the French East India Company in 1664. From this time on French wares imitated the imported wares more and more. As Louis XIV gradually succeeded in making France the arbiter of taste throughout Europe during the latter half of the century and the activities of the French East India Company increased, soon even French designs began to be demanded from the far eastern potteries and a mutual influence developed. Yet the blue-and-white decorations on porcelain from the Near and Far East remained *the* fashionable mode of decoration (Figure 18) for it was considered quintessentially Chinese, so that when the Sun King decided to build a little pleasure house for his mistress, the Marquise de Montespan, on the grounds of Versailles, it was a *Trianon de porcelaine* which his architect, Louis Le

Vau, produced in 1670-71. Looking singularly un-Chinese, it was decorated throughout with less expensive tin-glazed ceramic tiles, all, like the interior decorations as well, in blue-and-white — the epitome of the Chinese taste.[19]

ENGLAND

Although the English had long preceded the French in establishing their East India Company around 1600 and had treasured the blue-and-white wares of the Orient from that time on to the extent of often mounting them in silver for both protection against damage and as an embellishment, in manufacture they more or less followed the developments on the Continent, notably Dutch and Italian ones.[20] During the seventeenth century, and especially after the ascension of William of Orange to the English throne in 1690, the proximity of Holland as well as the steadily growing increase in English trade upon the seas, encouraged the vogue for Chinese and Japanese porcelain, and their imitation by local potteries, especially delftware, particularly at Southwark and Lambeth (Figure 19). But in Staffordshire, the main pottery making region, these Dutch-inspired versions of Oriental blue-and-white were never produced. There, the search for refinement of both material and form such as the Eastern wares inspired, had led by the eighteenth century to the development of a fine white salt-glazed stoneware, often decorated with blue.

105–109

Figure 19. *Mug.* England, Southwark. 1630. Probably by Chistian Wilhelm. Delftware. Inscribed: "James and Elizabeth Greene Anno 1630. The gift is small: Goodwill is all." London Museum.

NOTES

1. Indispensible to any study of European ceramics and its relationship to Eastern wares is the monumental "dictionary of factories, artists, technical terms, et cetera" of William Bowyer Honey, *European Ceramic Art from the end of the Middle Ages to about 1815*, London, 1952, under such rubrics as "blue-and-white," "Chinese and Japanese influences," "Delft," "English earthenware, maiolica, delftware and stoneware," "Florence, porcelain," "Frankfort-am-Main," "Lambeth," "Nevers," etc. The best introduction to the origins of the appreciation, and the attempts at imitation of Oriental porcelain is Friedrich Hoffmann, *Das Porzellan*, Berlin, 1932, pp. 9–46; Donald F. Lach, *Asia in the Making of Europe*, II, *A Century of Wonder*, I, *The Visual Arts*, Chicago, 1970, pp. 104–109; and Hugh Honour, *Chinoiserie*, London, 1961, pp. 33–40.

2. The best discussion of Italian pottery and porcelain is Bernard Rackham, *Italian Maiolica*, London, 1952, rev. ed. 1963, and Arthur Lane, *Italian Porcelain*, London, 1954, both in the series of the Faber and Faber Monographs on Pottery and Porcelain, edited by W. B. Honey, in which several other volumes dealing with the ceramics of other countries are also pertinent to the theme of this exhibition and its catalogue.

3. Luciano Berti, *Il Principe dello Studiolo*, Florence, 1967, p. 57, note 22.

4. Giuseppe Morazzoni, *Le porcellane italiane*, Milan-Rome, 1935, pp. 15–33.

5. Elizabeth Schleicher, *Die Kunst- und Wunderkammern der Habsburger*, Vienna-Munich-Zurich, 1979, pp. 73–136.

6. Alfons Lhotsky, *Die Geschichte der Sammlungen, Festschrift des Kunsthistorischen Museums zur Feier des Fünfzigjährigen Bestandes*, II, 1, pp. 237–298. For the English-speaking reader, see: R.J.W. Evans, *Rudolf II and his World*, Oxford, 1973, particularly Chapter 5: "Rudolf and the Fine Arts."

7. Rotraud Bauer and Herbert Haupt (herausg.), "Das Kunstkammerinventar Kaiser Rudolfs II., 1607–1611," *Jahrbuch der Kunsthistorischen Sammlungen in Wien*, 72, Vienna, 1976, entire issue.

8. Erwin Neumann, "Das Inventar der rudolfinischen Kunstkammer von 1607/11," *Analecta Reginensia*, I, (Queen Christina of Sweden, documents and studies), Stockholm, 1966.

9. Berti, *op. cit.*, pp. 43–59.

10. G. Liverani, *Catalogo delle porcellane dei Medici*, Faenze, 1936.

11. Mario Bucci, *Lo Studiolo di Francesco* I, Florence, 1965.

12. G. Morazzoni, *op. cit.*, pp. 3–8.

13. W. B. Honey, *op. cit.*, p. 495.

14. Eric Cochrane, *Florence in the Forgotten Centuries, 1527–1800*, Chicago and London, 1973, p. xiv.

15. W. B. Honey, *op. cit.*, p. 231

16. C. H. deJonge, *Delft Ceramics*, London, 1970, p. 32 ff.

17. Adolf Feulner, *Frankfurter Fayencen*, Berlin, 1935.

18. Arthur Lane, *French Faience*, London, 1948, p. 10 f.

19. Hugh Honour, *Chinoiserie*, London, 1961, pp. 53–63, and *passim*.

20. The literature on English wares is large and constantly enlarging. The various volumes in the Faber & Faber monograph series are recommended to the reader and student alike, especially W.B. Honey, *English Pottery and Porcelain*, London, 1933 (and later editions) and B. Rackham, *Early Staffordshire Pottery*, London, 1951.

Hispanic Blue-and-White Faience in the Chinese Style

Jean McClure Mudge

In the modern era, potters in Portugal, Spain and Mexico initiated the West's imitation of Chinese export blue-and-white porcelain thirty to forty years before their counterparts anywhere in Europe or England. From the late sixteenth and throughout the seventeenth century, Iberians and Mexicans added blue-and-white *majolica* clearly indebted to Chinese models to industries drawing upon a number of earlier styles. Three general categories were the result: faiences largely faithful to eastern prototypes, others which incorporated Chinese forms and decorations equally with national traditions, and still others which allowed the latter motifs to prevail with mere hints of an Oriental ancestry.

With a few exceptions, this variety of borrowings follows a chronological order from the 1580s to about 1700, when preferences for polychrome wares diminished demand for blue-and-white. In general, earlier objects closely echo the Chinese, in decoration if not always in form, while later ones more strongly announce their country of origin, although native elements were clearly present from the start. These national factors are incorporated with the Chinese so idiosyncratically that Portuguese, Spanish and Mexican blue-and-white faience in the Oriental mode are easily distinguished. The prevalence of Chinese models plays a primary role in their adaptation by each group of native potters.

PORTUGAL

The availability of late Ming dynasty export blue-and-white porcelain is still evident in Portugal and for good reason: from the late fifteenth century and into the sixteenth century, she pioneered Europe's trade in the Far East. Today that fact is commemorated by collections of porcelains in museums and private homes, but also quite dramatically by a gem of a room, the *Casa das Porçolanas* — so called in a 1704 inventory — in the Santos Palace, now the French Embassy in Lisbon.[1] Here in a space four meters square, a pyramidal ceiling (seven and a half meters high at its apex), is covered on all four sides with 261 dishes and plates, held in precarious place by iron clasps, on a ground of floral volutes of sculpted and gilded wood. Most of these are blue-and-white dishes of the sixteenth and early seventeenth centuries, attesting to the taste initiated by King Manuel I (1469–1521) from the first decades of the 1500s and continued by his successors. Many of the dishes are over fifty centimeters in diameter. A small number are of the late eighteenth century.[2] Only four enameled polychrome pieces appear, tucked in toward the top of a mid-sixteenth-century pendant largely decorated with blue-and-white.[3]

This *Casa* is a microcosm of a rich variety of high quality, though stock, blue-and-white, passing from trader to customer to Portuguese potter. Estimates of Chinese export entering the country in the sixteenth century are high (as early as the 1530s, 40–60,000 pieces of porcelain per year),[4] yet much of it was re-exported to northern buyers in Antwerp and increasingly, Amsterdam; also, it was expensive. If incentives to imitate were immediately present, probably such copying began right away. But the youthful state of Portugal's potting industry as well as the lack of documented near-copies of the early sixteenth century and of contemporary pottery records prevents attributing such imitation until the late 1500s.

Then, however, in 1582, King Philip II of Spain and Portugal (1527–1598), an avid ceramic collector and student of Asia, wrote from Lisbon to his daughters at home, referring to faiences, called "*porcelanas,*" or porcelains, which he said were "of a new style, at least I have not seen them until now."[5] Philip's reference helps to clarify a possible confusion: blue-and-white faience could be called porcelain, initially referred to in quotes, because it copies Chinese porcelain. He also implies that the Portuguese potter was making export imitations before the Spanish.

Using "porcelain" to denote Portuguese faience in the Chinese style apparently became common over the next decades. In 1619, nearly forty years later, the craft guilds of Lisbon erected arches for a visit of King Philip III (1578–1621) of Spain (II of Portugal) to the capital. The potters' monumental, ornately decorated arch included a number of pots and full-sized figures, some of saints, others allegorical. One of the latter held a "porcelain" vase "of the kind made in Lisbon, a copy of the Chinese." The quality of this ware was proudly celebrated in verse:

> Here most gracious Majesty
> We offer you the pilgrim art
> Made in the Lusitanian Kingdom
> Which formerly China sold us at such high prices!

As if to compete with China abroad as well as at home, the arch included a waterfront scene in which Portuguese ships unloaded Chinese porcelain and European vessels took aboard Portuguese ceramics. The harbor view was labeled: "Ours also go to various regions of the world."[6] Portugal's "pilgrim art," then, was soon exported as the first faience in the Chinese style to reach Europe. Though Persian "Kubachi" ware was contemporary with the Portuguese, it was not marketed for Europe in quantity.[7] Also contemporary, Mexico's Puebla ware was used almost exclusively in the New World. Portuguese "porcelain" was then a pioneer, appearing thirty or forty years before Dutch delftware was made in quantity and well before similar English and European blue-and-white.

Lisbon, port of entry for Chinese export ware and of exit for the country's faience copies, was the uncontested center of Portugal's production. Later, Oporto (today Porto) farther north and Estremoz on the Spanish border may also have produced some.[8] A small bowl (Figure 20) is the earliest dated Portuguese "porcelain" to survive. Less than twenty faiences similarly bearing Arabic numerals on their bases, or more rarely on the obverse side, are known for the whole seventeenth century.[9] They are indispensable for helping divide the blue-and-white into three, perhaps four groups, roughly corresponding to each quarter of the century.[10]

The first period, c. 1600–1625, includes wares which attempted to be faithful to the Chinese model, but which inevitably reveal their Portuguese nature. The painter's eye had been accustomed to Islamic, Italian, Spanish, even Flemish styles, especially from tilework, one of Portugal's most developed arts. Further, a lack of training in Chinese brushwork, the absence of pattern books and the ignorance of traditional associations of once symbolic themes and motifs made

Figure 20. *Bowl*. Portugal. Marked 1621. Faience. Height 11.3 cm. Diameter 21.5 cm. Museu Nacional de Soares dos Reis, Porto.

Figure 21. *Dish*. Portugal. 1600–1625. Faience. Diameter 38.5 cm. Mark on base: LA and a cross [possibly signifying the owner]. Museu Nacional de Arte Antiga, Lisbon.

Figure 22. *Plate*. Portugal. 1600–1650. Faience. Diameter 35 cm. The Victoria and Albert Museum, London.

any "copy" far from true. Also, from the start, certain domestic forms not produced in Chinese export were recipients of the new decoration, especially *albarellos* (drug jars) and two and four large-handled jars. Other native forms later to receive Chinese decoration were bottles, porringers, basins, tureens, oval or lobe-shaped boxes, inkwells and even buttons. (*Guan*-type jars and teapots, of course, were in imitation of Chinese shapes.) Despite the hybridization of the export ware, the results are vigorous, definite and appealing.

For the most part, carrack ware prototypes (c. 1580–1650) bore the decorations most imitated. (Interestingly, the Dutch gave the Portuguese word for ship, *carrack*, to this ware, acknowledging that Portugal was its first western importer.) As with the bowl in Figure 20, the dishes in Figures 21 and 22 follow a common Portuguese category of copying carrack's paneled borders with a central land-landscape view of animals, birds and flowers, and less often, small figures. But a fresh interpretation is clear: the linear emphasis despite at least two tones of blue, the enlarged subjects, the movement (the dishes are electric with curving lines; in Figure 21, one buck has a leg raised above the other's back while ribbons swirl about the border scrolls), and the freer spacing of the reserves (the interim ribbon and S-shaped line-panels are larger than their Chinese prototypes). The water fowl in Figure 22 is more clearly separated in its center than are the bucks in Figure 21, but both are more integrated with their borders than the usual Chinese dish. The latter often has a six or eight-sided central medallion elaborated with *ruyi* or cloud motifs in each corner. In the two Portuguese dishes one may compare two distinct qualities of ware made in the same period.

During the next quarter, the tendency increased to produce faience even less inspired by the Chinese. Once started, the Portuguese potter may have capitalized on the slow decline of Chinese models in the 1650s until a virtual end of quality export in the period 1660–1680. Figure 23, a bottle of semi-Oriental influence, is nonetheless thicker in body and bolder in design. In fact, were it not for its Chinese figure with parasol, other features of this piece would make it wholly Portuguese: its shape, flowers and dominant borders on neck, shoulder and base—all three akin to the Italianate borders of acanthus scrolls on local tiles. The parasol was now so inevitably paired with Orientals that none, it seems, left home without them. The parasolled Chinese is a clear mark of Iberian *chinoiserie*, not a borrowing from export.

On plates, borders still echoed carrack paneling (Figure 24), but like their predecessors, they were much more active in their vigorous scrollwork and bold lines. Central designs were wholly changed and now included knights, Portuguese arms, mythological nudes, women in farthingales, family names, native motifs such as lions and rabbits (the latter are equally Oriental or Hispanic) or the ubiquitous, and, for the Chinese, oversize figure-with-parasol, as on the bottle. Still another feature on plates of this period is a totally open border in which a typical design features tree trunks, rather than the entire tree, and Chinese either standing, seated or reclining. The center of such plates repeats the border motifs in a delicate painting style, a repetition rare in Chinese models of the period. The smooth edges of such dishes bear no resemblance to the foliate rims of carrack ware. Also, in some examples, aqua replaces the blue.[11]

The movement toward a national blue-and-white style only faintly echoing the Chinese could become, in the third quarter of the seventeenth century, inspired anecdote, as shown in one highly painted dish (Figure 25), dated 1660. Familiar but previously unpaired motifs appear in a whimsical whole. From the central nude at her toilette, a Renaissance subject, two concentric circles of

Figure 23. *Bottle*. Portugal. c. 1650. Faience. Height 25 cm. Museu Nacional de Arte Antiga, Lisbon.

Figure 24. *Plate*. Portugal. c. 1640–1660. Faience. Height 5 cm. Diameter 27.6 cm. Museu Nacional de Soares dos Reis, Porto.

kneeling or standing Chinese alternate with rabbits or small houses (possibly the formulaic façade of country Portuguese chapels).[12] At the outer base, a parasol shades one man while two in each circle are protected by trees with acanthus-leaved, "lampshade" branches. The detailed painting in two delicate shades of blue, as well as the thirteen flattened oval reserves dividing the two borders, just saves the design from excess. Its owner's initials, not the potter's, are on the reverse, as was customary.

This third period, which often blends with the fourth, also had more standard wares. Certain plate borders with *aranhoes* or "spiders" were so-called from leaf or diamond-shaped motifs arranged quarterly from which emerged curling lines akin to insect legs. Alternating with the "spiders" are paired pomegranates with palmettes sharing a stem and pair of leaves. A variant motif is a set or trio of paired, flattened fern leaves alternating with chrysanthemum "spiders." A similar fern style was popular in Spain, whether a model for the Portuguese or vice versa is unknown. Typically, with all these borders, a central Chinese figure sits or stands, or a Portuguese ship, lion or single bust is featured.

Shaped jars of this period, often imitating the *guan*, have divided areas of decoration from top to bottom, like the Chinese. However, their featured subjects may or may not be Oriental. Whatever they are — elephants, parrots, dogs or busts — they are outsize for eastern taste. And their borders are more Italianate than Chinese.

A late seventeenth-century plate in blue and yellow, now at the Museu de Arte Antiga, summarizes the preceding periods while it also points to the next century's predominant interest in polychrome faience.[13] Its border, paneled like car-

Figure 25. *Plate.* Portugal. 1660. Faience. Diameter 41 cm. Mark on base: D NE S 1660. Museu Nacional de Arte Antiga, Lisbon.

rack, nonetheless bears the "spiders" and ferns of the third period. In the center, Abraham with sword raised is about to sacrifice Isaac. But in this era, more purely Portuguese dishes were produced. Metalwork forms, especially scalloped edges or lobed bodies, joined flat ware. On these later pieces, the central design sometimes extends into the border area, reducing it to a thin decoration on the object's edge. Seventy-five years earlier, the height of Portugal's China trade had occurred, but not until the late seventeenth century did her production of "*porcelana*" in the Chinese idiom finally reflect that decline. She had produced a range of wares in that style which in the Hispanic world only Mexico could rival.

SPAIN

Even though Spain officially ruled Portugal in the period 1580–1640, the control was political, not cultural, and the two countries produced ceramics of a significantly different sort. From present knowledge, Spain's production of blue-and-white faience echoing Chinese export, which the Spanish also called "*porcelana*," was neither as wide-ranging in form nor as varied in decoration; in short, there apparently was less of it. Perhaps the ware was not as popular as that of Portugal. Choice must have played a strong role in a country with a venerable ceramic industry, active since the twelfth century, much older than that of her neighbor. Spain had the expertise to produce anything she might want, short of porcelain itself.[14]

Was there more export ware in Spain to satisfy demand without copying? From the best evidence, not as much Chinese export porcelain reached Spain as it did her colony in Mexico (see below). Only a few paintings show such wares, in contrast to the Dutch in whose still-lifes carrack ware is a favorite prop (Figure 12).[15] One should think, then, that potential Spanish demand for imitations would have been high. The Catholic scholar-priest Ajofrín, in writing of the potteries of Talavera observed, "...they procure Chinese porcelain in order to imitate them." But how much and how often? Further, a Talavera potter, Francisco Muñoz de la Ballesta, attempted to establish a kiln in Vaciamadrid, where he would monopolize "Chinese painting," but did so only by inciting endless protests and complaints, suggesting that at least in his time (unspecified in the source), such ware had a market.[16]

According to sherd finds, the Castilian centers of Talavera and El Puente del Arzobispo in central Spain were the major producers of imitation Chinese blue-and-white. Since both cities are quite near the Tajo (Tagus) River, which begins 250–300 miles to the west in the same bay as Lisbon, possibly Portuguese imports from China and Portuguese imitations influenced them. Though a substantial number of Spanish "*porcelanas*" may have been produced in their heyday, and many remain, these survivors exhibit a narrow range, especially in decoration. If other types are extant, they are in private hands and have not been well publicized.

Before the modern era, however, a certain taste for Chinese ceramics had been indirectly stimulated by the Arabs in Spain. Their caliphate once extended from Persia to most of the Iberian Peninsula, and Arabic influence, from the eighth to the fifteenth centuries, left a permanent mark. (In this era, Moslem ceramic technology and design was also brought to Spain but not to Portugal.) Doubtless Arab trade with China led to pieces of Tang dynasty *sancai*, three-color lead-glazed earthenware, being brought to Spain, influencing Iberian potters. Their *cuerda seca* ("dry cord" or "plain line") faience, first produced by Andalusians in the eleventh and twelfth centuries, isolated areas of honey-brown, green and blue with simple black or dark-red lines, the whole clearly echoing *sancai*.[17] In addition, the Arabs' exportation of cobalt blue to the West as well as to the East prepared the Spanish for China's own use of "Muhammadan blue." When Europe's trade with China began, the Spanish had long been accustomed to the beauty of blue-and-white. Perhaps because they preferred more familiar designs in the Hispano-Moresque or Mudéjar (combined Islamic and Christian), Italian or Flemish styles, carrack wares were less appealing in Spain than they were to the nascent Portuguese potters. The latter, on the coast, may also have seen a marketing opportunity the inland Spanish did not.

For whatever reason, and their usual rough potting is an additional one, the Spanish copies of Chinese wares appear to be few. Plates were the standard preferred form. Following Hispanic shapes, their sides slope smoothly to a rather deep interior. Besides plates, bowls, salts, inkwells, jugs, jars and chamber pots are known. Unlike Portuguese examples, only a few of the Spanish are dated, thus a specific chronology is difficult. Two-armed jars exist similar to the one in Francesco de Zurbarán's painting, *Saint Hugo in the Refectory*, decorated with the Franciscan emblem and the name of Sor. Ana Dorotea, the natural daughter of Emperor Rodolfo II, who confessed in 1628 and died in 1694. Zurbarán's dates are 1598–1662, providing a final year for the jar depicted, but still leaving a forty or fifty-year period of possible manufacture. Other Spanish carrack-like plates with the fern-and-daisy border described below bear the names of owners, as does one of about 1650. In the cavetto border at the top it reads, D [ON] BLAS DE FALERMOSA (Figure 26). But no Spanish "*porcelana*" has been recorded marked by a potter or kiln.[18]

As far as decorations are concerned, one late sixteenth-century style of Spanish blue-and-white has not previously been included in the "*porcelana*" category. However, the *mariposa* or butterfly pattern repeats in dark blue, rapidly painted strokes, typical Chinese motifs on a wide border with a central decoration, albeit in a particular Hispano-Moresque style. The central focus is usually birds, herons, deer and rabbits. (The Chinese and Spanish shared the bird and rabbit as subjects, but the spread-winged bird and the rampant or playful rabbit mark the Hispanic types.[19]) The whole composition and its subject matter are familiar late Ming designs. No Portuguese cousins are known. Probably the butterfly pattern derives its Orientalism via Arabic intermediaries (the deep form and lack of an orange glaze, an Italian contribution, indicate a Moorish heritage).[20] Not so, apparently, with other contemporaries. They are too close to Chinese prototypes or to Portuguese and Dutch copies. In fact, Talavera "*porcelanas*" have been nicknamed by the Spanish "Delft imitations," but some, like their Portuguese counterparts, apparently pre-date Delft and are therefore misnamed. Later ones could have been Dutch imitations, but if so, inexact. In fact, Spain's examples clearly differ from Delft but also, though less markedly, from the Portuguese. The Spanish stamp on blue-and-white "*porcelana*" is marked by a decided preference for one general border pattern with variations.

This dominant "*porcelana*" pattern, in imitation of carrack, is a border of six, eight, or sometimes ten lotus-shaped panels invariably containing three pairs of flattened fern leaves (Figures 26, 27). Separating the middle pair, is a *margarita* or daisy, possibly a westernized chrysanthemum. Between the panels are smaller ones with single ferns or ovals and dots. Later examples have a unified wreath border of stylized fern leaves alternating with birds or branches. (The earlier border bears some affinity with Portuguese examples, cf. Figure 20 and in Dos

Figure 26. *Plate*. Spain, Talavera. c. 1650. Faience. Diameter 38.1 cm. Mark on border of cavetto: D[ON] BLAS DE FALERMOSA. The Victoria and Albert Museum, London.

Figure 27. *Plate*. Spain, Talavera. 1700–1725. Faience, a fern-and-daisy variant. Diameter 25.7 cm. The Philadelphia Museum of Art, Philadelphia. Purchase: Special Museum Fund '07–46.

Santos 1960, p. 105, Figure 78.) Central decorations with the fern-and-daisy border include stylized landscapes of leafy vegetation with birds (especially swallows), deer, ducks and rabbits, these presumably on the earlier pieces (Figure 26). Later, busts and coats of arms replaced them. One large dish of the last sort is now at the Hispanic Society of America, unfortunately with its outer border removed but with similar leaves remaining, hinting that it was the fern-and-daisy. But the central coat of arms of De la Torre impaled with those of Bustamante and a plumed, grilled helmet above, denoting nobility, is minutely painted in light blue and is of exceptional quality. One Fausto de Bustamante, who married Eusebia de la Torre and in 1698 was knighted in the Order of Santiago, doubtless owned this dish.[21]

By the late seventeenth and early eighteenth centuries, blue-and-white ware was generally replaced by a polychrome aesthetic, also incorporating Chinese motifs. But the fern-and-daisy pattern continued, now debased on most samples, alongside the newer wares.[22] Of the two centers of production, sherds from Talavera are lighter blue than those from El Puente del Arzobispo.[23] Also, Talavera produced more expensive ware than the latter town, possible indicating better quality "porcelain."[24]

Unlike the Portuguese, Spanish *chinoiserie* blue-and-white is rare, or at least, not yet widely publicized. A jar of Chinese form now in Barcelona is one handsome example. Its wide central band of deer in an eastern landscape of lush vegetation wraps around the whole object. Its borders are also Chinese-inspired: at the neck, a meander; at the base, panels of stylized lotuses. The whole is exceptionally well-painted. If more such quality pieces are discovered, the story of Spanish wares modeled on Chinese blue-and-white will be much the richer.

MEXICO

In surprising contrast to the mother country, New Spain's production of Chinese-inspired faience was richly varied and long-lived. Yet the Baroque period in Mexico (late 1500s to 1800), brought forth a great *mestizo* or hybrid originality in art; thus unique, lively ceramics might be expected. Mexican faience is notable for its size and boldness, appropriate to the elaborately exuberant, or Churrigueresque style of art which was part of the period.

Within the general term *loza fina*, the Mexicans denoted the best of three grades of ware, including Chinese imitations; the latter was less often referred to as "*porcelana*." It was distinguished from *porcelana de China* which, records indicate, signified Chinese export ware. The Mexicans came to know export ware as well as the Portuguese, and evidently much better than the Spanish, as models for their own inspirations. Doubtless that availability helps explain Portugal's and Mexico's plentiful supply of contemporary imitations.

Chinese porcelain arrived in Mexico by two routes: first from Spain in small shipments because of its rarity and purchase through the Portuguese, then in much larger quantity after the Manila Galleon was regularized in the 1570s. Shiploads bought from the Chinese in Manila were unloaded in Acapulco, then divided between those which would go north to Mexico City and those to be sent to Spain. The latter amount, probably less than that kept in Mexico, especially large pieces—judging from travelers' accounts and what remains in Spain today—had to travel through Puebla de los Angelos en route to Veracruz, the port of embarkation for Seville.[25] Puebla, an historic pottery-making center even before the arrival of the Spanish, thus had a stream of examples of Chinese wares to stimulate its industry. (Mexico City also had a number of potteries;

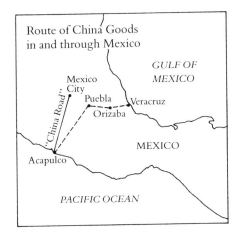

Route of China Goods
in and through Mexico

GULF OF
MEXICO

Mexico
City
Puebla
Orizaba
Veracruz

"China Road"

MEXICO

Acapulco

PACIFIC OCEAN

they, too, may have produced Chinese-style blue-and-white, but as yet, it has not been clearly identified.[26]) Porcelain's transport across the Pacific and overland through Puebla began only a decade before the first recorded potter was known to have been working there. In 1580, and again in 1582 and 1585, the town records listed Gaspar de Encinas as a master potter. He was joined in 1593 by Juan García Carillo and Gabriel Hernández. The list grew much longer after the turn of the century.[27]

Doubtless others were contemporary with Encinas; certainly he had predecessors. Traditionally, it has been thought that soon after the arrival of the Spanish, Dominican friars in Puebla working with Aztec potters requested that a handful of fellow friar-potters from Talavera de la Reina come to their aid. In doing so, the augmented group of Dominicans reputedly "trained a generation of workmen who for the first few succeeding years produced some excellent pieces."[28]

With this early relationship to Talavera in Spain, and with one of its styles similar to Talavera pots, no wonder Puebla's became known as "Talavera" ware. Perhaps the link determined that blue-and-white, tin-glazed faience rather than any metallic luster wares, as in the other major faience centers of Malaga and Valencia, would be made in Puebla. But even with a specific Talaveran heritage (and the influence of Sevillian potters who came over as well), Puebla pieces are a class apart, brilliantly combining a number of styles, but slavishly copying none. Nonetheless, for convenience, these sources of style have been divided into four different categories in overlapping chronological order: Moresque (1575–1700), Spanish or Talavera (c. 1600–1780), Chinese (c. 1650–1800) and Hispano-Mexican or Pueblan (c. 1800–1860).[29]

However, in light of the Manila Galleon's history (roughly 250 years from the 1570s to the early 1800s), the Chinese period is probably both earlier and and longer, c. 1590–1820, than previously thought. After all, not only were named potters at work who had a plentiful supply of models via Acapulco, but also in 1600, Puebla is described as having pottery "so perfected that with satisfaction we have seen pieces that rivaled foreign pottery, in form as well as in design."[30] In the best examples and excluding questions of thickness, one may agree.

Chinese from Manila often shipped as common sailors in the annual galleons. Some remained in Mexico as *chinos* to work in the silver mines with blacks and Indians. Some also reportedly worked as goldsmiths in Mexico City. Did any become part of the ceramic industry? If they did, then their duties were probably restricted to humbler chores such as mixing clays. The master potter's role, as defined by the Potters' Guild regulations of 1653, was reserved for Hispanics, excluding blacks, mulattos, "or any persons of mixed blood,"[31] in short, non-whites. The Chinese, lumped with these at the bottom of society, would certainly have been excluded. Also, the Chinese potter would have had no incentive to transplant from China where porcelain rather than pottery was being produced and where he was well-employed. Further, Chinese painters enjoyed a prestige at home they would not have had in Mexico. And finally, no Mexican faience exhibits a trace of an Oriental hand, only fanciful interpretations of it.

In any style, Puebla wares have their own aesthetic. Of forms, tiles may outnumber any other. The one in the exhibition instantly communicates exuberance, if not intended play, by its painter. On an under-size Oriental spotted deer, probably painted first, sits a Spanish soldier, his feet nearly touching the ground. He also has trouble staying inside the top frame of the tile; to do so, his head is radically tilted backward. The "F" in front of his nose, one of a number of potters' marks of the early seventeenth century, is not yet identified.[32] Such marks

110

became mandatory when the Guild was officially established in 1653 (lasting only until 1676)[33] but may, of course, have been used before.

At first, tiles had church-related purposes: architectural embellishment in friezes, panels, façades, domes, wall mosaics with lavatories and basins, and baptismal and holy water fonts. One famous example is a totally tiled kitchen, the convent of Santa Rosa in Puebla.[34] Tiles were then adapted to private houses for the same decorative purposes, with the addition of coats of arms over entrances. (Interestingly, few flat or hollow pieces of Puebla ware bear such coats of arms. Those that do are rarely for individuals but rather for distinguished clergy or religious communities and exhibit a range of quality.[35])

Flat and hollow wares were used for general domestic purposes, religious or secular. Shapes—a blend of East and West—included domed jars (whose lids are often long lost), cisterns, dishes, bowls, basins, beniters (small fonts), inkstands, sand-sprinklers, salt-cellars, candlesticks, flower pots in the form of barrels with three raised bands (copied from the Italian form and only reminiscent of Chinese garden seats by their decoration alone, since, of course, they served a different purpose), and *albarellos*. The *albarello*, or *canilla* in New Spain, was equally used for flowers, only a few have spaces for the names of drugs. The Mexican *canilla* might follow its Italian prototype with a flanged ring for fitting a shelf socket, but it could also splay in an unbroken line from center to base.[36]

In the 1653 guild regulations, it was stipulated that "in making the fine wares the coloring should be *in imitation of the Chinese ware*, very blue, finished in the same style and with *relief work in blue*, and on this style of pottery there should be painted black dots and grounds in colors."[37] Most of these requirements are evident on remaining examples. First, the best Puebla ware is of finer quality, taking inspiration from the more delicate and detailed Chinese export, especially those examples which were bright blue. Second, the blue's thickness on Mexican pieces is often in relief (in contrast to Spanish taste which required a smooth surface). But blue, not black, dots (the black dots of Spanish wares) are common. Interestingly, earlier Puebla ware not only has a relief blue painting but also depressions of the blue, smooth semi-circles in the surface. The fusing of the blue *into* the glaze during one single firing explains these sunken areas.[38]

The previous terms for this technique, "tattooed" or "intaglio," are essentially incorrect. They should be replaced, perhaps by "sunken" style.[39] The blue was neither punched nor carved into the glaze with a tool. As indicated, the kiln's action, not the artist's, affected the fusing of the blue with the glaze, thus its fallen appearance. In another contrast with Spanish practice, this sunken style was achieved in a single firing of the object, not as in Spain where the blue was painted over the glaze of the once-fired object before a second, lower-temperature firing. Another characteristic of Puebla ware is the outlining of subjects in black, indigo or light blue. All three methods of using the blue—in relief, depressed or in outline (not just the latter, as has been suggested)—were used in painting pieces inspired by the Chinese.

With this impressive array of techniques, the Puebla painter brought fresh conceptions to any size surface, but especially to the spacious areas of large jars, using them as canvases but with unique "landscapes." The jars, often of Chinese shape, as frequently exhibit eastern motifs as well combined with Mudéjar, Hispanic and sometimes hints of Aztec decoration. Such is the case with the *guan*-shaped *tibor* (Chinese large jar) in Figure 28 decorated with a great sense of fun and fancy. Each of its four panels is filled, sampler-like, with raised and depressed emblems of East and West. In one panel, a Chinese with streaming pig-

Figure 28. *Jar*. Mexico. 1600–1625. Faience. Height 46 cm. The International Museum of Folk Art, Santa Fe. Houghton Sawyer Collection.

tail is paired with a long-tailed bird, a doe and buck pose under a palm tree while below them a Moorish structure with a tower floats above cranes and floral motifs; in still another a figure pushes a child in a swing. Elsewhere are towered Hispanic buildings and poplar-shaped trees around which Hispanic rabbits gambol. All is pleasingly placed within borders of hybrid outline, Chinese lobe-and-lotus on the top, Mudéjar/Chinese on the sides, and Hispanic on the base border. Is an Aztec-inspired design reflected in the top border? The shoulders above the panels are diagonally arranged, broken Chinese meander patterns. In effervescence of spirit, execution and preservation, this example competes with the best of Puebla's survivors.

Figure 29. *Basin*. Mexico. c. 1600. Faience. Diameter 43.8 cm. The Metropolitan Museum of Art. Gift of Mrs. Robert W. de Forest, 1911, 11.87.27.

Another spacious form popular in the seventeenth century was the *lebrillo* or basin. The one in Figure 29, with its bicephal eagle of the Spanish Hapsburgs, an insignia adopted during the reign of Philip II (1556–1598), has borders in the carrack style. Shallow bowls similar to the ones brought up in the salvaging of the Dutch East Indiaman, "Witte Leeuw," sunk off St. Helena in 1613, may have suggested the quadrant composition and ogival and lobed reserves containing Chinese flower baskets and delicate Oriental adjacent scrolls.[40] The dots and leaf fillers are typical of an earlier Puebla style. For both historical and stylistic reasons, this basin probably is of the period 1600–1630, or from seventy to a hundred years earlier than previously thought.[41]

113   An Hispanic-shaped flower pot in the exhibition, wide-hipped and ribbed, may be of the same period, though of lesser quality than the basin. Nonetheless, each of the four landscapes between the ribs, done in sunken style of a mixture of western and eastern architecture and plant life, is an attempt at realism, even though its execution, in contrast to a Chinese model, is flatter, busy with leafy background, and lacking heavier or lighter strokes to indicate space. One section features a typically rendered Chinese with moustache, but without a parasol. Like the Portuguese working at the same time, Mexican artisans were creating a *chinoiserie* style all their own.

112   A plate in the exhibition indicates a shift of style, a borrowing from new Chinese models which replaced carrack ware in the late seventeenth century. Kangxi export porcelain (1660–1722) often featured the "Chinese aster" (stylized chrysanthemum or palmette) in panels. In this plate, twelve unpanelled flowers resembling the Chinese are still contained by groups of parallel lines, their leaves. In the center two long-tailed birds, imitation pheasants or possibly swallows, soar amidst cross-hatched rocks and the dots and dashes of an earlier style.

A crisper Chinese mode, contemporary with the one just discussed, was also quite popular (Figure 30). On a vase of Oriental shape, once with a lid, are bold white reserves containing symmetrical floral sprays on a dark blue ground. Light blue lines at the edges soften the contrast and serve as stems as well. The shoulder and vertical band scrollwork, Chinese in inspiration, is bolder in effect. The neck and base borders are the familiar Hispanic clusters of dots, which also play a minor role within the reserves. The whole has the pristine effect of its model, a clarity unlike Puebla's earlier faience. The two bottles in Figure 31 show the continuation of old forms and decorations with the new. The smaller double gourd-shaped bottle on the left echoes a form familiar in China since Yuan times, but adapted to late seventeenth-century Mexico, doubtless from a contemporary export model. A New World innovation, however, is its indented upper sphere for easier grasping. The light and dark blue foliage and flowers of its decoration are more purposefully spaced than the "old-fashioned," Mudéjar/Chinese animal-bird-leaf-dot/dash style of the larger Hispanic bottle-vase.

Figure 30. *Vase*. Mexico. c. 1685–1700. Faience. Height 36.8 cm. The Metropolitan Museum of Art. Gift of Mrs. Robert W. de Forest, 1911, 11.87.36.

Figure 31. *Two bottles.* Mexico. c. 1700. Faience. *Left*: Height 18.4 cm. *Right*: Height 27.3 cm. The Metropolitan Museum of Art. Gift of Mrs. Robert W. de Forest, 1911, 11.87.27.

An Oriental form widely used in Mexico, as it had been in the Philippines and elsewhere in south-east Asia, was the "Money Jar" or *chocolatero*. Its iron lid with key, also Mexican made, gave the vessel its name, since it could then safely store cacao beans, used as small change. Also, of course, it protected anything valuable, especially spices. The diagonally paneled, strongly scrolled and lined decoration is in the Talaveran tradition. But the featured bird may be hybrid. It has a much more elaborate tail than in earlier examples. Possibly this one is a simplified phoenix, a bird readily accessible to Mexican buyers of "Swatow" export wares available in Manila throughout the seventeenth century.[42]

The heydey of Puebla ware in the Chinese style may now be given an earlier beginning date of 1600 and extended to the late eighteenth century. This lasting indebtedness to the Chinese potter is another factor distinguishing Mexican blue-and-white from the Portuguese and Spanish. In 1745, Father Juan Villa Sanchez commented on both the glass and ceramics of Puebla:

> The pottery, of which great quantities are made in Puebla, is similar to the glassware, being so fine and beautiful that it equals or excels that of Talavera, or of Cartagena of the Indies, the ambition of the Puebla potters being to emulate and equal the beauty of the wares of China. There is a great demand for this product, especially for the most ordinary qualities, which are most in demand throughout the kingdom.[43]

Two examples of Puebla ware from the early and late eighteenth century show how well blue-and-white kept to the hopes Sanchez described as they also competed favorably with polychromes which were the coming fashion.

The first, a basin in the exhibition, shows the white reserve on blue style in a linked border. In the center, in curious combination, is a kneeling figure with pigtail, thus probably Chinese (yet with the large nose of the typical Aztec face, especially on tiles). Over his right shoulder, a snake slithers, symbolic of an Aztec deity (the snake is part of Mexico's state seal today). The figure kneels before a fancifully symmetrical stream spotted with regularly-spaced, dotted stones surrounded by clusters of dots. At the stream's left edge is a tower with banners, representing a complete Moslem building, possibly a mosque, found on other Puebla ware. Only in America could one put a Chinese of this size in such an improbable intercultural position, surely a humorous concoction.

A second late eighteenth-century blue-and-white piece is a platter, one of a pair, each with a Chinese musician.[44] Though the border is separated into alternating diaper and floral panels, familiar from Chinese export of the mid-eighteenth century, the oval shape is handled vertically rather than horizontally, the common practice in both West and East. It focuses upon a mustachioed Chinese beating his drum while airily sporting scroll-toed shoes. The floral scroll frame, groups of triple dots in the background, and tiled floor put him solidly in an Hispanic setting. Combining Spanish, Chinese and Mexican elements, this platter is an excellent example of the long-lived nature of a purely American *chinoiserie* style. Later, nineteenth-century Puebla wares also drew upon Chinese blue-and-white for inspiration, but by then, the vitality of inspiration and quality had considerably declined. What Mexico accomplished at its height, however, surpassed Spain in variety and quantity while its two hundred years of production of blue-and-white of Chinese inspiration continued much longer than Portugal's equally rich and inventive "*porcelana*."

1. Daisy Lion-Goldschmidt, "Les porcelaines chinoises du Palais de Santos," *Arts Asiatiques* (XXXIX, 1984), pp 5–72.

2. *Ibid.*, pp. 6–8.

3. *Ibid.*, p. 8, fig. 4.

4. Ilda Arez, *et. al.*, *Portugal and Porcelain* (New York: The Metropolitan Museum of Art Exhibition Catalogue, 1984–1985), p. 18.

5. Reynaldo dos Santos, *Faiences Portugueses* (Alvaro, Portugal: Livraria Galacia, 1960), p. 143.

6. *Ibid.*, 115; also Arez, p. 22.

7. Robert C. Smith, *The Art of Portugal, 1600–1800* (New York: Meridith Press, 1968), p. 261.

8. Florence C. and Robert H. Lister, "Majolica, Ceramic Link Between Old World and New," *El Palacio* (Vol. 76, No. 2, Santa Fe, N.M., 1969), p. 9.

9. Dos Santos, p. 38; Smith, *op. cit.*

10. Dos Santos, p. 142.

11. Dos Santos, Pl. XI, f.p. 66.

12. Smith, p. 262.

13. Dos Santos, Pl. XXII, f.p. 118.

14. Lister and Lister, p. 9. In 1627, Chinese porcelain is mentioned in a government price regulation. Letter to author, Florence C. Lister, October 27, 1983.

15. Alice Wilson Frothingham, *Talavera Pottery* (New York: The Hispanic Society of America, 1944), Fig. 26, p. 35; Fig. 50, p. 57.

16. Balbina Martinez Caviro, *Cerámica de Talavera* (Madrid: Instituto Valencia de Don Juan, 2nd ed., 1984), pp. 23–24.

17. Balbina Martinez Caviro, *Cerámica Española en el Instituto Valencia de Don Juan* (Madrid: Instituto Valencia de Don Juan, 1978), pp. 71–72.

18. Martinez Caviro, *Talavera*, p. 24.

19. Illustrated, Frothingham, Fig. 16, p. 21; also, Martinez Caviro, *Cerámica Española*, figs. 130, 131.

20. Frothingham, p. 16.

21. Frothingham, p. 123.

22. Illustrated, Lister and Lister, p. 10.

23. Martinez Caviro, *Talavera*, p. 14.

24. Frothingham, pp. 68–69.

25. William Lytle Schurz, *The Manila Galleon* (New York: E.P. Dutton and Company, 1959), p. 384.

26. Elizabeth Wilder Weismann, trans., Manuel Touissant, *Colonial Art in Mexico* (Austin, Texas, 1967), pp. 175–176.

27. Enrique A. Cervantes, *Loza Blanca Y Azuelo de puebla*, I (Mexico, 1939), 197; II, 185–186.

28. A.M. Gottscholk, U.S. Consul-General in Mexico City, report to the State Department, as quoted by Edwin A. Barber, *The Emily Johnston De Forest Collection of Mexican Maiolica* (New York: The Hispanic Society of America, 1922), x.

29. Edwin A. Barber, *The Maiolica of Mexico* (Philadelphia: The Pennsylvania Museum, 1908), p. 46.

30. Barber, p. 16.

31. Barber, p. 19.

32. Cervantes, I, 72.

33. Barber, p. 18.

34. Illustrated, Touissant, p. 375.

35. Charlotte Wilcoxen, "Tin-glazed Pottery of Puebla, Mexico," *Antiques* (April 1977), CXI, No. 4, p. 793.

36. Alejandra Peon Soler and Leonor Cortina Ortega, *Talavera de Puebla* (Mexico: Ediciones Comermex, 1973), p. 3; also, Edwin A. Barber, *The Pottery and Porcelain of the United States* (New York: G.P. Putnams, 1909), p. 585.

37. Barber, *Maiolica of Mexico*, p. 27.

38. Barber, *Mexican Maiolica in the Collection of the Hispanic Society of America* (New York: The Hispanic Society, 1915), p. 5.

39. Barber, *Ibid.*, pp. 7–8.

40. C.L. Van der Pijl-Ketel, ed., The Ceramic Load of the *"Witte Leeuw"* (1613), (Amsterdam: Rijksmuseum, 1981), pp. 104 ff.

41. Barber dates the basin c. 1680–1700, *Mexican Maiolica*, Figure 61, p. 21. A smaller one (Diameter 30 cm) with a similar double-headed eagle has a continuous cavetto border with two European mounted figures each with an attendant, one pair hunting a deer, another, a boar. Soler and Ortega, No. 1, n.p.

42. Barbara Harrisson, *Swatow in het Princessehof* (Leeuwarden, the Netherlands: Gemeentelijk Museum Het Princessehof, 1979), pp. 92–102.

43. Barber, *Maiolica of Mexico*, p. 17.

44. Both the flautist who is this drummer's companion and the latter are illustrated in Barber, *Mexican maiolica*, xvii.

Catalogue of the Exhibition

1 Cowry shells

a. Five cowries from Male, Maldive Islands. Modern, collected in 1974.
b. Four cowries from Mantai, Sri Lanka. Tenth century A.D., excavated in 1984.

The five modern cowry shells were collected on Male, the capital of the Maldives, in 1974. Of the variety known as *Cypraea moneta,* cowries were widely used as currency throughout India, Africa and the Far East, including China, from at least the ninth century onward. Numerous writers mention the Maldives as the source of the cowries as, for instance, the Arab merchant Sulayman who listed them among Maldivian exports in 851 A.D. (Ferrand 1922, pp. 31, 33, 50).

The four older cowries from the 1984 excavations at Mantai, an international trading emporium at the northern tip of Sri Lanka (Ceylon), pre-date the demise of the site in the late tenth century as a result of the Chola invasions. They are representative of the cowries used as currency mentioned by numerous writers, such as Sulayman, Al-Biruni, Ibn Battuta and Pyrard de Laval (Carswell 1977a).

It was such cowries that Marco Polo called *porcellana* ("little pigs"), also using the same word in China to describe pottery, thus initiating the use of the word *porcelain*. Having a shiny white shell-like surface like the cowries, it is not difficult to see how the word was transferred to the pottery.

The lacquered box of coconut-wood is a modern example of a traditional Maldivian product, mentioned as early as the seventeenth century by the French sailor Pyrard de Laval, who was shipwrecked and spent several years on the islands (*ibid.,* p. 140).

1a

2a

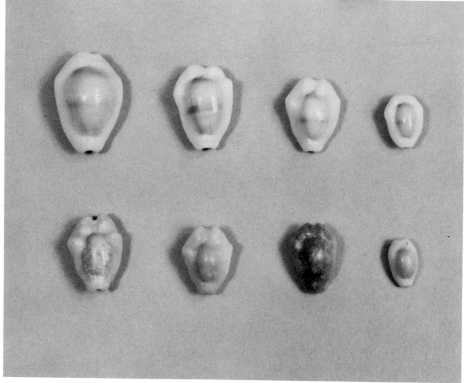

1a (top row), 1b

2 Imitation cowries and porcelain money

a. Two gold-plated, real and bronze imitation cowries. Kn 157, 963.
b. Two bronze imitation cowries. Kn 169, 170.
c. Seven stone imitation cowries. Kn 160 (green stained), 161, 162, 165, 166, 167, 168.
d. Two pieces of porcelain money. Large, Kn 266; small, Kn 267.

Buffalo Society of Natural Sciences, Buffalo Museum of Science.

The use of cowries in China as currency is described by Marco Polo and other commentators in the early middle ages. Cowries have been found on late Neolithic sites in China. Imitations of them in bone, stone and mussel-shell in Shang dynasty contexts (1600–1100 B.C.) suggest they were already being used as currency in the second millenium B.C. Later bronze imitations of cowries appear about 500 B.C. (Pelliot 1959–1973, pp. 533–4).

The gold-plated cowries include both real shell and bronze imitation; Marco Polo's description of the use of cowry shells as currency in the province of Yunnan also contains the information that this area was the source of gold in profusion (Polo 1938, 1, p. 278).

The two bronze imitation cowries reproduce the vulva-like opening on the underside fairly faithfully, while the seven stone copies reduce it to a simple slit, some with hatching on either side and some plain. One is stained green, presumably to imitate a bronze cowry.

The two pieces of porcelain money are octagonal in shape, with molded characters and underglaze cobalt blue marks; the larger piece is also molded with an animal motif, colored green.

SMALL COIN:
Octagonal; stamped white porcelain, with underglaze blue.
obverse: raised double border, two Chinese characters in relief, *Shui li,* "water flows very smoothly."
reverse: plain surface, inscribed in underglaze blue with the Chinese character *fang.*

LARGE COIN:
Octagonal; stamped white porcelain, with green and blue underglaze painting.
obverse: raised double border, two Chinese characters in relief, *Xingli,* "prosperous."
reverse: impressed circular frame, animal and disc in relief, the animal stained green and the disc inscribed in underglaze blue with the Chinese character *fang.*
fang could be a surname, or classification symbol.

(translation by Dr. James Cheng)

The use of porcelain money was noted in Siam in the late nineteenth century (Pelliot 1959–1973, pp. 555–6).

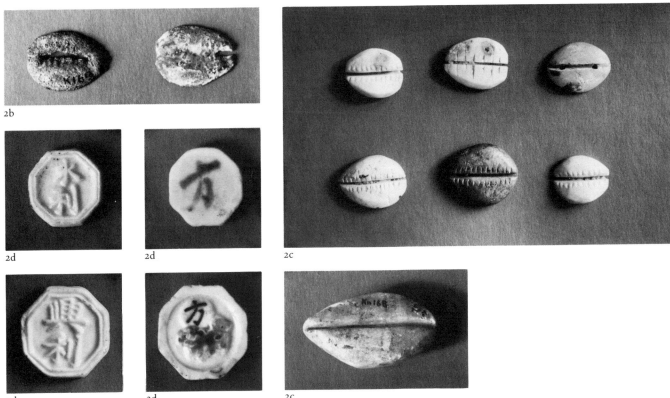

2b

2d   2d   2c

2d   2d   2c

3 Small jar

China, Tang dynasty (618–906 A.D.) Early eighth century.
Off-white earthenware body, thick white slip and underglaze blue
  decoration.
Height 4.5 cm. Diameter 4.5 cm.
Indianapolis Museum of Art. In memory of Franklin B. Mead,
  gift of Mr. and Mrs. John Mead, 81.458.

4 Small bowl

Mesopotamia, Abbasid dynasty. Eighth/ninth century A.D.
Cream-colored earthenware, with opaque gray glaze, decorated in
  cobalt blue.
Height 5 cm. Diameter 14.8 cm.
The Oriental Institute Museum, The University of Chicago.
  A 24768.

3

4

Globular jar with a short spout, rolled rim and splayed foot; the
lower part of the body is unglazed. Decorated with splashes of
cobalt blue.

Cobalt blue was one of the three colors (*sancai*) used to decorate
lead-glazed earthenware during the Tang dynasty. The cobalt ore
was of west Asiatic origin, probably from Persia (Garner 1956).
The first recorded use of blue in China is on a lid from a tomb
dated 664 A.D. (Watson 1984, p. 50). An unpublished sherd excavated at Mantai in Sri Lanka in 1984 is decorated with ochre/
brown and blue splashes, and is similar to a bowl from a Tang
tomb dated 706 A.D. (Watson 1973b, p. 141, no. 282).

This small bowl of "Samarra" type ware was excavated by Erich
F Schmidt at Istakhr near Persepolis during his 1937 Iranian expedition. The bowl has an everted lip, and a narrow ring base apparently ground down after firing, perhaps to remove traces of glaze.
Of cream-colored fine earthenware, the opacified warm gray tin
glaze covers most of the bowl and part of the base. Decorated in
dark cobalt blue under the glaze. There are eight segmental motifs
at the rim, each with rough double outlines. At the center is a single Arabic word written in Kufic-like script.

The segmental motifs are also found on Tang dynasty Chinese
painted stoneware bowls from Changsha, known to have been exported to southeast Asia, Sri Lanka, India, the Gulf, Iraq and Iran,
and which may well have influenced the design of early Islamic
pottery (Whitehouse 1970; Whitehouse and Williamson, 1973).
Known as "Samarra" ware after its discovery at that site (Sarre
1925, Plate XVIII). The painted decoration was felicitously described by Arthur Lane as "like ink on snow." The shape is a response to imported Tang white ware of similar form; and the use
of cobalt blue in both Mesopotamia and the Far East at about the
same time can hardly have been fortuitous; the blue was probably
introduced into China by western Asiatic merchants.

PUBLISHED: Erich F Schmidt, *The Treasury of Persepolis and other Discoveries
in the homeland of the Achaemenians,* Oriental Institute Communications,
21, The University of Chicago, Chicago, n.d., p. 115, Figure 81.

5 Bowl

China, Song/Yuan dynasty. Twelfth/thirteenth century.
White porcelain with *qingbai* glaze, carved and combed
    decoration.
Height 7.1 cm. Diameter 20.1 cm.
The Art Institute of Chicago. Bequest of Russell Tyson, 64.847.

6 Bowl

China, Yuan dynasty. Early fourteenth century.
Shufu white ware with opaque glaze, molded decoration.
Height 9.7 cm. Diameter 20.8 cm.
The Art Institute of Chicago. Gift of C. T. Loo, 25.39.

5

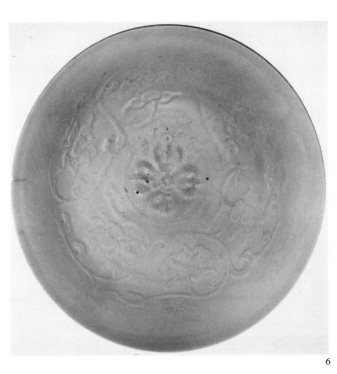

6

Finely constructed bowl with six indentations on the rim, V-shaped foot-ring. Bluish-green sparkling *qingbai* glaze pooling to an even deeper tone in the indentations, such as the stepped ring at the center. The base is partly glazed, and the unglazed area is fired orange-brown, with iron impurities; there appear to be traces of a cylindrical kiln support; the foot-ring is completely glazed.

The inside of the bowl is carved with an elegant spray of a peony and leaves with delicately combed details.

Three similar bowls were excavated in Sri Lanka, and are now in the National Museum in Colombo (Carswell 1979a, Figure 2).

Bowl of *shufu* ware, with slightly everted rim, sturdily cut foot-ring unglazed on the bottom and inside; the conical base is also unglazed except for a spot of glaze at the center; the unglazed areas have fired a light orange color. Measurement of the bowl shows the base to be exceptionally thick.

Inside, in the cavetto, is a molded wreath of six composite flowers of different types on an undulating stem with flame-like leaves and bud-like terminations. At the center inside a raised ring is a double *vajra*. At the top of the wreath on opposite sides of the bowl are two molded characters, *ji* and *fu*.

The inordinately thick base is a feature found on a number of fourteenth-century blue-and-white bowls with everted rims from Syria, now in the Pharaon and Larsson Collections. The foot-ring and base were probably carved while the bowl was still on the mold. The very thin section of the upper part of the bowl would never have been strong enough to support the weight of the base.

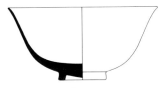

7 Bowl

China, Yuan dynasty. Early fourteenth century.
Shufu white ware with opaque glaze, molded decoration.
Height 7.8 cm. Diameter at rim 17.3 cm.
The Cleveland Museum of Art. Anonymous gift, 53.122.

The thinly-potted bowl has a warm gray-green glaze with a dull luster. The bottom of the sharply angled foot-ring and the base are unglazed and fired light orange; there are unfired spots on the lower body and the rim. The bowl is molded on the inside with three tiers of chrysanthemum petals, the two upper tiers with forty-six petals and the inner tier with thirty-nine petals; in the center is a molded ring enclosing a spiral of faintly raised dots. On the opposite side of the bowl in the upper tier of petals are two molded characters, *fu* ("prosperity") and *lu* ("emoluments of office").

Shufu ware, so named after the characters *shu* and *fu* on many pieces of this type, was made at the Jingdezhen kilns. The distinguishing feature is an opaque white glaze of dullish tone, differing markedly from the sparkling glaze on *qingbai* ware. The molded decoration derives from a silver prototype, and is also found on *qingbai* pieces, such as the Fustat sherd in the exhibition, with underglaze-blue decoration (12a).

Another bowl with the characters *fu* and *lu* is in the Barlow Collection (Sullivan 1963a, p. 118, Plate 121a); and an almost identical bowl is in the Ashmolean Museum (Swann 1963, no. 157).

An early fourteenth-century date for *shufu* ware has been suggested by a piece in the British Museum, bearing an inscription on the base in the short-lived Phags'pa script (Gray 1955, p. 45, Plate 95). A sharply-carinated bowl of *qingbai* porcelain with three similar molded tiers of petals was found on the Sinan wreck, before 1323 (Sinan 1977, no. 214).

PUBLISHED: Sherman Lee, "Janus in Limbo," *Cleveland Museum of Art Bulletin*, 50, Cleveland, 1963, pp. 2–6. Wai-kam Ho and Sherman Lee, *Chinese Art under the Mongols: The Yuan Dynasty (1279–1368)*, Cleveland, 1968, Plate 119. Yoshiaka Yabe, *Betonam no toji, (Ceramics of Thai and Vietnam)*, Tokyo, Heibonsha, 1978, p. 112, Figure 60. Duncan Macintosh, "Shu-fu wares: Their Origins, Development and Decline," *Bulletin of The Oriental Ceramic Society of Hong Kong*, Hong Kong, 4, 1978–80, p. 43, Figure 18. The most complete discussion of this piece is by Henry J. Kleinhenz, *Pre-Ming Porcelains in the Chinese Ceramic Collection of The Cleveland Museum of Art*, Case Western Reserve University, Cleveland, 1977, (unpublished PhD. thesis), pp. 614–7.

7

8a

8 Two jarlets

China, Yuan dynasty. First half of fourteenth century.
White porcelain of *shufu* type, one decorated in underglaze blue.
a. Height 5 cm. Diameter 5.5 cm.
b. Height 5.1 cm. Diameter 5.5 cm.
Indianapolis Museum of Art. Gift of Mr. and Mrs. Daniel
  Henkin, 79.515, 79.511.

a. Jarlet with globular body, rolled rim, and two loop handles
  (one repaired). Thick gray *shufu* type glaze; the bottom is
  unglazed, fired gray with faint orange patches.
b. Jarlet, with globular body and rolled rim, and two loop
  handles. Thick gray *shufu* type glaze, gray-blue underglaze
  decoration. The disc base is unglazed, fired buff color. The
  jarlet is painted with a single chrysanthemum spray encircling
  the body, the flower with a spiral center, and v-shaped leaves.

Jarlets of this form were commonly exported to south-east Asia in
the fourteenth century, and plain, underglaze blue, underglaze
copper-red and iron-spotted examples have been published (Jingdezhen 1984, nos. 42, plain; 73, iron-spot; 144, copper-red; 109,
blue; 104, blue, no handles; 107, four vertical sprays of blue
flowers with spiral centers separated by beaded bands. Hong
Kong 1979, nos. 78, 79, 80, blue; 73, with two birds, crayfish and
flowers. Locsin and Locsin 1967, pp. 99–104, nos. 80, 81, 82, 85,
87, for sprays of chrysanthemum with spiral centers. Guy 1980,
for jarlets with *qingbai* glazes, nos. 42, with iron spots; 48, with
prunus spray, crescent and full moons in blue).

9 Small jar

China, Yuan dynasty. First half of fourteenth century.
White porcelain with *shufu* type glaze, underglaze blue
  decoration.
Height 7.8 cm. Diameter 9.5 cm.
Indianapolis Museum of Art. Gift of Mr. and Mrs. Daniel
  Henkin, 79.512.

Small jar of miniature *guan* form, of *shufu* type ware with a dull
bluish opaque glaze and underglaze gray-blue decoration. The
concave, recessed base is unglazed and fired an orange-buff color.
The potter's finger-marks are visible inside the jar, which appears
to have been made in two parts luted together. The rim has been
ground down and is unglazed; the jar probably once had a lid.

Outside, on the shoulder between two rings is a band of freely
drawn classic scroll. On the body between single and double rings
are two chrysanthemum sprays, the flowers with spiral centers.
Below, a sketchily drawn band of large and small scallops, and
leafy spirals.

Similar miniature *guan* jars have been published (Jingdezhen
1984, nos. 115, 116; no. 113, for a jar twice the size, 14.8 cm. high,
with a cover; and Lee and Ho 1968, no. 129, for a similar jar 11.6
cm. high from the Garner Collection with a lotus-leaf cover and
similar scalloped band at the bottom. See also, Jingdezhen 1984,
no. 76, and Guy 1980, no. 41, for iron-spotted jars with covers.
Hong Kong 1979, no. 76, and Locsin and Locsin 1967, nos. 85,
87, for blue decorated jars, the latter with cover).

8b

9

10 Stem-cup

China, Yuan dynasty. First half of fourteenth century.
White porcelain with underglaze blue decoration.
Height 9.4 cm. Diameter 11.7 cm.
The Dayton Art Institute. Gift of Mrs. Virginia W. Kettering,
     69.42a.
Formerly in the collection of Mr. and Mrs. John A. Pope.

10

10

The stem-cup has an everted rim, and the stem three convex
moldings, each finely incised with a double ring. The unglazed
foot is sharply beveled and fired orange-red. The cup is decorated
in grayish blue under a greenish glaze.

On the inside at the rim is a sketchily drawn classic scroll. At
the center is a flaming pearl inside a single ring. In the cavetto is a
wreath of molded flowers, four chrysanthemums alternating with
four marguerites, with leafy sprays between them.

On the outside of the cup a dragon vigorously chases a flaming
pearl; the dragon has a cross-hatched body, triple claws and a
spiky spine.

A number of stem-cups of this type are known, and it has been
argued that they were produced over an extended period of time
during the fourteenth century. This would at first glance appear to
be corroborated by a similar stem-cup from a Chinese tomb dated
1371. But the tomb also contained southern Song pottery, and is
cited by the Chinese as a prime example of the burial of heirloom
pieces, and the stem-cup may well have been one such (Addis
1978, 31a).

Two fragmentary stem-cups from Beijing in the present exhibition (11a, b) are closely linked to the Dayton stem-cup, and also
painted in a simplified, sketchy style. The stem-cup can be linked
to other early blue-and-white by the molded flowers with cross-
hatched centers, such as on the outside of a *qingbai* stem-cup in the
David Collection (Ayers 1957, Figure 24), and on the inside of a
brown-painted stem-cup in the British Museum (Jenyns 1961, pp.
107–111, Plate xxxviii). Discussing the latter piece Jenyns sup-
ports a date in the second quarter of the fourteenth century for
such stem-cups. Another stem-cup of this type is painted with a
chrysanthemum spray similar to the Fustat sherd (12a) in the exhibition (Lee 1949, no. 6). An almost identical stem-cup to the
Dayton example was sold in Hong Kong in 1978 (Sotheby/Hong
Kong 1978, no. 51); and a similar fragment of one was among the
sherds excavated at Kharakhoto in Mongolia (Pope 1956, Plate
133, 1, 2).

PUBLISHED: Rhonda Cooper, *The Asian Collection, Gallery Guide*, The
Dayton Art Institute, Dayton, Ohio, 1979, p. 24, Figure 35 (in color). Jean
Gordon Lee, *Ming Blue-and-White: The Philadelphia Museum Bulletin*,
XLIV.223, Philadelphia, 1949, no. 6.

11a–e A group of fourteenth-century sherds from Beijing

11a Fragment of a stem-cup

White porcelain with *qingbai*-type greenish glaze; dark blue underglaze decoration.
Height of stem 6.2 cm. Diameter of foot-ring 3.4 cm.
Freer Gallery of Art Study Collection (Smithsonian Institution).
  SC-P 925.

The sherds were collected by John A. Pope in Beijing in 1945–46, and now form part of the study collection in the Freer Gallery. Along with a number of other sherds from the capital, they are indicative of the type of blue-and-white ware made for the home market. The prevalence of Cizhou painted pottery has been noted among material from the Yuan capital, Dadu, at Beijing (Addis 1984, p. 20); the blue-and-white represents a continuing taste for painted ware.

The bottom of the foot-ring and the inside of the stem are unglazed and fired orange-red; there is an irregular glazed ring at the bottom of the inner stem. Inside the cup is a single flower with a spiral center, with a spray of short, pointed leaves. The stem of the cup has lightly incised rings on each convex molding.

EXHIBITED: Jean Gordon Lee, *Ming Blue-and-White, The Philadelphia Museum of Art Bulletin*, XLIV.223, Philadelphia, 1949, no. 3 in the supplementary list of sherds lent by Dubosc and Pope.

11a

11a

11b Fragment of a stem-cup

White porcelain with *qingbai*-type greenish glaze, underglaze blue decoration.
Height of stem 7.2 cm. Diameter of foot-ring 4 cm.
Freer Gallery of Art Study Collection (Smithsonian Institution).
   SC-P 926.

11c Fragment of a vase

Buff-colored porcelain, dark blue decoration under a warm glaze.
Height of sherd 8.6 cm. Diameter of disc base 5.3 cm.
Freer Gallery of Art Study Collection (Smithsonian Institution).
   SC-P 930.

Similar to (11a), but larger. The floral spray is enclosed in double rings. The bottom and inside of the stem are unglazed and fired a buff color, orange on the foot.

EXHIBITED: Jean Gordon Lee, Philadelphia, *loc. cit.*, supplementary list no. 3.

The two stem-cups are respectively larger and smaller than the Dayton stem-cup on exhibition (10). The decoration is characteristic of early fourteenth-century blue-and-white, and the floral spray similar to one on a stem-cup lent to the 1949 Philadelphia exhibition, no. 6. It is seen in more elaborate version on the Fustat sherd (12a).

The body is luted together, the junction showing on the outside as a faint horizontal ridge. The inside and the rough disc base are unglazed, fired buff color and faintly orange at the edge of the glaze; the glaze has run onto the foot at several points. Painted a dark cobalt blue, the pigment is unevenly applied and fired blackish where thick. Washes of blue show how the leaves were built up with a series of strokes. A single lotus is surrounded by pointed lobed leaves with single or double spikes. There is no ring below the floral design.

This fragment displays a number of unusual features. The disc base is unique on any early blue-and-white piece known to the writer, but a similar base was found by him among sherds from a wreck off the coast of Sri Lanka in 1984, which otherwise contained celadon closely paralleling that from the Sinan wreck of 1323 A.D. The Sri Lanka sherd was unglazed. The loose painting of the lotus-spray, its odd diagonal placing on the body, and the lack of any marginal definition is very unconventional. Could this be an early experimental piece?

As the Freer Gallery registration card does not explicitly give the provenance of the sherd, it is not certain that the piece is from Beijing. This may have simply been an oversight on the part of the cataloguer, as sherds in immediate numerical sequence both before and after this one are specifically registered as such, and the "P" of the registration number appears to stand for Peking (Beijing).

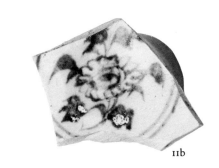

11b

11b

11c

11d Fragments of a vase

White porcelain, with vivid underglaze blue decoration.
Diameter at widest point of body 14 cm.
Freer Gallery of Art Study Collection (Smithsonian Institution).
SC-P 929a, b, c.

11e Fragment of a stem-cup

White porcelain with *qingbai*-type glaze, decorated in underglaze
    copper-red.
Height 8.6 cm. Diameter of foot-ring 3.4 cm.
Freer Gallery of Art Study Collection (Smithsonian Institution).
SC-P 923.

The interior of the vase is unglazed, showing how the body was made in two parts luted together. The foot-ring has broken cleanly away from the base of the vessel. Decorated with a landscape scene, on the right is a running deer, with leaves and stick-like motifs below; to the left is a rock, bamboo, a fungus spray and the right leg of a figure with bare foot and leggings and part of a flowing robe. Below, a diaper ring with almond-shaped segments. On the lower body is a ring of lotus-panels, with thick outlines, filled with pendant spiral scrolls.

The deer and figure in a landscape suggest that this is another vessel of the type known to have been painted with scenes from Yuan dramas (Saito 1967a, pp. 25–41, one bottle illustrated has a deer in a similar position; Saito 1967b, pp. 52–74, especially Figure 14). The diaper band is of the same type as on a *guan* wine-jar in the David Foundation decorated with incised panels and blue and copper-red; the pendant spirals are also similar (Medley 1974, Plate B). Pendant scrolls are also on a faceted sherd from Kharakhoto (Pope 1956, p. 134, no. 28).

In his publication of these sherds Pope drew attention to the clean break of the foot-ring, showing that on vessels of this type it was made separately and luted on, rather than carved out of the body of the pot.

PUBLISHED: John Pope, "Two Chinese Porcelains in the Umezawa Collection," *Far Eastern Ceramic Bulletin*, June 1959, p. 17, Plate IV).

EXHIBITED: Jean Gordon Lee, Philadelphia, *loc. cit.*, supplementary list no. 1.

The bottom of the foot-ring and inner stem are unglazed and fired a light buff color; there is a narrow band of glaze inside the stem at the foot. Decorated on the outside of the cup with irregular splotches of copper-red, with a pale band on the inner rim. Inside the cup is a molded design of a flying goose encircled by a fine line, with a small loop at one point enclosing a character.

This kind of loosely applied copper-red decoration is on a vase in the David Collection; and there is a molded goose on a *shufu* bowl in the Barlow Collection (Ayers 1957, Figures 13, 14, 27). A stem-cup in the British Museum, sketchily painted in a brownish-red, has a molded floral design inside (Jenyns 1961, pp. 109–110, Plate XXXVIII).

PUBLISHED: W. J. Young, "Discussion of some analyses of Chinese underglaze blue and underglaze red," *Far Eastern Ceramic Bulletin*, II.2, December 1949, p. 19, Plate III.

EXHIBITED: Jean Gordon Lee, Philadelphia, *loc. cit.*, supplementary list no. 5.

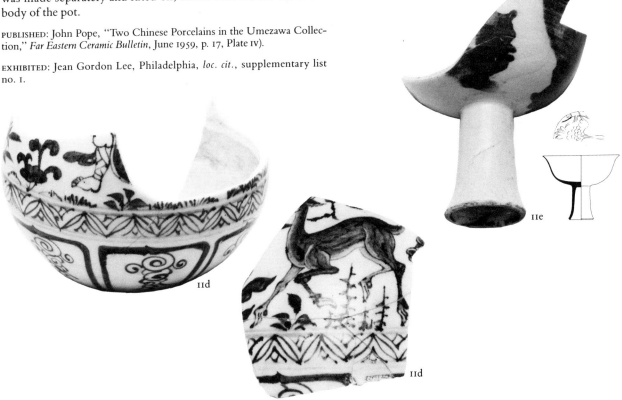

11e

11d

11d

12a–c A group of fourteenth-century sherds from Fustat

12a Fragment of a bowl

China, Yuan dynasty. Second quarter of fourteenth century.
White porcelain with *qingbai* glaze, underglaze blue decoration.
Diameter of foot-ring 6.4 cm.
Private Collection, London.

Fustat (old Cairo) in Egypt has been dug intermittently since 1912 by a number of excavators, the most active of whom has been George Scanlon; see his reports in the *Journal of the American Research Center in Egypt*, from 1965 onward. A select bibliography is given in Mikami 1980–81, p. 88, n. 4.

Purchased in Cairo, the three sherds described are from the rubbish mounds at Fustat.

Part of a bowl with a slightly flaring foot-ring, the bottom and inside of the foot-ring and the base unglazed and fired a buff color, with some iron spotting.

Inside, the bowl is molded with three tiers of chrysanthemum petals, with a double ring at the center. The inner tier has thirty-four petals and the second tier, forty-one. A spray of chrysanthemum with shaded petals and cross-hatched centers, buds and short pointed leaves is painted in underglaze blue inside double rings, in an arbitrary manner on top of the first tier of molded petals.

On the outside of the bowl there is a ring of breaking, serpentine waves, inside pairs of concentric rings. The bowl has been broken and once riveted.

The similarity of the molding to that on the inside of the *shufu* bowl from Cleveland in the exhibition (7), but with a *qingbai* glaze and underglaze blue decoration, suggests that this is an early piece of blue-and-white, utilizing an existing type of Jingdezhen molded ware. The breaking waves are a slightly cruder version of the type of waves seen on the David vases.

PUBLISHED: John Carswell, "A fourteenth-century Chinese porcelain dish from Damascus," *American University of Beirut Festival Book, (Festschrift)*, Beirut, 1967, ed. F Sarruf and S. Tuqan, pp. 39–59, Plate 4D, Figure 1D.

12a

12a

12b Fragment of a bowl

China, Yuan dynasty. Second quarter of fourteenth century.
White porcelain with *qingbai* glaze, underglaze blue decoration.
Diameter of foot-ring 6.2 cm.
Private Collection, London.

12c Fragment of a bowl

China, Yuan dynasty. Second quarter of fourteenth century.
White porcelain with *qingbai* glaze, underglaze blue decoration.
Height 8.1 cm. Diameter 16 cm.
Private Collection, London.

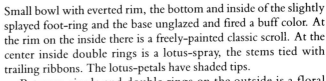

Part of a bowl with slightly flaring foot-ring, the bottom and the inside of the foot-ring and the base unglazed and fired light orange, with traces of hard black, slag-like material adhering to the foot. The center of the base has a conical depression. Written in ink on the base is an inscription in Arabic/Persian.

Painted in pale blue on the inside of the bowl within double rings is a spray of two lotuses tied with trailing ribbons. The petals have shaded tips. On the outside is the lower part of a ring of lotus-panels, each with a pendant pointed lobed leaf at the center.

The shaded tips of the lotus-petals can be traced back to the painted wares of the Cizhou kilns, along with other motifs such as the breaking waves, and the knobbed scrolls.

PUBLISHED: John Carswell, "A fourteenth-century Chinese porcelain dish from Damascus," *American University of Beirut Festival Book, (Festschrift)*, Beirut, 1967, ed. F. Sarruf and S. Tuqan, Plate 4C, Figure 1C.

Small bowl with everted rim, the bottom and inside of the slightly splayed foot-ring and the base unglazed and fired a buff color. At the rim on the inside there is a freely-painted classic scroll. At the center inside double rings is a lotus-spray, the stems tied with trailing ribbons. The lotus-petals have shaded tips.

Between single and double rings on the outside is a floral wreath with flame-like pointed lobed leaves on a thin undulating stem. Below, between single rings, a ring of lotus-panels with thick and thin outlines, and pendant lobed leaves at the center of each.

It is unusual to find small bowls of this type in the Near East, a larger variety of the same kind being much more common. The cobalt blue varies considerably on this piece, due to uneven exposure to the heat source in the kiln. Under the rim outside it is a vivid, violet-blue, whereas lower down on the body the blue is almost gray. Where thickly applied the cobalt has fired a greenish-black, with dull spots; this is a characteristic of early blue-and-white.

In his discussion of the analysis of the cobalt blue used in Chinese porcelain, Garner (1956, p. 50) pointed out that the color of the blue depends not only on its purity but on firing conditions.

Sketchily painted small bowls are common in southeast Asia, but of quite a different type to this specimen; compare *Jingdezhen Wares... 1984*, nos. 119, 120, 122, 123, 125.

PUBLISHED: John Carswell, A fourteenth-century Chinese porcelain dish from Damascus," *American University of Beirut Festival Book, (Festschrift)*, Beirut, 1967, ed. F. Sarruf and S. Tuqan, Plate 4B, Figure 4B.

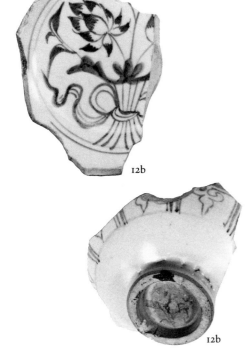

12b

12b

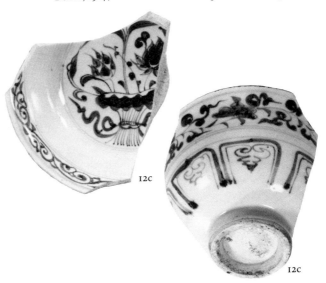

12c

12c

13a

13a

68

13b

13b

13a Large dish

China, Yuan dynasty. Mid-fourteenth century.
White porcelain with underglaze cobalt blue decoration.
Height 7.5 cm. Diameter 39.5 cm.
Museum of Fine Arts, Boston. Gift of Mr. and Mrs. F. Gordon
 Morrill, 1982.456.

This classic example of a well-known fourteenth-century type is of fine white porcelain, the bottom and inside of the foot-ring and the base are unglazed; the base has traces of radial chatter and concentric wheel marks. On the plain, flat rim is a diaper band between single and double rings. In the cavetto, between pairs of double rings, a lotus-wreath with six flowers of two different types, on an undulating stem with pointed, lobed leaves with single spikes on either side, and smaller lobed leaves. At the center inside double rings is a lotus-pond, across which glide two ducks, male and female, the one in front with head turned back. Around them are lotus-sprays, the flowers with shaded tips to their petals.

The outside of the dish is painted with sixteen lotus-panels, with thick and thin outlines, each with a scalloped leaf within a single ring.

Parallels to this dish can be found in the Topkapu Saray Collection (Pope 1952, Plate 4) and at Ardebil (Pope 1956, Plate 7, different rim pattern of overlapping concentric waves, but identical scalloped leaves in lotus-panels on the reverse; Plate 8, two similar dishes but without the ducks). The lotus-spray design was popular in the Near East (12b, c, in the present exhibition, from Fustat, Egypt) and the lotus-pond design with ducks found on a number of fourteenth-century dishes and bowls from Syria (Carswell 1967, Plates 1, 2. Sotheby 1981, Lot no. 185. Carswell 1979b, for an elaborate version with a number of ducklings). The type has also been identified among many fourteenth-century Chinese porcelains found in Delhi, before 1398 and probably before 1388 (Smart 1977, Plates 75a, b; 76b, 77a, 79d, 81c(i) (ii), d; 83a, 84b, 85a, 86b, c(i) (ii), d; 87b, c; 88a, b, d; 89a b, c, e, f; 90a, b). The lotus-spray was widely copied on Syrian and Egyptian pottery of the Mamluk dynasty; in highly stylized form, it also occurs in mid-fifteenth century Ottoman tilework (Carswell 1972b, Plates 2, 3, E7, E11, E20).

13b Large dish

Syria, Mamluk dynasty. Before 1401.
Off-white earthenware, decorated in cobalt blue under a crackled
 glaze.
Height 7.5 cm. Diameter 35.5 cm.
National Museum, Damascus. From excavations at Hama, Syria,
 C917.

This large dish of off-white earthenware is painted under the glaze in dark cobalt blue. The lower part of the body, foot-ring and base are unglazed.

On the plain, flat rim between pairs of rings is a pattern of jagged serpentine waves and diagonal hatching. In the cavetto is a wreath of simplified flowers with large and smaller pointed, lobed leaves. At the center inside double rings is a large spray of lotuses, the long stems below the lotus-leaf being tied together with flame-like ribbons. The lotus-flowers have petals with shaded tips, and to the left and around the central spray are water-plants of different types.

On the back of the dish are eleven panels between two rings, each separated by three radial strokes, with a plant at the center.

The parallel between the Syrian copy and the Chinese original, such as (13a) in the present exhibition, is obvious. The breaking-wave pattern on the rim has been garbled, and the flowers in the cavetto of indeterminate type, where one would have expected more carefully rendered lotuses. In the central panel, the lotus-leaf has become dominant, rather than the flowers. The lotus-panels on the back have become attenuated and far removed from the original. The form and size of the dish are however surprisingly close to the Chinese prototype; the foot-ring is of smaller diameter than would be found on a Chinese dish, and is closer in its square-cut section and size to the type of Chinese bowl of the same period of which a number of examples have been found in Syria.

The real importance of the dish lies in its provenance. Hama was destroyed by Timur in 1401 during his campaign southwards through Syria, just before he marched down the Bekaa valley and turned eastwards to ravage Damascus. The top of the *tell*, or steep-sided mound, at Hama was never extensively reoccupied after its devastation by Timur, and the later medieval town grew around its foot, along the banks of the Orontes. The material excavated by the Danish campaign may therefore be safely assumed to predate 1401 (Riis and Poulsen 1957). A number of other Syrian blue-and-white sherds were excavated, as well as a few fragments of Chinese porcelain.

14a Small plate

China, Ming dynasty. Fourteenth century.
White porcelain with underglaze blue decoration.
Height 2.4 cm. Diameter 19.6 cm.
The Art Insitute of Chicago. Gift of Russell Tyson, 54.475.

14b Small plate

China, Ming dynasty. Fourteenth century.
White porcelain with underglaze copper-red decoration.
Height 2.4 cm. Diameter 19.6 cm.
The Art Institute of Chicago. Gift of Russell Tyson, 54.476.

14a

14b

Small plate with flattened rim and stepped ring at center; short rounded foot-ring and the base are unglazed but fired a shiny orange color. The decoration is in grayish-cobalt blue, with blackish spots.

Inside, on the rim is a band of thunder-pattern between rings. The cavetto is plain. In the center, inside double rings, is a wreath of peonies, alternately in profile and full face, finely shaded and with five-pointed leaves. In the middle, inside single and double concentric rings, is a single chrysanthemum with a cross-hatched center and three buds.

The outside is decorated with thirteen lotus-panels with one thick and two thin outlines, and a pendant lobed leaf and circle within. The lotus-panel frame is more attenuated and less bold than the thick-and-thin outlines of the earlier fourteenth-century Yuan examples.

Virtually identical to the small plate (14a) except it is decorated in underglaze copper-red instead of blue. The foot-ring and base are also unglazed and fired a lighter, shiny orange color. The drawing is slightly cruder than that on the blue plate, and there are fourteen lotus-panels on the back instead of thirteen.

15 Flask

China, Ming dynasty. Xuande period (1426–1435 A.D.).
White porcelain, decorated in underglaze cobalt blue.
Height 32 cm. Diameter at center 21 cm.
Indianapolis Museum of Art. Gift of Mr. and Mrs. Stanley
    Herzman, 1984.273.

15

The flask is of fine white porcelain, painted in cobalt blue with a heaped-and-piled effect under an open crackled glaze. The body of the flask is circular, with two convex faces and flat sides. The base is recessed and the bottom of the foot-ring is unglazed, fired orange at the edge of the glaze. At the bottom of the short concave neck is a raised molding; the upper half of the neck is convex and contracts to a narrow rim. On either side of the neck are two loop handles, joined to the sides of the body with a raised heart-shaped panel.

Painted on the globular upper neck between two pairs of rings are thin stems bearing two types of tiny flower, rosettes and flowerets with four serrated petals, and little feathery trefoil leaves. There are double rings on the raised molding at the base of the neck. The two loop handles have double blue outlines and the heart-shaped terminal is decorated with a symmetrical peony spray with tiny feathery leaves. On each convex side, at the edge is a chevron ring inside two pairs of concentric rings; at the center is an eight-pointed stellar motif with thick and thin outlines, with interlocking scrolls between them, each with a crown of lotus-petals. At the center is a ring of scalloped petals inside double rings, enclosing a *yin yang* symbol. Both sides are identically decorated.

The shape has long been considered to derive from a Near Eastern glass form (Pope 1956, pp. 86–7), which inspired the *yue ping* ("moon flask"), here further modified with bulbous neck. In fact the form is much closer to a metal shape, of which a rather grand thirteenth-century Mamluk example is in the Freer Gallery (Atil 1975, pp. 68–73, no. 28) which in turn inspired an equally splendid fifteenth-century Chinese blue-and-white copy (Pope 1959a, pp. 357–375). The heart-shaped terminals to the handles where they are affixed to the body, and the raised molding at the base of the neck, leave no doubt about the metallic origin of the form. The bulbous upper neck is also a feature of the Freer flask, which has an engraved geometric interlace between double lines at exactly the same point as the Indianapolis flask.

Other similar examples bear the six-character mark of Xuande (1426–1435) in a horizontal line just below the neck (Garner 1954b, Plate 31A: Lee 1949, no. 69), and the distinctive band of tiny flowers with feathery leaves on the neck is repeated on the Indianapolis bowl (19) in the exhibition, which also has a six-character Xuande mark on the base.

The curious central motif of interlocking scrolls and petals is more difficult to analyze, and has no immediate parallel in Near Eastern metalwork.

The form is also found in Syrian unglazed pottery, again equally likely to have been based on a metal model (Atil 1981, p. 190, no. 96, for an example found at Aleppo).

15

16

17

16

17

16 Bowl

China, Ming dynasty. Early fifteenth century.
White porcelain, underglaze cobalt blue decoration.
Height 7 cm. Diameter 14 cm.
The British Museum. Mrs. Walter Sedgwick Bequest,
1968.4–22.28

17 Bowl

China, Ming dynasty. Early fifteenth century.
White porcelain with underglaze blue decoration.
Height 10.2 cm. Diameter 21 cm.
Indianapolis Museum of Art. Gift of Mr. and Mrs. Eli Lilly,
60.107.

Bowl with curving sides and narrow foot-ring, painted in shades of dark cobalt blue under a crackled glaze. Inside at the rim between pairs of rings, a band of chevron pattern with groups of four semi-circles arranged to form triangles; below, a ring of pendant half-rosettes. In the cavetto, a wreath of eight carnation-like flowers with shaded petals, linked to each other by arabesque stems bearing long blade-like leaves and shorter curved trefoil leaves. At the center is an eight-pointed star with trefoil finials weaving in and out of a ring of eight ovals, with a single petal and a pair of hook-like leaves between. At the center between pairs of concentric rings, eight more half-rosettes each between a pair of tiny trefoil leaves, facing alternately inwards and outwards. In the middle, a four-petal flower forming a cross with pairs of curved spikes between the petals.

Outside, between pairs of rings at the rim, an undulating stem bearing tiny lily-like flowers with scrolling lobed leaves. Below, a ring of arches with tiny pendant lobed leaves. On the body, four floral sprays with auspicious emblems between them above a ring of sixteen blade-like pointed leaves, with double outlines, each with a trefoil finial. On the outer foot-ring between a pair of rings, a classic scroll.

The dotted blue and slightly finicky nature of the ticky leaves suggest a date in the early fifteenth century, before the suave assurance of most Xuande pieces. The central four-pointed flower-like motif could be a simplified double *vajra* like that on the Brundage basin (28).

The pattern beneath the outer rim of the bowl is paralleled on two large dishes in the Ardebil Collection of typical early fifteenth-century style, where it occurs on the inner rim (Pope 1956, Plate 36, 29.113, 29.117). A bowl of similar shape and with a rather more open and elegant version of the central design in the Dubosc Collection has a Xuande mark (Lee 1949, no. 50), as does a bowl similar in design to the British Museum specimen but much more finely executed (T.O.C.S. 1972, no. 108).

The beautifully proportioned bowl with curving sides of *lianzi* shape is painted in cobalt blue with a "heaped and piled" effect. Inside at the rim between single and double rings there is a vigorous band of tossing waves, with white spray breaking among them. Below in the cavetto is a wreath of six flowers, three chrysanthemums and three camellia-like blossoms, with smaller buds and two kinds of leaves. At the center inside double rings is a stiff spray of fruit, the berries each with a cross at the center, with serrated leaves. Outside, there is a band of thunder pattern at the rim between single and double rings. Below, solid blue spear-like petals radiate from the base, producing a striking contrast with the inner decoration of the bowl. On the outer foot-ring there is a single ring.

John Pope tentatively identified the fruit in the center with similar fruit in the cavetto of a large fifteenth-century dish at Ardebil as cherry (Pope 1956, Plate 42, 29.310), but the serrated leaves would seem to argue against this. More likely is his identification of a similar fruit spray on another fifteenth-century dish in Topkapu Saray as loquat, *Eriobotria japonica* (Pope 1953, p. 41). Bowls of this type directly inspired an early sixteenth-century group of Iznik pottery (Pope 1972, p. 136, nos. 22, 23); there are many sherds of such bowls in the Benaki Museum study collection (unpublished) of which two are included in the present exhibition (65a, b).

PUBLISHED: Yutaka Mino and James Robinson, *Beauty and Tranquility: The Eli Lilly Collection of Chinese Art*, Indianapolis Museum of Art, Indianapolis, 1983, p. 234, Plate 91.

18

19

19

18 Bowl

China, Ming dynasty. Xuande mark and period (1426–1435 A.D.).
White porcelain with underglaze blue decoration.
Height 8.1 cm. Diameter 20.3cm.
The Art Institute of Chicago. Bequest of Henry C. Schwab,
    41.554.

Bowl with sloping sides with six indentations in the rim; the bottom of the sharply cut foot-ring is unglazed and fired a buff color. The inside of the foot-ring and the base are glazed. The bowl is decorated in shades of dark cobalt blue with blackish spots where thickly applied.

Inside the bowl at the rim between pairs of foliate and plain rings are twelve sprays of flowers, fungus and a single cross composed of four trefoils; the stems of all the sprays curl back to form a hook. In the cavetto are six larger floral sprays of three kinds: peony, lotus and chrysanthemum, with appropriate leaves; the chrysanthemum has a cross-hatched center. At the center of the bowl inside triple concentric rings is a fruit spray.

Outside, there are double foliate rings at the rim. On the body are six fruit sprays, of peaches, [unidentified], pomegranate, grapes, [two unidentified]. Below and between the fruit sprays are six smaller floral sprays, of peony (two), lotus, chrysanthemum, [unidentified] and fungus. On the outer foot-ring between single rings is a finely drawn band of classic scroll.

On the base inside double rings is a six-character mark of Xuande. A classic example of Xuande porcelain, with its "heaped and piled" use of cobalt blue; a similar bowl is in the Brundage Collection (Asian Art Museum 1985, no. 9).

19 Bowl

China, Ming dynasty. Xuande mark and period (1426–1435 A.D.).
White porcelain, underglaze blue decoration.
Height 7.9 cm. Diameter 17.4 cm.
Indianapolis Museum of Art. Gift of Mr. and Mrs. Stanley
    Herzman, 1984.290.

The small bowl has an everted rim, and is finely glazed, with brilliant cobalt blue painting; much repaired and refired; the bottom of the foot-ring is unglazed.

Inside at the rim, within single and double rings, is an undulating stem bearing tiny rosettes and short pointed leaves. In the cavetto is a wreath of five flowers, including chrysanthemum, lotus and peony, with appropriate leaves. At the center inside double rings is a lotus on a curving stem, with two smaller blossoms.

Outside at the rim, between single and double rings, a band of thunder pattern. On the body is a wreath of five lotuses and blossoms between, on an undulating stem bearing lobed leaves with flame-like tips. Below, from the foot-ring radiate thirty-two petal-panels, filled in with solid blue. On the outer foot-ring between double and single rings, is a neatly drawn band of classic scroll.

On the bases inside double rings, a six-character mark of Xuande.

Two similar bowls were exhibited at Philadelphia in 1949, one with a Xuande mark and one unmarked, also with the formal band of petal-panels on the lower outside body (Lee 1949, nos. 45, 46). Again, like the motifs on (15) and (16) in the present exhibition, the question arises of the possible metallic origin of the ornament. If so, from where did the influence come? There is no immediately detectable Islamic source.

20 Dish

China, Ming dynasty. Xuande mark and period (1426–1435 A.D.).
White porcelain, decorated in underglaze blue.
Height 5.5 cm. Diameter 27 cm.
The Art Institute of Chicago. Gift of Russell Tyson, 55.1204.

The dish has a vigorously bracketed rim, with ten points, and a raised edge; the bracketed form continues down into the cavetto. The bottom and sloping inner face of the foot-ring and the base are unglazed and fired a salmon color. The dish is painted in shades of warm cobalt blue.

On the rim between pairs of bracketed rings is a floral scroll with twenty lily-like flowers and little feathery leaves. In the cavetto are ten radiating sprays of flowers of six types, arranged in pairs opposite each other across the dish. At the center inside a pair of bracketed rings is a lotus spray tied with a ribbon, with the flowers, leaves and buds of various other water-plants.

On the outside there are bracketed rings on the underside of the rim, with a six-character Xuande mark written horizontally between them. On the body are ten more floral sprays like those in the cavetto, and double rings on the outside of the foot-ring.

This Xuande dish is painted with great delicacy, particularly evident in the writing of the reign mark, and the floral scroll on the rim. The cobalt blue is softer than the blue on Yongle pieces and more subtle in its application.

20

20

21 **Dish**

China, Ming dynasty. Early fifteenth century.
White porcelain, with underglaze blue decoration.
Diameter 31.5 cm.
The Nelson-Atkins Museum of Art, Kansas City, Missouri
(Nelson Fund), 64.4/1.

Inside, at the rim between rings is a band of classic scroll. In the cavetto is a wreath of thirteen flowers on an undulating stem, including chrysanthemum, lotus, camellia and peony, the flowers being placed in pairs. At the center, inside double and single rings, is an airily composed bouquet of flowers, with a flame-like ribbon tied in a bow. Below the knot, three stalks curve to the left, and five undulate to the right. The flowers include lotus, a seed pod, sagittaria and various other water plants.

This dish exemplifies the stylistic break with the fourteenth-century style, and the sinicization of blue-and-white; the informal, asymmetrical arrangement of the central bouquet and the generally naturalistic feeling, and the odd number of thirteen flowers in the cavetto, show a new spirit in the concept of decorating the surface of the piece. Even when the floral elements are more consciously placed in a geometric arrangement, the open

quality of the design remains. It should be noted, however, that when fifteenth-century blue-and-white was a source of Near Eastern designs, the Islamic potters tended to re-establish the sense of symmetry and order (Carswell 1972a: 1972b). In the Ardebil Collection there are thirty-four examples of this type of plate alone, and Pope stresses how instructive they are when studied as a group, showing the considerable variation there is in the drawing of individual details (Pope 1956, pp. 91–93, Plates 30, 31).

21

22 Large dish

China, Ming dynasty. Early fifteenth century.
White porcelain, with underglaze blue decoration.
Height 8 cm. Diameter 41 cm.
The Art Institute of Chicago. Gift of Russell Tyson, 54.463.

The dish has a sloping plain rim raised at the edge, with a molded step at the bottom of the cavetto, and a rounded, V-shaped short foot-ring. The bottom and inside of the foot-ring and the base are unglazed, with a smooth, light gray surface. The decoration is in dark cobalt blue with blackish spots, slightly blurred in the glaze.

On the rim is a stylized pattern of breaking waves, a simplified version of the fourteenth-century motif. In the cavetto are eleven flowers of different kinds on a thin undulating stem, with various kinds of leaves. At the center, inside double rings, is a single flower, with shaded, scalloped petals, on a fine, wire-like spiral stem, from which branch off other stems bearing three more flowers, and three smaller blossoms, all of different types with a variety of leaves.

The design has an open, naturalistic quality typical of early fifteenth-century blue-and-white. On the outside there are single rings below the rim, and at its junction to the body. On the body there are eleven flowers of different kinds on an undulating stem, again with many varieties of leaves.

This type of disk was widely exported to the Near East, and examples are in both the Topkapu Saray and Ardebil Collections (Pope 1956, Plates 34, 35, 36). Many of the hexagonal blue-and-white tiles in the Murad II mosque at Edirne, of the mid-fifteenth century, show the influence of such dishes in their design, which can also be traced in Persia, Syria and Egypt (Carswell, 1972a: 1972b: 1979). Although this is generally considered to be the period of the "sinicization" of blue-and-white and a break with the fourteenth-century style, the export of these finely painted wares shows that they were by no means confined to the home market.

22

22

23 Large dish

China, Ming dynasty. Early fifteenth century.
White porcelain decorated in underglaze blue.
Height 7 cm. Diameter 38 cm.
Collection of Mr. J. Chase Gilmore.

Large dish of white porcelain with a greenish-tinged glaze, the bottom and inside of the foot-ring unglazed, with a smooth gray finish, the foot-ring with salmon-pink patches and some grits adhering to the inner surface. The dish has a flattened sloping rim with a raised edge, and a faint raised molding at the intersection of the cavetto and the center. The underglaze cobalt blue has many darker blue spots, and is blackish where thickly applied.

On the rim between single and double rings is a pattern of breaking waves. In the cavetto is a wreath of twelve flowers of different kinds on an undulating thin stem with pointed leaves. At the center, inside double rings, are three bunches of grapes on a knotty stem, with vine leaves, stalks and tendrils.

Outside between a single ring and double rings on the outer foot-ring is another wreath of twelve flowers like those in the cavetto, including lotus, peony, chrysanthemum, fungus and morning glory.

23

23

24 Brass stand

Syria/Egypt, Mamluk dynasty. First half of fourteenth century.
Brass stand, with engraved decoration.
Height 17.7 cm. Diameter of rim at top 16.3 cm.
The Metropolitan Museum of Art. Bequest of Edward C. Moore,
1891, 91.1.568.

The brass stand consists of two parts, the upper half including the
median convex molding, the lower half with part missing at the
top and soldered onto the upper half; a disc inside above the foot
appears to be a later insertion, as are three holes drilled through
the foot.

The upper surface of the rim is engraved with four rosettes
with whorling petals, their frames linked to the borders of a ring
of leaves on an undulating stem.

The two sloping sides of the stem are each engraved with a
large wheel-like medallion, with a radiating Arabic inscription,
with a smaller roundel at the center with one word inscribed in it
horizontally. Between the roundels is another inscription in two
parts against a spiraling leafy background. On the convex molding at the center of the stand are four more rosettes like those on
the rim, separated by two bands of three diamonds with a cross at
the center, and a further inscription in two parts. The base is engraved in similar fashion to the upper rim.

INSCRIPTIONS:
upper half: The high excellency, the lord, the wise, the governor,
   the victorious
medallions: The high excellency, the lord, the wise, the royal,
   (center) the king
center: The high excellency, the lord, the wise, the master
lower half: The high excellency, the lord, the wise, the great, the
   royal   (translation by Yassir al-Tabba)

PUBLISHED: John Carswell, "An Early Ming Porcelain Stand from
Damascus," *Oriental Art*, New Series, XII, Autumn 1966, pp. 180, 182, H.

24

24

25 Stand

China, Ming dynasty. Early fifteenth century.
White porcelain, with underglaze blue decoration.
Height 17.2 cm. Diameter at rim 17 cm.
The British Museum. Brooke Sewell Bequest Fund, 1966.12.15.1.

The porcelain stand has a slightly concave cylindrical body with a convex molding at the center and a wide rim at the top and bottom. There is an unglazed ring 7 mm. wide on the inside, at the junction of the foot to the body. The stand is decorated in dark cobalt blue with blackish spots where thickly applied.

The rim and upper surface of the foot are painted with a ring of elongated almond-shaped petals, with blue outlines. The petals on the rim are on a blue ground with white chevrons between them; on the foot, the ground is white and the chevrons blue. Under the rim are four rosettes flanked by palmettes, with four single rosettes between them. The central molding is painted with two rings of slanting petals.

The upper and lower halves of the body are painted with horizontal bands of pseudo-Arabic against a background of leafy spirals, separated in two parts by roundels. The roundels with a six-armed motif at the center surrounded by leafy spirals, are placed so that each roundel falls midway between the two roundels on the other half.

The porcelain stand is based on an engraved Mamluk metal prototype, like the example in the exhibition (24), copying both the form and the ornament of the original. The stand, however, is not unique. A second virtually identical example has been found in China, and is now in the Tientsin Municipal Museum (Tenshin-shi 1982, no. 238). The British Museum stand was previously in the collection of Dr. Joseph Aractingi in Damascus, who bought it many years ago in the *suq*.

Unlike later Zhengde porcelain with Arabic/Persian inscriptions made for the Moslem market in China, the Arabic on the two stands is quite unintelligible, although both are based on the same original inscription. The faithful rendering of the engraved ornament and the placing of the roundels strongly suggest that it was an actual Mamluk metal stand that was copied at Jingdezhen. The only Chinese element in the decoration are the rosettes beneath the rim; these link the stand to a series of early fifteenth-century dishes with similar motifs (Pope 1956, nos. 29.271, 29.83, 29.113, 29.58). The rosettes are very similar to those beneath the rim of two cups in the Beijing Palace Museum, the only two pieces of porcelain bearing the mark of the emperor Yongle, 1403–25 A.D. (Addis 1978, pp. 82–4, 35a, b). It should be noted that the bottom of the wide foot-ring of these two cups was unglazed, and that they were probably fired, like the stands, on some kind of cylindrical support.

PUBLISHED: John Carswell, "An Early Ming Porcelain Stand from Damascus," *Oriental Art*, New Series, XII, Autumn 1966, pp. 176–182. Basil Gray, "Chinese porcelain of the fourteenth and fifteenth centuries and the John Addis gift," *British Museum Yearbook II*, London, 1977, p. 164.

25

26

27

26 Glass basin

Syria/Egypt, Mamluk dynasty. Fourteenth century.
Glass basin with enameled decoration.
Height 16.6 cm. Diameter 29.3 cm.
The Metropolitan Museum of Art. Bequest of Edward C. Moore, 1891, 91.1.1532.

27 Brass basin

Syria/Egypt, Mamluk dynasty. Fourteenth century.
Brass basin with silver inlay, and engraved decoration.
Height 21.3 cm. Diameter 46 cm.
The Metropolitan Museum of Art. Bequest of Edward C. Moore, 1891, 91.1.589.

Glass basin with widely flaring rim, of bubbled, greenish-brown glass, with tooled rim and pontil mark on the concave base. Enameled in opaque, dull blue, gray, dull red, light brown and green.

Inside at the rim are six blue floral motifs and six circles within single and double rings, with scribbles between them. At the center of the basin is a circular design of eight radiating triangular petals with a circle in the center and between the tips of the petals.

Outside, an Arabic inscription in large *thuluth* script in four parts, separated by roundels with scalloped borders, with smaller roundels at the center between pairs of rings.

INSCRIPTION: Glory to our lord, the sultan, the king, the wise, the wise, the wise.

Both in form and decoration, the glass basin is clearly a crude derivative of the brass prototype.

PUBLISHED: M. Jenkins, *The Renaissance of Islam: Art of the Mamluks, Checklist of Additional Objects Exhibited at the Metropolitan Museum of Art,* New York, 1981, no. 28. M.S. Dimand, *Handbook of Muhammadan Art,* Metropolitan Museum of Art, New York, 1944, p. 248. *A Handbook of Mohammadan Decorative Arts,* Metropolitan Museum of Art, New York, 1930, p. 198. Lamm, *Mittelalterliche gläser...*, 1930, I, p. 419; II, Plate 184, no. 3. Pier, "Saracenic glass," *Orientalisches archiv...*, I, 1910–11, p. 189, Plate XXXVII, Figure 3. Lavoix, "La collection Albert Goupil, II: L'art oriental," *Gazette des Beaux-Arts,* II, 1885, p. 303. *Catalogue de la collection Goupil,* 1888, p. 37, no. 37. John Pope, *Chinese Porcelains from the Ardebil Shrine,* Freer Gallery of Art, Smithsonian Institution, Washington, D.C., 1956, p. 89, Plate 135B.

Brass basin with a widely flaring rim, with engraved decoration and silver inlay. Inside, at the rim, a band of flying ducks; below, an undulating leafy scroll interspersed with four rosettes; a wide band of Arabic with a floral background, in four parts separated by four large medallions; the medallions have scalloped borders, with rosettes at the center surrounded either by flying ducks, or by six lotuses. Below, a band of interlocking leafy stems, with almond-shaped pendant motifs.

Outside, an inscribed band in four parts, in *thuluth* script, separated by medallions whose scalloped borders interlace with the horizontal borders of the inscription. The medallions, with rosettes at the center, are surrounded by lotuses and smaller rosettes. At two points there are traces of the preliminary engraving of the inscription, showing how the Arabic text was lightly engraved before being deeply incised.

On the base is a mark, possibly of the owner: ربانرمداع

INSCRIPTIONS:
inside: Glory to our lord, the sultan, the king, the fighter for the faith, the wise, the governor, the aided, the victorious, the aided to victory, the sword of Islam, 'Ali, may his victory be glorious.
outside: Glory to our lord, the sultan, the king, the fighter for the faith, the wise, the governor, the aided, the victorious, the aided to victory, the master of kings and sultans, the killer of infidels and polytheists,... the widows, the sword of Islam 'Ali the commander of the faithful, may his victory be glorious.

(translation by Yassir al-Tabba)

A large silver-inlaid brass tray with similar decoration in the Louvre is inscribed with the name of Sultan al-Malik al-Mujahid Saif as-Din 'Ali ibn Dawud (ruled 1321–63 A.D.). The name of the same Sultan is on a brass candlestick, and an enameled glass bottle, both once in private collections in Paris.

PUBLISHED: M.S. Dimand, "Unpublished metalwork of the Rasulid sultans of Yemen," *Metropolitan Museum Studies,* III, 2, 1931, p. 234, figure 4. Max Van Berchem, "Notes d'archéologie arabe...," *Journal Asiatique,* Series 10, III, 1904, p. 60 (brass tray in Louvre), pp. 64–8 (brass candlestick, and glass bottle, in Paris).

28 Basin

China, Ming dynasty. Early fifteenth century.
White porcelain decorated in underglaze cobalt blue.
Height 13.9 cm. Diameter 30.5 cm.
Asian Art Museum of San Francisco. The Avery Brundage
  Collection, B60 P33 +.

This magnificent piece with its deep, rounded body and flaring rim, owes its form to a Near Eastern prototype, of either glass or metal, of which examples are in the exhibition (26, 27). Of these, it is probably closer to the glass shape, less angular than the large inlaid brass basin.

The decoration is wholly Chinese, painted in dotted cobalt blue characteristic of the early fifteenth century with a vivacity and calm assurance which makes this basin unique.

On the gently curving inner rim is a wide band of delicately painted flowers of carnation type, between single rings. The flowers spring from an undulating stem, which also bears tiny trefoil leaves and flame-like tendrils. In the cavetto is a lotus-wreath with eight flowers, smaller blossoms and pointed, lobed leaves with flame-like tips.

At the bottom is a ring of thunder pattern inside double rings, and in the center an elaborate design with a double *vajra* inside triple rings, an outer ring of scalloped petals and eight lotus-panels radiating outwards. The frames of the lotus-panels have lobed, foliate points and inside at the base form cloud-collars. At the center of each panel is one of eight auspicious objects, a pair of interlocking rings, a silver ingot, crossed rhinoceros horns, a pair of crossed books, a pair of interlocking lozenges, three pearls (?), a coral branch and an umbrella (?). The shading of the whole of the central design is such that it has an organic, three-dimensional quality, emphasizing its iconographic content.

On the outside of the basin between pairs of rings, the body is decorated with a wreath of eight flowers, including chrysanthemum, peony, convulvulus and lotus, with smaller flowers between and various kinds of leaves. Below is a ring of alternating cash and lozenge-shaped motifs.

One of the more remarkable elements is the wriggling tendril-like form repeated on the inner rim; one writer has suggested that its calligraphic nature might have been an attempt to imitate the Arabic of the Islamic model that inspired the form of the basin (Lion-Goldschmidt 1978, p. 70). Cursive Arabic, however, is not a feature of Mamluk glass or metalwork; but it should be noted that this form closely resembles the word [A]llah but without the initial *alif.*

Related examples of the basin are in the National Gallery, Melbourne; the Hakone Art Museum, Japan; the National Palace Museum, Taibei; and the Topkapu Saray Museum, Istanbul.

Fourteenth-century examples of similar wheel-like central designs with radiating lotus-panels (varying in number from six to fourteen) filled with auspicious objects are in the Ardebil Collection (Pope 1956, Plate 19, 29.49; 21, 29.127, 29.48; and for a central double *vajra*, mutated into a four pointed cloud-collar motif, Plate 23, 29.319). In Istanbul, a most elaborate version is a dish with an inner ring of six panels, and an outer ring of eighteen panels, all with auspicious objects (Pope 1952, Plate 9; see also Plate 15; and Plate 26, a bowl with no less than twenty-six panels). More examples are among the fourteenth-century pieces in Delhi (Smart 1977).

PUBLISHED: Y. d'Argencé, *Chinese Ceramics in the Avery Brundage Collection,* The deYoung Museum Society, San Francisco, 1967, p. 144, Plate LII. D. Lion-Goldschmidt, *Ming Porcelain,* London, 1978, p. 70, Plates 29, 29a. S. Little, "Cross-Cultural Influences in Asian Ceramics," *Apollo,* August 1980, p. 110, Figure 9. C. Shangraw, *Orientations,* May 1985.

28

28

29 Small vase

China, Ming dynasty. Jingtai period, c. 1453 A.D.
White porcelain, underglaze blue decoration.
Height 15.4 cm. Diameter of body 8 cm.
Buffalo Society of Natural Sciences, Buffalo Museum of Science.
  Ch 456.

29

Small vase with trumpet-shaped neck and pear-shaped body with a flaring foot and two handles. The vase is covered with a crackled, milky glaze and decorated in grayish-blue. The bottom and inside of the foot and the base are unglazed and fired a buff color. The vase was made in four separate parts luted together, the joints showing clearly as ridges on the outside. The splayed foot was made separately and luted onto the body.

The neck is decorated with leafy sprays between the handles, themselves outlined in blue. On the body between loosely-drawn double rings, a sketchily painted but vivacious rendering of flowers and leaves on an undulating stem. On the foot, two more horizontal floral sprays.

This vase would be difficult to date except for the existence of two groups of pottery from tombs near Jingdezhen excavated in 1974 (Ouyand and Huang 1981). The first tomb, dated 1453 A.D., contained seven pieces of blue-and-white, including two pairs of vases closely related to the Buffalo vase in size and decoration, and similarly constructed. The contents of these tombs are of particular importance as they demonstrate the kind of pottery being made during the Interregnum period, 1436–1464 A.D. when the adverse political situation, famine and government prohibition had a disastrous affect on the ceramic industry (*ibid.*, p. 36).

30 Bowl

China, Ming dynasty. Fifteenth/sixteenth century.
White porcelain, underglaze blue decoration.
Height 6.5 cm. Diameter 13.9 cm.
Indianapolis Museum of Art. Gift of Mr. and Mrs. Daniel
   Henkin, 79.507.

30

30

Small bowl with curved sides, painted in gray-blue under a milky gray-blue glaze. The bottom of the sharply-angled foot-ring and part of the inner foot are unglazed. Inside, there is a ring at the rim, and at the center a roughly drawn conch shell inside sketchy rings.

Outside, a much simplified band of serpentine waves breaking to the left, between sketchy rings; below, a ring of vertical, sharply pointed plantain-like leaves with serrated edges, and double rings on the outer foot-ring.

Crudely made but not without a certain lively charm, this type of blue-and-white porcelain, probably the product of a south Chinese provincial kiln, was widely exported to south-east Asia. The origin of the type can be seen in the *lianzi* bowl (17). Large collections of this type of export ware can be studied in the Museum of Anthropology, The University of Michigan; and the Field Museum, Chicago.

For two related bowls, Aga-Oglu 1982, p. 71, nos. 155, 156.

31 Large dish

China, Ming dynasty. Fifteenth/sixteenth century.
White porcelain, grayish blue underglaze decoration.
Height 4.8 cm. Diameter 24 cm.
Indianapolis Museum of Art. Gift of Mr. and Mrs. Daniel
Henkin, 79.502.

32 Bowl

China, Ming dynasty. Late fifteenth/early sixteenth century.
White porcelain, underglaze blue decoration.
Height 14.2 cm. Diameter 33 cm.
Private Collection, London.

31

Dish with a narrow, flattened rim, the bottom of the recessed foot-ring is unglazed and fired orange. Painted in blue which has fired a gray color, in a loose, sketchy style with considerable verve. At the rim, between single and double rings, a narrow band of diagonal hatching. In the cavetto, a ring of trailing arabesque stems and feathery intertwining leaves, and spirals. At the center inside single and double rings, a phoenix rises in the air with outspread wings, head turned to the right. In the background are more trailing leaves, and heart-shaped flowers above and below.

On the outside, between double rings below the rim and at the base, five highly simplified lotuses with dotted petals on an arabesque stem, with pointed lobed leaves and tendrils.

The origins of many late fifteenth/early sixteenth-century pieces are found in fourteenth-century wares; the later pieces are often clearly pastiches of elements in the earlier wares. For this dish, compare with one from Ardebil (Pope 1956, 28.128); even closer parallels for the rising phoenix are on two Delhi fragments (Smart 1977, Plate 80b (upside down), 87d).

Large bowl with everted rim, of white porcelain freely painted in shades of cobalt blue, fired in blackish spots where thickly applied. The bottom of the inward-sloping foot-ring is unglazed and fired a salmon-pink color.

Inside at the rim between pairs of rings is a classic scroll. In the cavetto are five peonies on an undulating stem, with pairs of smaller blossoms between, and leaves. The flowers appear to have been blocked in first with large smudges of cobalt blue, the details added afterwards. At the center inside single and double rings, a lotus-spray with two flowers and other water-plants, a large lotus-leaf and water rippling to the right.

Outside between pairs of double rings, a wreath of six lotuses in profile on a double undulating stem rising above and below the margins, with short pointed, lobed leaves. Below, a ring of twelve lotus-panels, each filled with three spirals grouped in a pendant triangle, and three ticks. Below, double rings, and double rings on the upper foot-ring.

This bowl and (33) can be compared with the two bowls in Giovanni Bellini's *The Feast of the Gods*, for which they provide close parallels, and therefore are before 1514. This type of bowl and other associated shapes were widely exported to south-east Asia and the Near East. Many examples have been noted in Syria, as well as in the Topkapu Saray and Ardebil Collections; some large dishes even got as far as Portugal (Lion-Goldschmidt 1984, Figures 1–3, 12–17) suggesting the style was still current by the time the Portuguese arrived in India and the Far East at the beginning of the sixteenth century. It is not known when this style began; in theory a key piece should be the large vase in the David Foundation, dated 1496 A.D., but the stiff drawing has little of the fluency of the wares under consideration (Garner 1954b, p. 26, Plate 58).

For close parallels to this bowl from south-east Asia, see Aga-Oglu 1982, nos. 93, 94: and Yeo and Martin 1978, no. 74. Both works illustrate numerous other examples from the same family of blue-and-white.

Dr. A. Spriggs was the first scholar to draw attention to the bowls in the Bellini painting, in his pioneer paper on blue-and-white in western paintings (Spriggs 1967).

32

32

Figure 32. *The Feast of the Gods,* 1514. Giovanni Bellini, The National Gallery of Art, Washington, D.C., Widener Collection (details). Commissioned by either Isabella or Alfonso d'Este, this painting was Giovanni Bellini's last great work, for he died two years later. Among the studio props used in the painting are three pieces of blue-and-white, two bowls and a dish with a gilt mount. Bellini's dated painting provides a useful *terminus ante quem* for this type of porcelain, widely exported to south-east Asia and the Near East towards the end of the fifteenth century.

33 Bowl

China, Ming dynasty. Late fifteenth/early sixteenth century.
White porcelain, underglaze blue decoration.
Height 12.4 cm. Diameter 31.4 cm.
Private Collection, London.

Large bowl with curved sides, of white porcelain decorated in dark cobalt blue under a greenish-tinged glaze. The center had sandy grits adhering to the glaze. The lower half of the inward-sloping foot-ring is unglazed, and fired a salmon-orange color at the junction with the glaze.

Inside, there are double rings at the rim; below, in the cavetto are six flowers in profile on a thin, undulating stem rising above the upper margin, with smaller blossoms and tight spiral leaves. At the center inside single and double rings, a peony spray with large veined leaves.

Outside, at the rim between pairs of rings is a band of classic scroll. Below, on the body, on a double stem rising above and below the margins, six more flowers like those in the cavetto, with similar spiral leaves. Below, between pairs of rings, a ring of twenty pointed motifs, designed as if based on half a *ruyi* head, with spirals between. There is a single ring on the outer foot-ring.

Like (32), this bowl in form resembles the bowl in the Bellini painting, held aloft by one of the nymphs (see Figure 32).

34 Box and lid

China, Ming dynasty. Late fifteenth/early sixteenth century.
White porcelain, underglaze blue decoration.
Height with lid 12.5 cm. Length 27.5 cm. Width 15 cm.
Private Collection, London.

The box and lid have slightly curved sides and rounded ends. There is a raised rim on both the box and the lid. The inside of the rims of the lid and the box are unglazed, as is the underside of the foot; the base also has a large patch of yellow, sandy material adhering to it. At the junction of the glazed and unglazed areas there is an orange line. The box is painted in dark cobalt blue, which has fired a blackish tone where thick.

The top of the box is painted with a symmetrical design, with a lotus flanked by irises on a spiraling stem, and tightly-drawn, lobed leaves with a double outline. Around the lid, between the edge of the molding and the rim decorated with classic scroll, there is a band of *ruyi* lappets, with a scalloped band above. The box itself has a band of classic scroll at the rim; below, an undulating stem bears lotuses and flowers, each of the latter with six veined, fleshy petals, one of which has a dotted outline. On the same stem are more lobed and pointed leaves with double outlines.

The form of the box is fairly common in late Mamluk metalwork, often fitted together in sets of two or three, and designated as "lunch boxes" (Allan 1971). Such composite boxes are used to this day in the Near East by workmen, to contain a variety of cold food for the midday meal. The translation of the form from metal to porcelain is singularly inappropriate, and the Chinese potters must have been unaware of the original purpose. They may, of course, have been conceived in porcelain with some other purpose in mind than an *alfresco* meal. A sixteenth-century Persian manuscript shows a bath scene, with similarly-shaped containers of silver and gold, some with lids; perhaps they were soap dishes, or contained a depilatory (Robinson 1959, no. 910).

A smaller version of the box and lid has been noted in Beirut (Carswell 1979, p. 21, Plate XXV, Figure 6). Of the same date, it is painted with a fish and a variety of water-plants. Related boxes with lids have been published from south-east Asia (Yeo and Martin 1978, no. 29, with an internal division and without a lid, this one certainly a pen-box: Aga-Oglu 1982, no. 126).

PUBLISHED: John Carswell, "Sin in Syria," *Iran,* XVII, 1979, p. 21, Plate XXIV, Figure 5.

33

34

34

35 Bowl

China, Ming dynasty. Mark and period of Zhengde (1506–1521
A.D.).
White porcelain with underglaze blue decoration.
Height 9.3 cm. Diameter 20.6 cm.
The Cleveland Museum of Art. Anonymous Gift, 57.359.

36 Fragment of a bowl

China, Ming dynasty. Mark and period of Zhengde (1506–1521
A.D.).
White porcelain, underglaze blue decoration.
Height 12.3 cm. Diameter 28 cm.
Freer Gallery of Art Study Collection (Smithsonian Institution).
SC-P940.

35

Part of a bowl with an everted rim; inside at the rim is a band of
thunder pattern. At the center is an Arabic Quranic inscription:

ash-shukr-u bi ni'matihi

"thanks for his favors"

Encircling the inscription is a wide ring of thick, leafy scrolls.

Outside below the rim is another band of thunder pattern. On
the body were six roundels, of which three remain. These contain
a Persian inscription, the full text of which can be reconstructed
from a similar, intact bowl in the Freer Gallery (Figure 8):

/ [igbal] / va daulat-e / khudavanda / [cavid bad] / [keh har ruz]
/ bar mazid ast /

"May the good fortune and power of the prince which is daily
on the increase be eternal"

Between the roundels are pairs of leafy floral motifs. Below is a
ring of open pointed petals. On the base inside double rings is a
six-character Zhengde mark.

Found in Beijing in 1945–6, by John Pope, this fragmentary
bowl with its Arabic-Persian inscriptions reinforces the argument
that similarly inscribed wares of the Zhengde period were
intended for the resident Moslem population rather than for export. This fragment, and the complete bowl in the Freer Gallery,
are the only two pieces known to the writer which combine both
Arabic and Persian inscriptions on the same piece, as well as a
Zhengde mark.

This simply adorned but elegant bowl is decorated in warm cobalt blue. The bottom of the foot-ring is unglazed and fired a faint
buff color; the foot-ring slopes slightly inwards.

Inside, the only decoration is a pair of rings at the rim. Outside, at the rim between single and double rings is a finely drawn
band of classic scroll, each pair of spirals with tendril-like leaves.
Below, there are four sprays of lotus on the body, alternating with
four more sprays of lotus-buds, springing from ripples of water
flowing to the right.

Below is a ring of eight interlocking *hui hui wen*, "Mohammadan scrolls," so called by Chinese writers, and frequently oc-
curring on Zhengde blue-and-white porcelain with Arabic/
Chinese inscriptions (Garner 1954b, pp. 28–30). The scrolls are
painted with single strokes of the brush, an exception to the general practice for this type of decoration, where the scrolls are
drawn in outline and then filled in with a blue wash.

Broad bands of interlocking arabesques and geometric ornament are a feature of late Mamluk metalwork, and may have been
a source for these distinctive scroll patterns (see Atil 1981, p. 102,
no. 35, on a bowl c. 1470–90). A much closer and more probable
inspiration would have been Mamluk textiles; for instance, a fourteenth century silk with rings of such interlocking scrolls, and a
slightly later silk with a more complex variant of the same design
(Atil 1981, nos. 115, 118).

There are double rings on the outer foot-ring, and a four-character mark of Zhengde inside double rings on the base.

An almost indentical bowl is in The Metropolitan Museum of
Art (Valenstein 1970, p. 63, no. 35).

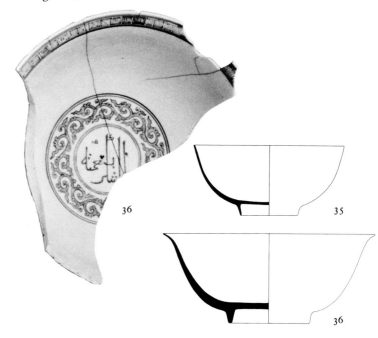

36

35

36

37 Tripod censer

China, Ming dynasty. Mark and period of Zhengde (1506–1521 A.D.).
White porcelain, underglaze blue decoration.
Height 10.3 cm.
Benaki Museum, Athens. From the Eumorphopoulos Collection, 119.9.V.D20.

37

The tripod censer has a globular body molded with six convex panels, a short neck and a vertical rim. The three stepped feet have oval unglazed bases; there is a wide unglazed ring on the bottom of the censer fired a pale orange color. The glaze has the texture of orange-skin, and the decoration is in cobalt blue with darker outlines.

The rim is painted with a horizontal band of blue spots between double and single rings. On the neck, in the middle and at the joints of each molded panel, there is a blue lappet. On each face of the body, there is a cartouche with four ogival points with a double outline, from the two horizontal points of which spring symmetrical leafy scrolls with scalloped borders, almost encircling the cartouche. The upper part of each foot is outlined in blue and below there is a pair of spirals.

Each of the six cartouches contains part of a Persian inscription, which reads:

an keh ba 'attar / migardad / qarib / u hami yabad / ze bu-ye khod / nasib

"He who gets close to a perfume seller he acquires a share of his own scent"

On the bottom on the glazed circle inside the unglazed ring is a six-character Zhengde mark.

Another censer of different shape in the British Museum (38) also has a Zhengde mark, circular instead of ogival panels, and an Arabic instead of Persian inscription. An unmarked censer in the Ashmolean of plain white porcelain (40) has a carved Arabic inscription in three parts. The spots on the rim may derive from rivets on a bronze censer, such as one with Arabic inscriptions and a Xuande mark in the Victoria and Albert Museum (Bushell 1924, p. 58, Figure 43).

PUBLISHED: R. L. Hobson, *Catalogue of the George Eumorfopoulos Collection of Chinese and Corean Pottery and Porcelain*, IV, London, 1925–8.

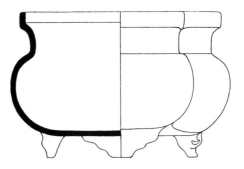

38 Tripod censer

China, Ming dynasty. Mark and period of Zhengde (1506–1521 A.D.).
White porcelain, underglaze blue decoration.
Height 12.4 cm. Diameter 14 cm.
The British Museum. 1973.7–26.367.

38

The tripod censer has a flattened globular body, short vertical neck and square rim, and stands on three tall feet. It is decorated in two shades of cobalt blue. There is a wide unglazed ring on the bottom of the censer, and the circular base of each foot is also unglazed. The censer once had two handles, now missing.

On the outside of the rim is a band of thunder pattern. On the neck are two symmetrical scrolling bands, each with a *ruyi* head at the center. On the body are six circular panels with double ring frames, from the top and bottom of which spring wing-like pairs of leaf scrolls. In between each panel are pairs of opposed *ruyi* heads separated by a diamond.

Each circular panel contains part of an Arabic inscription:

ana l–hannan /	"I am the Tender-hearted /
fa–utlubni /	so seek Me [and] /
tajiduni /	thou shalt find Me /
sulh[?] ilayya /	. . . [?] to Me /
la taqsud /	Thou shalt not desire /
siwaya /	[anyone] but Me" /

On the bottom, on the glazed circle inside the unglazed ring, a six-character Zhengde mark inside double blue rings.

The form has an earlier prototype; a bronze inlaid censer in the Musée Cernuschi, Paris, of the same shape has a Chenghua mark; it also has a band of thunder pattern on the rim and classic scrolls on the neck (Jenyns and Watson 1963, p. 137, no. 60).

Similar inscriptions inside double rings are on a vase in Philadelphia, and a covered rectangular box in Toronto; the *ruyi* heads with symmetrical flanking scrolls are on an inscribed plaque in the David Foundation (Garner 1954, Plates 43A, B, 45).

EXHIBITED: *Chinese Blue and White Procelain from the 14th to the 19th centuries*, Oriental Ceramic Society, at Arts Council, London, December 16, 1954 – January 23, 1954. Then belonging to Mrs. Seligman, the censer is referred to by Garner in his notes on the exhibition, "Blue and White of the Middle Ming Period," *Transactions of the Oriental Ceramic Society*, 1951–53, London, 1954, p. 64. He also discusses Zhengde wares with Arabic/Persian inscriptions at length.

39 Two bronze censers

China, Ming dynasty. Xuande dates (1430 A.D. and 1431 A.D.); but
   questionably of the period.
Bronze, coated with a lustrous brown polish.
a. Height 11.2 cm. Diameter 16.5 cm.
b. Height 9.6 cm. Diameter 17.7 cm.
Field Museum of Natural History, Chicago. a. 117602 b. 117601.

39a

a. Bronze censer with flattened globular body, concave neck and
everted rim, two upsweeping loop handles, and triangular feet
round in section. An inscription in Arabic in raised letters against
a punched ground, in three parts, each framed in an ogival
medallion with rounded ends. The inscription reads:

afdalu al-dhikr /	"The best confessional invocation [is]: /
la ilaha illa Alahhu /	There is no god but God /
Muhammad rasul Allah /	Muhammad is the apostle of God" /

大明宣德
五年監督
工部官臣
吳邦佐造

On the underside of the censer cast in a recessed square in archaic
seal script in four rows of four characters is a Chinese inscription.
Transcribed at right into modern Chinese it reads:

   "Made in the fifth year of the period Xuande [1430 A.D.] of the
   great Ming dynasty by his majesty's servant Wu Bangzuo, who
   held office in the Board of Public Works with the title of super-
   intendent or director"

b. Bronze censer of flattened globular form, concave neck and flat
everted rim with two upsweeping loop handles and three peg-like
feet round in section. The cast decoration includes two dragons
on each handle, a basket-like pattern on the vertical side of the
rim, thunder pattern on the neck, and a raised ring. On the body
are two pairs of five-clawed dragons, and below, three more four-
clawed dragons. Flaming pearls rest on a cloud motif between the
dragons, and the outsides of the tripod feet also have spiraling
cloud designs on them. On the base in a square raised frame is a
Chinese inscription in four rows of four characters:

   "Made in the sixth year of Xuande [1431 A.D.] of the great Ming
   dynasty under the supervision of his majesty's servant Wu
   Bangzuo, president of the Board of Public Works"

The background of the ornament and inscription is punched.

PUBLISHED: Berthold Laufer, "Chinese Muhammedan Bronzes," *Ars Isla-mica*, I.2, Ann Arbor, Michigan, 1934, pp. 133–147. Soame Jenyns and William Watson, *Chinese Art: The Minor Arts*, Fribourg, 1963, p. 91. For a discussion of these two bronzes and other bronze and porcelain censers with Arabic inscriptions, see p. 97.

39b

40

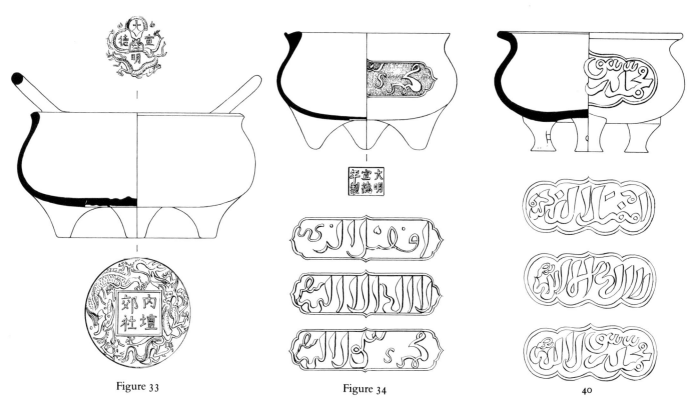

Figure 33   Figure 34   40

40 Tripod censer

China, Ming dynasty. Sixteenth century.
White porcelain with carved decoration.
Height 9 cm. Diameter 15 cm.
Ashmolean Museum, Oxford. 1980.405.

Tripod censer of white porcelain, with flattened globular body, concave neck and everted rim, standing on three short feet, round in section and hollow inside, with holes on the inside to allow air to escape when firing. The base of the censer is concave and unglazed.

The body of the censer is carved with three panels with ogival and rounded frames, and inscribed in Arabic with the letters standing in relief:

afdalu al-dhikr /	"The best confessional invocation [is]: /
la ilaha illa Alahhu /	There is no god but God /
Muhammad rasul Allah /	Muhammad is the apostle of God" /

This type of porcelain censer, unlike the two underglaze-blue examples, more obviously derives from a metal prototype. Precisely the same type of ogival frame with rounded ends can be seen on a bronze censer in the Field Museum, the Arabic again in relief against a punched background (39a). The bronze censer has the same invocational inscription, though in more attenuated script. It also has on the underside a Chinese inscription in archaic seal script.

Another censer in the Field Museum (39b) is elaborately decorated with dragons and other decorative motifs, but no Arabic; it does, however have a similar Chinese text on the base, this time in modern characters.

Bernard Laufer, who published both the bronze censers, was convinced that Wu Bangzuo was a Moslem and supervised the production of the censers for the emperor. He explained away the Arabic as a conscious attempt to impress the sovereign in favour of Islam, and accepted the bronzes unequivocally as of the period of Xuande (Laufer 1934).

Before examining this attribution, there are two other pieces which have some bearing on the question, both belonging to private collectors once living in Beirut. The first (Figure 33) belonged to the archaeologist, the late Gerald Lankester Harding, who although he spent his life in the Near East, was actually born in Tientsin, from whence the censer came. This bronze censer has a four-character Xuande mark inside, in a dragon frame. On the underside in a more elaborate dragon frame is a Chinese inscription:

"Palace altar for sacrifices to the God of the Soil"

The second piece belongs to Professor Yussif Ibish (Figure 34). This censer has tripod feet very similar in style to the Harding censer, whose shape it also resembles except for the two sloping handles. This one has three panels of Arabic against a punched background, the cartouches of more attenuated form and rather like stretched-out versions of the ogival frames on the Benaki censer. The Arabic is very strange, particularly the writing of the word Muhammad, but the text is again the same invocation as on the Ashmolean and Field Museum censers. It also has in common with the Ashmolean example swollen forms for the *alif*-like vertical strokes. This censer has a six-character Xuande mark on the base.

What can we conclude from this group of porcelain and metal censers? The only fixed points are the two Zhengde blue-and-white pieces, which are marked and obviously of the period, having all the features of this family of porcelain with Arabic/Persian inscriptions. The third porcelain piece is unfortunately not marked. If it is also Zhengde, then there must have been some metal prototype, and it certainly shares a number of features with the Xuande bronze censers, not least of all the same text. With the propensity for the Chinese to copy works of the Xuande period, they could of course be later (and so could the Ashmolean censer). But it is curious that the two Field Museum bronzes have such specifically historic inscriptions on them, and that the Harding censer should also make reference to an imperial context for the altar which it was supposed to adorn. If they are later, one explanation might be that they were made by Moslems to reinforce their claim to historical credibility and importance during the Ming dynasty.

In discussing Xuande bronzes and the later bronzes with Xuande marks, Watson considered the Field Museum censer with its Arabic inscription and Xuande 1430 date to be an isolated example, and possibly a later product (Jenyns and Watson 1963, p. 91). But as noted above, there are at least two more censers with Xuande marks inscribed with Arabic; a third in the Victoria and Albert Museum was published by Bushell (Bushell 1924, pp. 57–58, Figure 34); and Laufer mentions a fourth, once in the collection of C. Shefer (Laufer 1934, pp. 134, 136). Watson also published a rectangular censer in the British Museum with an Arabic inscription, with precisely the same frame and type of Arabic script as both the Field Museum censer and the Ashmolean porcelain censer. This he describes as Zhengde (Jenyns and Watson 1963, pp. 87–91, Plate 59).

41 Dish

Vietnam. Fifteenth/sixteenth century.
Off-white ware, underglaze blue decoration.
Height 7.2 cm. Diameter 35.4 cm.
Collection of Mr. and Mrs. Robert McCormick Adams.

41

Deep dish of off-white ware, decorated in shades of dark cobalt blue. The dish has a narrow rim with a raised edge, and rounded, V-shaped foot-ring. The raised rim and the lower part of the foot-ring are unglazed and fired a cream color; the base is also unglazed with swirls of dark brown dressing applied to the surface.

Inside on the rim within single and double rings is a sketchy chain pattern. In the cavetto there are five flowers, with leafy sprays between them springing alternately from the upper and lower margins. At the center of the dish inside pairs of double concentric rings are seven wave-like motifs, with hooked leaves between them. In the middle is a large peony with shaded and hatched petals, surrounded by large pointed leaves.

Outside, between double and single rings, there are thirteen lotus-panels with widely-spaced outlines, each filled with three spirals, a circle and three ticks forming a pendant.

Vietnamese ware (referred to until recently as "Annamese ware") has in the past few years been the subject of intensive research (Frasché 1976. Brown 1977. Guy 1980. Vietnamese 1982). Vietnamese underglaze blue and/or iron-brown decorated wares appear in quantity throughout south-east Asia about the middle of the fourteenth century. The underglaze blue ware derives stylistically from Jingdezhen blue-and-white, but the designs and individual motifs are interpreted with a new vitality and freedom. Often the style of painting is reminiscent of Cizhou ware; flowers, particularly the peony, are strongly modelled.

Vietnamese wares were also exported to the Near East, and there are examples in the Topkapu Saray and Ardebil Collections, and a number of pieces have also been recorded from Syria.

For dating a key piece is a large Vietnamese flask in the Topkapu Saray Collection, with an inscription of 1450 A.D. (Hobson 1934. Garner 1954b, pp. 8, 54, Plate 84A. Vietnamese 1982, p. 32, Figure b). There is also a splendid *guan* jar and a large dish in the Ardebil Collection (Pope 1956, Plate 56, 29.496; Plate 57, 29.143). The influence of Vietnamese ceramics on Near Eastern blue-and-white can be seen on a hexagonal tile in the Murad II mosque at Edirne in Turkey, of the second half of the fifteenth century (Carswell 1972b, p. 100, Plate 3, EII).

The present dish falls into the fifteenth/sixteenth century group of related pieces (Vietnamese 1982, nos. 106, 108, 125, 152, 189). Chronological divisions seem to be based at the moment on the assumption that the more simply painted pieces in less brilliant blue are later. A very distinctive feature of Vietnamese ceramics is the dark brown dressing on the base, the purpose of which is far from clear (d'Argencé 1958).

42 Large dish

China, Ming dynasty. Mark and period of Jiajing (1522–1566 A.D.).
White porcelain with underglaze blue decoration.
Height 7.2 cm. Diameter 32.2 cm.
The Art Institute of Chicago. Gift of Russell Tyson, 54.465.

43 Large dish

China, Ming dynasty. Late sixteenth century.
White porcelain with underglaze blue decoration.
Height 8 cm. Diameter 38.2 cm.
Collection of Mr. J. Chase Gilmore.

The large dish has curved sides, and the bottom of the undercut foot-ring is unglazed and fired orange at the junction with the glaze. Painted in shades of vivid cobalt blue.

On the inside there are widely spaced double rings at the rim. The cavetto is plain. At the center inside a pair of concentric rings, two dragons are clawing up and down, with a flaming pearl and cloud-scrolls around them. The dragons have five claws.

Outside on the body are two more dragons chasing flaming pearls round the dish, with more cloud-scrolls. There are double rings below the rim, and on the outside of the sloping foot-ring. On the base inside double rings is a six-character mark of Jiajing.

Large dish, with the bottom and inside of the undercut foot-ring and the base unglazed, and fired a warm gray. The base shows traces of spiral and radial chatter-marks, and the inside of the foot-ring, diagonal chatter-marks.

The dish is simply and boldly painted in two shades of cobalt blue with darker outlines. Inside at the rim within single and double rings is an undulating stem bearing six chrysanthemum-like flowers and six cross-like flowers, with both scrolling and plain five-pointed leaves. The cavetto is plain. At the center inside double rings is a watery landscape with a boat on a river, with two figures under a rectangular canopy, a mast in front and a single oarsman at the stern. All around are rocky islets, pagodas, shrines, a pine tree, mists and swirling clouds. The scene is composed of direct and simple images.

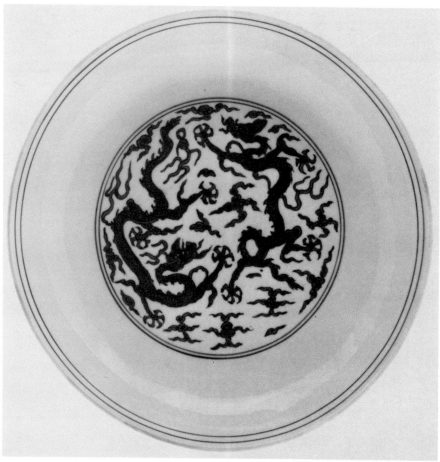

42

44 Large bowl

China, Ming dynasty. Mid-sixteenth century.
White porcelain, underglaze cobalt blue decoration.
Height 16 cm. Diameter 35 cm.
Private Collection, United Kingdom. From Syria.

The large bowl has been broken in three, part of the rim is missing and restored, and it was once riveted. The bottom of the footring is unglazed and fired orange at the edge of the glaze.

Inside, at the rim between pairs of concentric rings, ten pointed medallions each containing a flying crane and cloud-scrolls, with diaper pattern between them on a blue ground. The cavetto is plain. At the center inside double rings is a *qilin* with head turned back, parapet to the right, flaming scrolls, a pine tree and rocks, clouds, grass and the moon.

Outside, at the rim, between pairs of rings, a band of vine scroll with grapes and little ferret-like animals, all reserved on a blue ground. Below, seven large medallions, six with three cranes and cloud-scrolls and the seventh with two phoenixes and cloud-scrolls, all reserved on a blue ground. Between the medallions are pairs of three-armed cloud-scroll motifs. Below, a band of twelve lotus-panels with a lobed leaf reserved on a blue ground at the center of each, and three bars below. On the outside of the footring between double rings is a band of linked spirals. On the base is a four-character seal mark:

Fu gui jia qi
"fine vessel for the rich and honorable"

44

44

45 Bowl

China, Ming dynasty. Mark and period of Jiajing (1522–1566 A.D.).
White porcelain, underglaze blue decoration.
Height 13.5 cm. Diameter 28.9 cm.
Private Collection, London.

45

45

The bowl is decorated in shades of brilliant cobalt blue. Inside, at the rim are pairs of rings. The cavetto is plain. At the bottom inside double rings, a white hare crouches with right forepaw raised and head turned upwards, against a background of grass and fungus.

On the outside, between single and double rings at the rim, there are six fruit sprays and six berriboned auspicious objects. On the body are five roundels, of birds and animals in a landscape. Below, a ring of highly formalized lotus-panels, and a single ring on the foot.

On the base, the six-character mark of Jiajing.

According to Chinese tradition, the hare lives on the moon and sits under the shade of an *olea fragrans* tree, pounding the elixir of life with a pestle and mortar (Bushell 1899, p. 595).

An exact parallel to this bowl was exhibited in Singapore (Yeo and Martin 1978, no. 99, Plate 57).

46

47

47

46 Dish

China, Ming dynasty. Sixteenth century.
White porcelain, underglaze blue decoration.
Height 8.4 cm. Diameter 45.8 cm.
The Metropolitan Museum of Art. Rogers Fund, 1967, 67.21.

Large dish with sloping flattened rim. White porcelain painted in shades of cobalt blue. The bottom of the sharply-angled, undercut foot-ring and the base are unglazed and fired a light buff color. Some grits adhere to the base, with faint traces of chatter-marks.

Inside, on the rim are eight peony sprays, with eight emblems: the conch, pair of books, cymbals, iron pot, drum, fan, sounding stone and lozenge of victory. The cavetto is plain. At the center inside double rings is a leaping fish above breaking serpentine waves, with flames, clouds and the moon above.

Outside, there are four branches of prunus blossom below the rim. On the body are three stems of flowers and fruit, separated by roughly-drawn circles. On the outer foot-ring is a ring of linked spirals.

A similar dish was exhibited in Singapore (Yeo and Martin 1978, no. 80).

47 Bowl

South China, Ming dynasty. Sixteenth/seventeenth century.
White porcelain, underglaze blue decoration.
Height 9.5 cm. Diameter 20.5 cm.
Indianapolis Museum of Art. Gift of Mr. and Mrs. Stanley
    Herzman, 80.456.

The lower part of the foot-ring and the base are unglazed and fired a pinkish-buff color, with grits adhering. Loosely painted in a dingy gray-blue, under a slightly opaque, dingy glaze, pitted and crackled on the outside.

Inside, at the rim between two rings there is a crudely drawn classic scroll. The cavetto is plain, and at the center inside concentric rings a fish leaps up from breaking waves with clouds on either side and the moon above.

Outside are six sprays of water-plants and lotuses with three ducks swimming among them. Three cranes swoop down from above.

Technically inferior and pictorially inept, the bowl is a typical "Swatow" product, so named after the south China port from which much of this ware was shipped to south-east Asia and further afield. The kilns were in northern Guangdong province and the wares included slip-decorated and enameled pottery besides blue-and-white. "Swatow" ware has been found in Japan, southeast Asia, India and the Near East, and in spite of its crudity appears to have been a popular export product (Aga-Oglu 1955).

The central motif on the bowl derives from the leaping fish design on a sixteenth-century dish like (46). It is also seen on a Wanli dish (Garner 1954b, Plate 55 A).

48 Dish

China, Ming dynasty. Late sixteenth century.
White porcelain, underglaze cobalt blue. English silver-gilt
    mounts, c. 1585
Height 10.2 cm. Diameter 36 cm.
The Metropolitan Museum of Art. Rogers Fund, 1944, 44.14.1.

The dish is of white porcelain painted in shades of cobalt blue. Inside, at the rim, there is a landscape frieze, with eleven herons facing to the right and left silhouetted against a background of lotuses and water-plants. The cavetto is plain. At the center of the dish within double rings is an elaborate landscape scene. A large barge-like vessel approaches land; it has latticed sides and a rectangular canopy raised on four poles; the stern is raised and a boatman with a coolie-hat manipulates the steering oar. Under the canopy are four seated figures, and at the front of the barge are two standing figures with tall hats, their arms concealed in the sleeves of their long gowns. Three similarly clad figures await them on a spit of land. In the background between two rocky pinnacles is a two-tiered shrine inside a crenellated wall; two more robed figures stand outside the gateway, one gesturing to the other. To the left is a thatched stable, with two more figures and two saddled horses. Above, the moon behind clouds, with flocks of birds and to the right a seven-tiered pagoda. In the foreground is another rocky island, with trees and a two-storied house.

On the back of the dish are four sprays of fruit. It was not possible to examine the base.

The rim of the dish is capped with a silver-gilt mount, and secured to the elaborately stamped and decorated base by four hinged clasps. The clasps are in the form of a bearded figure with a naked torso, with a monkey's head between volutes below, on a pedestal base. The mount is marked with three trefoils voided in a shaped shield.

The history of this famous dish and four other pieces of blue-and-white with silver-gilt mounts is traditionally linked to William Cecil, Lord Burghley, Lord Treasurer under Queen Elizabeth. William Cecil (1520–1598) was a secretary of State under Edward VI, and in 1558 he assumed similar office under Elizabeth, becoming a key figure in her reign. He was made Lord Treasurer in 1572, and appropriate to his stature, he had a house in London, and two in the countryside, one in Hertfordshire and the other in Northamptonshire. The latter, Burghley House at Stamford, has remained in the family to this day. William Cecil added to the house and its furnishings when he was created Baron of Burghley in 1571, and it is to this period that the five mounted pieces of Chinese porcelain belong. The mounts on four of them bear the same mark, three trefoils within a shield. This belonged to a silversmith working in London, and although his name is not known, his mark appears on two other pieces with a London hallmark dated 1585–86, and a third dated 1587 (Avery 1944, pp. 266–272).

An almost identical mounted piece to the Burghley dish appears in a still-life by Willem Kalf (1619–1693); the blue-and-white dish is of the same type, with white herons at the rim and fruit sprays on the outside, and the only difference is that the mount has two additional handles (Spriggs 1967, p. 75, Plate 61 *a, c;* Hackenbroch 1955).

A descendant of Lord Burghley, the fourth Marquis of Exeter, put the pieces up for sale in 1888. They were bought by William Agnew, the London dealer, and in turn passed into the hands of J. Pierpoint Morgan. They were acquired from his son for the Metropolitan Museum in 1944.

The fashion of mounting Chinese blue-and-white is almost as old as blue-and-white itself. Louis duc d'Anjou possessed a blue-and-white bowl with silver-gilt mounts in 1365, which must have been Yuan, and which was described in an inventory of 1379–80 as an *escuelle pour fruiterie* (Watson and Wilson 1982, p. 3). Both *qingbai* porcelain and celadon acquired European mounts; the Gagnières-Fonthill vase with its late fourteenth-century mounts has been referred to above (p. 28); and the Warham Bowl, of mounted celadon, was given by Archbishop Warham to New College, Oxford, in 1530.

The first recorded reference to *porcelain* in England is in a letter from the Surveyor of customs at Southampton, Henry Hutoft, to Thomas Cromwell, announcing the arrival of a present of Novelties for Henry VIII, including:

"Two musk rats, three little munkkeys, a marmozet, a shirt, or upper vesture, of fine cambric, wrought with white silk in every part, which is very fair for a such-like thing; a chest of nuts of India, containing xl. which be greater than a man's fist [coconuts], and three potts of erthe payntid, called Porseland. Hobeit, the merchant saith, before they shall be presented, there shall be to every one of these things certain preparations, such as chains of gold and silver, with colours and other things, for the furniture of the same."

(Strickland 1885).

Thus the gift of porcelain to Henry VIII was also to be mounted. And Lord Burghley himself, on New Year's Day, 1587, presented Queen Elizabeth with a white porcelain bowl mounted in gold.

PUBLISHED: Louise Avery, "Chinese Porcelains in English Mounts," *The Metropolitan Museum of Art Bulletin*, 11.9, May 1944, pp. 266–272. F. J. B. Watson and Gillian Wilson, *Mounted Oriental Porcelain in the J. Paul Getty Museum*, Malibu, California, 1982, pp. 4–6. Dr. A. I. Spriggs, "Oriental Porcelain in Western Paintings," *Transactions of the Oriental Ceramic Society*, 1964–66, London, 1967, p. 75.

48

48

48

49

50

49 Dish

China, Ming dynasty. Late sixteenth century.
White porcelain, underglaze cobalt blue.
Height 7.6 cm. Diameter 34.4 cm.
Private Collection, London. From Syria.

50 Dish

China, Ming dynasty. Late sixteenth century.
White porcelain, underglaze cobalt blue.
Height 7 cm. Diameter 34.3 cm.
Private Collection, United Kingdom. From Syria.

Similar to the Burghley dish, this dish and (50) were purchased in Damascus. The dish has curved sides, and the bottom of the foot-ring is unglazed. Several parts are missing, and it has been extensively repaired with rivets on the underside.

At the rim inside, there are thirteen herons — two more than on the Burghley dish — and they face each other in pairs, except for the thirteenth which is taking off in flight. There is also considerable variation in their stance.

The central scene is also not quite the same as on the Burghley dish. The sides of the boat are decorated with *ruyi* heads, and there are four figures seated around the table, two of them possibly women, and a servant to the left with a top-knot. A robed figure advances to the prow of the boat, which in this case is pointed, not square. On the spit of land there are two figures with their backs turned to the boat, but looking at it over their shoulders. They also appear to have packages with them. In the background a two-tiered shrine between pinnacles of rock; in front of it, a figure on horseback rides across a causeway, preceded by a coolie with an umbrella. To the left and right are two-storied houses, a six-tiered pagoda, trees and rocks with flights of birds in the sky and the moon against clouds above. In the foreground are more shrines and the top of a pagoda, rocks and trees. The narrative scene is intriguing; even more than the Burghley dish, it seems to tell a tale. On the back of the dish are four fruit-sprays, and double rings at the rim and on the outside of the foot-ring. There are also double rings on the base, but no mark within them.

Seven dishes of this type are recorded from Ardebil, the two illustrated much cruder in painting and detail (Pope 1956, Plate 93). A finer example has a foliate rim and very animated characterization of the birds (Garner 1954b, Plate 57). A number of similar dishes were exported to Portugal, now set in the ceiling of the Palace of Santos-o-Velho, once inhabited by Manuel I. This ceiling, in pyramid form and encrusted with export porcelain, was added at the end of the seventeenth century (Lion-Goldschmidt 1984). More examples of these dishes are in south-east Asian collections (Hong Kong 1979, no. 113).

PUBLISHED: John Carswell, "China and the Near East: the recent discovery of Chinese porcelain in Syria," *The Westward Influence of the Chinese Arts from the 14th to the 18th century,* Percival David Foundation Colloquies on Art and Archaeology in Asia, 3, London, 1972, pp. 21–25, Plate 6d.

A variant of dishes (48) and (49), on this dish there are nine herons at the rim, facing either right or left. The landscape at the center is dominated by a pine-tree, growing from behind one of two rocky pinnacles in the foreground, and straggling diagonally across the surface of the dish. A figure on a donkey crosses a three-arched bridge between the rocks; there is a thatched hut and parts of houses half-concealed on the islets. On the right is a fishing boat, with its rectangular sail up, and two fishermen. Unlike the other two dishes, here the water is indicated with hatched lines. Above, there are clouds and the moon(?). On the back are three fruit-sprays and three leaves.

This is a simpler concept, more related to the kind of landscape on (43) in the exhibition, and a dish in the Ardebil Collection (Pope 1956, Plate 93); a close parallel is in the Palace of Santos-o-Velho in Portugal (Lion-Goldschmidt 1984, no. 124, Figures 28, 29).

51 **Still life**

Willem Kalf (1619–1693). Dutch.
Oil on canvas. 60.4 x 50.2 cm.
Signed and dated lower left: "W.KALF 1663."
The Cleveland Museum of Art. Purchase, Leonard C. Hanna Jr.
 Bequest, 62.292.

Still life on a marble table with three glasses of wine, two amber
and one rose-colored. On the right a blue-and-white dish with an
orange and a sprig of orange-blossom, and two peaches, on a silver tray with a crystal-handled knife and a walnut. Under the
tilted dish is a Turkish carpet, in red, white, blue-gray, pale yellow
and green, with a fringed border.

 The blue-and-white dish closely resembles the dish in the exhi-
bition(52); it has a foliate rim, with T-fret pattern, and scalloped
oval panels in the cavetto separated by radial stripes; on the underside, oval panels with fruit sprays, with radial panels with a single
cursive stroke.

 An identical dish was recovered from the wreck of the "Witte
Leeuw," inv. no. 6422. Like the dish in the painting, the border of
the T-fret panel has a diagonal, straight edge; immediately to the
right are three linked spirals falling above the end of the oval panel
in the cavetto. The "Witte Leeuw" sank in 1613, off St. Helena,
on its homeward voyage (Witte Leeuw 1982, p. 107).

 See also color plate, Figure 12, p. 36.

51 (detail)

51

52 Small dish

China, Ming dynasty. Wanli period, early seventeenth century.
White porcelain, underglaze blue decoration.
Diameter 21 cm.
The Metropolitan Museum of Art. Rogers Fund, 1919, 19.136.13.

53 Drinking vessel

China, Ming dynasty. Late sixteenth/early seventeenth century.
White porcelain, decorated in underglaze blue.
Height 20.3 cm. Width 17.8 cm.
Private Collection, United Kingdom. From Syria.

52

53

Small dish with sloping foliate rim, decorated in shades of cobalt blue. The rim has four panels with rounded ends filled with fruit or floral sprays, separated by panels of T-fret or scale pattern and *ruyi* heads in the cavetto, four larger scalloped panels with fruit sprays, separated by four panels with pendant thick and thin leaf-like strokes. At the center, inside a four-pointed ogival frame, a group of beribboned symbolic objects, including an artemisia leaf.

Only one of the similar dishes from the wreck of the "Witte Leeuw" illustrated in the publication has a four-pointed ogival frame at the center, and identical rim and cavetto patterns, inv. no. 6449. The central design is quite different, a typical bird-on-rock landscape (Witte Leeuw 1982, p. 115).

PUBLISHED: Martin Lerner, *Blue and White, Early Japanese Export Ware*, The Metropolitan Museum of Art, New York, 1978, no. 9.

Kendi or drinking-vessel in the shape of an elephant. The base is unglazed, and the vessel is decorated in shades of light and dark cobalt blue. The *kendi* has a tall neck with a prominent molding at the top, painted with concentric rings and two lucky emblems with streamers on top of the molding, with three spots between them. The neck is painted with the "three friends": prunus, bamboo and pine. At the base of the neck is a slightly raised molded band, painted with sprays of chrysanthemum and scroll-like leaves. The body is roughly rectangular, with a patterned cloth over the elephant's body, and tasseled strings round it. The tail is raised in low relief and placed to one side. The elephant has twin nostrils from which the water may be poured and a ring of tassels round the neck. Other *kendis* of various forms are known to have reached the Near East (Pope 1956, pp. 117–8, 132, Plates 97, 137), and an elephant *kendi* was found in the "Witte Leeuw" shipwreck of 1613 (Witte Leeuw 1982, p. 133).

54 Drinking vessel

China, Ming dynasty. Late sixteenth/early seventeenth century.
White porcelain, underglaze blue decoration.
Height 19 cm. Diameter of body 15 cm.
The Metropolitan Museum of Art. Rogers Fund, 1919, 19.136.4.

54

White porcelain *kendi*, or drinking vessel, painted in shades of cobalt blue. The bottom of the stubby foot-ring is unglazed with some grits adhering. The *kendi* has a tall flaring neck, cut in at the top to a narrow vertical rim. The globular body is molded into five convex facets, and the shoulder is also convex. On one side is a mammiform spout. The top of the neck is decorated with five lappets, and the sides with two floral sprays. The rounded shoulder is painted with two oval panels each with a fruit spray at the center, with T-fret hatching between them. The body of the vessel is divided vertically into five panels, with indented grooves; the panels are filled with either fruit sprays or symbolic objects; under the spout is a *ruyi* head. The spout is decorated with two fruit sprays and a beribboned lozenge.

The *kendi* is a drinking vessel common to south Asia, the principal being that the vessel should not touch the lips. It has been suggested that the word derives from the Indian *kundikā*, or Buddhist monk's drinking vessel, dating back to at least the third century B.C. (Willetts 1965, p. 269). The Indian unglazed prototype was faithfully copied by the Tang potters in glazed earthenware (*ibid*, Plate 165). In Chinese blue-and-white, the shape varies considerably, both in the treatment of the neck rim and the form of the spout. Vietnamese *kendis* have exaggerated spouts of udder-like form (Locsin and Locsin 1967, Plate 145). *Kendis* also come in a variety of fantastic forms, being shaped like toads, phoenixes, white oxen and elephants such as (53) in the exhibition (Pope 1956, pp. 116–118, Plates 69, 97; De Flines 1969, Plates 44, 45 [dragon spout], 57, 92. Yeo and Martin 1978, Plates 27, 30, 33, 37, 78, 118). *Kendis* were recovered from the wreck of the "Witte Leeuw" (1613) of the same form and style of decoration as the Metropolitan example; there was also part of an elephant *kendi* (Witte Leeuw 1982, pp. 130–133).

PUBLISHED: Martin Lerner, *Blue and White, Early Japanese Export Ware,* The Metropolitan Museum of Art, New York, 1978, no. 47.

55 Small bowl

China, Ming dynasty. Late sixteenth/early seventeenth century.
White porcelain, underglaze blue decoration.
Height 10.8 cm. Diameter 21 cm.
Private Collection, London. From Syria.

55

55

Small bowl with curving sides, of fine white porcelain and painted in shades of underglaze blue. This is a carefully drawn example of a type which varies enormously in quality.

Inside at the rim, double rings. The cavetto is plain. At the center inside double rings is a circular floral medallion, with a single peony in the middle and groups of veined leaves radiating in the form of a cross. On the outside of the bowl there is a band of classic scroll at the rim. Below, four more similar floral medallions, interspersed with four tiny lotuses with trailing leaves, and one of the Eight Precious Things above. Single rings on the lower part of the body, and at the junction with the foot, and pairs of rings on the outer foot-ring. The base is plain.

The concept of decorating blue-and-white with designs in roundels would appear to have begun in the early sixteenth century during the Zhengde period, and became common by the middle of the century under Jiajing, when the floral medallion with cross-like leaf sprays first appears on dishes such as one at Santos-o-Velho, Portugal (Lion-Goldschmidt 1984, no. 38, Figure 43); the same medallions appear on the reverse of a dish from Syria recorded by the writer, with a Jiajing mark. Both small and large bowls have been recorded from Syria with floral medallions. Many have a six-character Chenghua mark, though not of the period.

Many of the Syrian pieces are crude versions of the type, as are examples in south-east Asian collections (Yeo and Martin 1978, no. 215). The design was widely copied by the Armenian Christian potters of Kütahya in the early eighteenth century. It was also copied in Persia, and at Frankfurt in the seventeenth century; see note to catalogue entry on the Persian copy (85), below.

56

57

56 Bowl

China, Ming dynasty. Late sixteenth/early seventeenth century.
White porcelain, underglaze blue decoration. Silver-gilt mounts.
Height 10.5 cm. Diameter 14.8 cm.
The Metropolitan Museum of Art. Avery Fund, 1923, 23.263.

Tall bowl with a high foot in engraved, twin-handled silver-gilt mounts. Painted in delicate shades of cobalt blue. Inside, at the rim there is a waterscape with eight white herons standing silhouetted against a background of water-plants, all facing right. At the center inside a single ring is a fishing-boat with two sailors, with the sail down, surrounded by large clumps of lotus.

The outside of the bowl is painted with an elaborate continuous landscape, with rocky islands, a large boat with tall platforms of square section at the prow and the stern with figures on top, and banners flying from the masts; smaller boats, rocky islands with pagodas, houses and shrines, pine trees, flights of birds and breaking waves in the foreground.

On the base is a seal mark, with the characters *fu* and *shou* ("happiness" and "long life"):

The rim is capped with an engraved and scalloped band. The two handles of Baroque design are molded with tiny masks on the outside. The pedestal base is also engraved, with an oval and cross design, and pendant scrolls. The mount is probably German, of the first half of the seventeenth century.

PUBLISHED: Martin Lerner, *Blue and White, Early Japanese Export Ware,* The Metropolitan Museum of Art, New York, 1978, no. 3. Suzanne Valenstein, *A Handbook of Chinese Ceramics,* New York, 1975, Plate 106.

57 Cup

China, Ming dynasty. c. 1613.
White porcelain, underglaze blue decoration.
Height 6.8 cm. Diameter 10.4 cm.
The Metropolitan Museum of Art. Gift of Mildred R.
Mottahedeh, 1980, 1980.141.9.

This little cup was recovered from the wreck of the Dutch East-Indiaman "Witte Leeuw," which sank off the coast of St. Helena on its return voyage from the Far East in 1613. It was excavated in 1976 by Robert Sténuit.

The cup has a foliate rim and the bottom of the foot-ring is unglazed and fired faint orange color. The cup was broken and has been restored.

Inside, there are six vertical panels, each filled with a single flower on a long stem, with narrower panels between with five blue spots. At the center inside a single ring, a bird on a rock with its head turned to the right, with curving leaves behind.

On the outside, six more large panels, filled either with bamboo shoots, a large bug above leaves, or a bird on a rock like the one inside. Narrow panels with five spots between.

A number of differently decorated cups were found in the "Witte Leeuw" wreck, described in the publication as "high bowls." Known in Dutch as *kraaikoppen,* "crow cups," because of the resemblance of the bird at the center to a crow. Volker states that this variety of cup was used for drinking *kandeel,* a mixture of eggs, milk, wine, sugar and cinnamon, served when a child was born, and the word *kandeelskoppen* appears frequently in V.O.C. lists (Witte Leeuw 1982, pp. 121–127). The cup closest to the Metropolitan example is inv. no. NG1977–125W.

The number of pieces of porcelain exported to Holland grew by leaps and bounds in the first half of the seventeenth century. After the excitement of the first sales of the cargoes of captured Portuguese carracks in 1602 and 1604, the market soared. For instance, in 1610 the ship "Roode Leeuw met Piglen" arrived in Holland with 9227 pieces of porcelain. By 1636, records from Batavia state that a fleet of six ships set sail from Batavia with 259,380 pieces on board (Volker 1954, pp. 25, 39).

58 Cup

China, Ming dynasty. Late sixteenth/early seventeenth century.
White porcelain, underglaze blue decoration. Silver-gilt mounts.
Height 6 cm. Diameter 12 cm.
The Metropolitan Museum of Art. Purchase by subscription,
    1879, 79.2.163.

59 Ewer

China, Ming dynasty. Wanli period, late sixteenth century.
White porcelain, underglaze cobalt blue decoration. Silver
    mounts. England, c. 1610, by unidentified maker, "E I."
Height 28 cm.
The Art Institute of Chicago. Gift of Mrs. Medard W. Welch,
    1966.133.

58

Small cup with foliate rim, decorated in shades of cobalt blue. Inside, at the rim, clumps of loosely-drawn splayed leaves, with insects between them, within a foliate and double rings. At the center, a bird on a rock framed by leaves, and the moon(?) above.

On the outside, two birds on a rock with flowers and leaves, and two more birds in flight to the left, above a landscape frieze, with insects and the moon(?).

The two handles are clipped to the rim, which is not capped. On the top of each handle is a grotesque animal head; the straps of the handle are engraved with a diamond-and-bar pattern. The underside of the mount is marked 91111.

Two related cups with foliate rims and continuous landscape friezes on the outside, and a bird on a rock at the center, were excavated from the "Witte Leeuw" wreck (Witte Leeuw 1982, pp. 141–142).

Silver-mounted globular shaped ewer, composed of a white porcelain *kendi* decorated in underglaze cobalt blue. Flowering prunus branches decorate the neck. Round-ended panels with floral and fruit sprays, divided by patterned bands, cover the lobed shoulder, bulbous body and dome-shaped spout.

The mounts consist of a low domed lid with a baluster finial. Cut card attachment. Flat scroll thumb-piece. S-curved handle. Serrated strapwork around body, spout and neck. Spout in the shape of a phoenix's head. Splayed reeded foot with serrated lip.

Drinking vessels of this *kendi* shape originated in south-east Asia. Chinese blue-and-white export porcelain *kendis* were highly valued and sought after in Near and Far Eastern markets, as well as in Europe. *Kendis* were mounted in the seventeenth century for utilitarian as well as aesthetic reasons. A similar mounted Wanli style *kendi* is in the Victoria and Albert Museum, London (M.220.1916).

The prototype for the silver spout in the shape of a phoenix head is not know. A Qing dynasty (late Shunzhi or early Kangxi period) *kendi*-based ewer in the Metropolitan Museum of Art in New York (24.80.229) with a porcelain spout in the shape of a phoenix head indicates the existence of this particular decorative device in the Chinese potter's vocabulary. These spouts may be an indigenous Far Eastern convention or a hybrid form resulting from the influences of Indo-European trade. (M.P.)

PUBLISHED: Christies, London, *Important Old English Silver*, (sale catalogue), 26 May 1965. Frank Davis, "Talking About Sale-Rooms: A View of Westminster," *Country Life*, CXXXVIII.3578, September 30, 1965. *Apollo*, July 1965, p. i (illustrated in advertisement of N. Bloom & Son, Ltd., London). *The Art Institute of Chicago Annual Report*, Chicago, 1965–66, p. 38.

59

60 Bowl

China, Ming dynasty. Late sixteenth/early seventeenth century.
White porcelain, underglaze blue decoration.
Height 6.4 cm. Diameter 21.7 cm.
The Metropolitan Museum of Art. Fletcher Fund, 1924, 24.170.1.

61 Dish

China, Ming dynasty. Seventeenth century.
White porcelain, with underglaze blue decoration.
Height 5.3 cm. Diameter 27.2 cm.
Anonymous loan. Formerly Georgia Burnett Collection,
  Winnetka. From the Hatcher wreck.

Dish with a sloping, foliate rim, the cavetto molded with four cartouches, and radial convex ribs between them. The bottom of the foot-ring is unglazed, with fine grits adhering. Faint chattermarks on the base. Painted in delicate shades of cobalt blue.

Inside on the rim within foliate and double rings, a landscape scene with leaves, flowers and winged insects. In the cavetto four cartouches filled with either fruit or floral sprays, with triangular devices at the corners, and vertical ribs with auspicious emblems at the center with pairs of dots and semi-circles above and below.

At the center an eagle is perched on a rock which conceals his lower body, head turned to the left, with a background of rocks, waves, spiraling clouds and the moon. Outside, below the rim, two loosely painted floral sprays. On the body, two more cartouches, each filled with a single fruit. Vertical ribs between are filled with a flame-like motif with an arrow head.

This unusual piece is extremely finely painted. The pictorial conception is also striking, with leaves seen behind open roots and the bird half-concealed by the rock on which it perches, giving a feeling of depth.

On the base is a finely drawn stork:

Clare Le Corbeiller has suggested the stork mark might derive from a Dutch faience mark.

PUBLISHED: Clare Le Corbeiller, *China Trade Porcelain, A Study in Double Reflections,* China Institute in America, New York, 1973, p. 22, no. 7.

The dish has a soft, grayish glaze with a dull tone, due to submergence in the sea. The base is unevenly glazed and shows traces of radial chattermarks; some grits adhere to the unglazed foot-ring.

Inside, the flat rim with a foliate edge and the cavetto are decorated with eight radiating panels, with thick and thin outlines, filled with either floral or fungus sprays. Between them are narrower panels with beribboned motifs and patterned panels above and below. In the center of the dish in an octagonal frame, a bird perches perkily on a rock, with clouds and a large spray of chrysanthemum in the background.

On the outside are five freely-drawn circles, with radiating lines between them. There are roughly drawn circles under the rim and on the outside of the sloping foot-ring.

This dish is from a wreck excavated in 1983 by Captain Michael Hatcher, twenty miles off the coast of Singapore. Several thousand pieces of intact porcelain were recovered, as well as a number of European and other artifacts. From their form, many of the pieces were obviously intended for the Far Eastern market, and the ship would have been bound for a south Asian destination. One piece was reputedly dated 1643, and the cargo as a whole provides a rich inventory of mid-seventeenth-century Chinese blue-and-white. Numerous variants of the bird-and-rock design as well as many other panel-style dishes with more unusual central motifs came from the wreck. The bird-on-rock design was commonly copied in European pottery.

REFERENCE: Christies, Amsterdam, *Fine and Important Late Ming and Transitional Porcelain,* intro. C.D. Sheaf, (sale catalogues), a. 14 March 1984, and b. 12–13 June 1984.

60

61

61

61a Baluster jar and cover

Chinese, Ming dynasty. Second quarter of seventeenth century.
White porcelain, underglaze blue decoration.
Height 29.7 cm., with cover 34.8 cm. Diameter of body 21.5 cm.
The David and Alfred Smart Gallery, The University of Chicago.
 Gift of the Smart Gallery Vienna Tour, 1985, 1985.2.
 From the Hatcher wreck.

61a

Baluster jar and cover of white porcelain, decorated in shades of soft cobalt blue under a greenish-gray glaze. The bottom of the octagonal foot-ring and the base are unglazed, with a light gray dressing. The foot-ring appears to have been shaped with a knife. The jar has eight facets, and was molded in four sections luted together: the foot, the body (two parts), and the octagonal neck rim. The cover also has an octagonal lip, with a circular rim, and a knob on top. The rim and interior of the cover are unglazed.

The jar is decorated with a crenellated band at the rim, and a horizontal line at its junction with the body. On the shoulder are eight overlapping pendant cloud-collar panels, each with a lotus-spray reserved on a blue ground. The body is painted with three large and four smaller sprays of flowers, trailing independently across the molded sides. The flowers include camellia, peony and prunus blossom. There are also grass and twigs, insects and individual fluttering leaves.

At the bottom between single and double rings are loosely drawn pendant blade-like leaves.

The cover has a chrysanthemum painted on top of its knob. There are floral sprays on the upper surface, between double and single rings at the base of the knob and an octagonal border at the edge of the cover.

From the Hatcher wreck no less than one hundred and twenty jars of this shape were recovered, all decorated with slightly different details: they are exceptional in having kept their covers. A similar baluster jar, but with a landscape panel, is in the Tcherepnine Collection, New York (Little 1984, no. 28); another, also with a landscape scene with figures was exhibited in Singapore (Yeo and Martin 1978, no. 248). A jar of the same form was copied in Nevers faience as early as 1644 (Lane 1948, pp. 7, 11, Plate 10).

62 **Large dish**

South China, Ming dynasty. Seventeenth century.
White ware, underglaze blue decoration.
Height 10.4 cm. Diameter 47 cm.
The Cleveland Museum of Art. Gift of Osborne and Victor
   Hauge, 54.579.

Large dish of "Swatow" type painted in shades of dark cobalt blue under a greenish glaze. The bottom and inside of the foot-ring and the base are covered with large gritty patches. The base is glazed in milky opaque smears on an orange surface; there are concentric and spiral wheelmarks.

Inside at the rim are double foliate painted rings, although the rim itself is plain. In the cavetto are six ovoid panels with scalloped tops, each filled with a chrysanthemum plant or a camellia. Between the panels the ground is painted with a square diaper pattern. At the center inside double rings a peacock perches on a peony bush, with rocks and grass below and a background of leafy scrolls, with the moon above. The bird has his head turned back and downwards.

On the outside, there are rings at the rim and on the lower body, and three loosely scrolling lines.

A variation on the bird-on-rock theme, the almost three-dimensional effect of the diaper pattern on the rim in place of the narrow radiating panels one would expect to find on the Chinese prototype is most unusual. A similarly patterned dish belonged to Soame Jenyns (Garner 1954b, Plate 88B).

The base of this piece, with its messy swirls of opaque white glaze, is typical of "Swatow" ware.

Three pieces of "Swatow" ware are among the collection at Santos-o-Velho (Lion-Goldschmidt 1984, pp. 62–63, Figures 110, 111).

62

63

63

63 Bottle

China, Transitional period. Mid-seventeenth century.
White porcelain, underglaze blue decoration.
Height 37 cm.
Indianapolis Museum of Art. Gift of Mr. and Mrs. Eli Lilly,
60.127.

Bottle with a tall, flaring neck and a globular molding. Spherical body and short foot ring. Painted in brilliant shades of cobalt blue with carefully graded washes of color.

On the upper neck, there are three symmetrical floral sprays, with wing-like leaves with tendril tips, and a tulip-like flower. On the molding is a ring of pendant trefoils, with four more horizontal, symmetrical sprays. On the lower neck, three symmetrical sprays of flowers and leaves, more elaborate versions of those on the upper neck, the flowers this time resembling lotuses. On the shoulder of the bottle, a ring of daisy-like flowers with wing-like leaves.

The body is painted with a rocky landscape in typical Transitional style. The Emperor stands in front of a sage-hermit with an ox and a calf; behind the Emperor is his servant, holding the imperial parasol above his head. To the right are two servants holding banners with streaming pennants, and behind them is the ruler's saddled horse and groom.

In his publication of a Transitional brush-holder with similar scene, Little identified it as an encounter between the Emperor and a sage-hermit, in which the Emperor offers his throne to the hermit, who refuses it (Little 1984, pp 64–5, no. 20).

As Mino and Robinson have pointed out, the form appears to be of Ottoman Turkish inspiration, copying either a metal flask, or *surahi*, or an Iznik pottery version of the same shape of the mid-sixteenth century (Mino and Robinson 1983, pp. 264–5: Petsopoulos 1982, nos. 30, metal; 70, pottery [c. 1530]). Certainly, ewers with tall pedestal feet and basins with pierced removable covers for ablutionary purposes were made to order in China for the Near Eastern market (Carswell 1972d, II, Plates 34a, b; 35a, b).

The decoration of symmetrical floral sprays with tulip-like flowers is also Ottoman. This presents the intriguing possibility of the export of Turkish metalwork, pottery and textiles to the Far East, a subject about which we know absolutely nothing.

A further possible link between China and Turkey is through "Swatow" slip-decorated monochrome ware. This could well be in imitation of Iznik slip-decorated pottery, which would certainly appear to predate the Far Eastern product.

PUBLISHED: Yutaka Mino and James Robinson, *Beauty and Tranquility: The Eli Lilly Collection of Chinese Art,* Indianapolis Museum of Art, Indianapolis, 1983, pp. 264–5.

64 Dish

Iran, Nishapur. Fifteenth century.
Buff-colored earthenware, white slip and underglaze blue and
 turquoise decoration.
Height 8.3 cm. Diameter 40.2 cm.
The Metropolitan Museum of Art. Rogers Fund, 1935, 36.20.4.
 Purchased in 1935, during the course of the Museum's
 excavations at Nishapur.

The large dish has a flattened rim with a raised edge, a wide, shallow foot-ring apparently ground down after firing, and an
unglazed base. Grainy, buff-colored ware painted in dull cobalt
blue under a degraded glaze, with faint traces of turquoise in the
cavetto; heavily restored.

Inside, on the rim is a pattern of opposed diagonal lines resulting in a tartan-like effect. In the cavetto, alternate single and double turquoise radial lines. At the center is an elaborate eight-
pointed motif, based on a flower with eight petals reserved on a
blue ground, with dotted trefoils between the points. The wide
border framing the flower extends into a series of overlapping
loops, from each of which hangs a pendant trefoil, the shape deriving from the Mongol cloud-collar. Inside and outside the interlacing bands the ground is patterned with overlapping scales, or
dots.

Outside, there is a single ring below the rim, and on the body
between two rings, two rows of curlicues. There is a single ring
on the outer foot-ring.

The dish is inspired by a fourteenth-century Chinese prototype, both in its form and its overall patterning. The rim is a free
interpretation of a diaper band, and the central panel is an Isla-
micized version of interlocking Chinese cloud-collar panels, here
amalgamated with an eight-pointed star based on two rotated
squares. For the type of Chinese dish that inspired the central design, see Jingdezhen 1984, no. 137; for the flattened, raised rim
and diaper pattern, the same publication, no. 138. Charles Wilkinson has noted (personal communication) that blue-and-white
wares were found during the course of the excavations, and that
although its exact provenance is unknown, this dish may also well
be a Nishapur product.

64

65 **Three sherds**

a, b. Turkey, Iznik, Ottoman dynasty. Early sixteenth century.
c. Egypt, Mamluk dynasty. Fifteenth/sixteenth century.
Benaki Museum, Athens. 20118, 20106/20108, 16705.

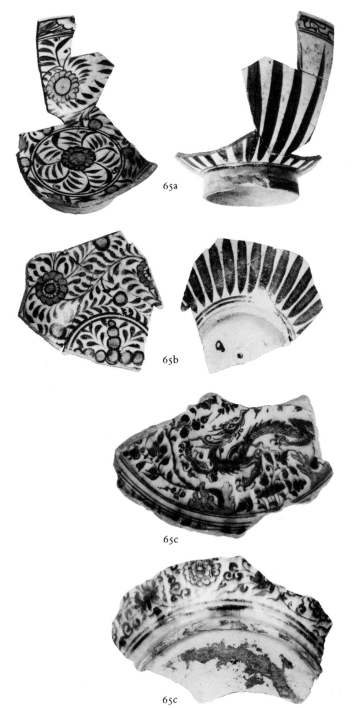

65a

65b

65c

65c

a. Fragment of a bowl, of buff-colored ware, with white slip, and decorated in cobalt blue and turquoise under a transparent glaze. The inner foot-ring and base glazed directly on the body, with no slip.

On the inside, between single and double rings at the rim, a stylized breaking-wave pattern. In the cavetto, chrysanthemum and round buds on curving stems with blade-like leaves. At the center inside double rings, a single chrysanthemum with seven radiating leafy stems and tiny spirals.

Outside, between single and double rings at the rim, a band of chain-like pattern. Below, slender pointed lotus-petals radiating from two rings at the junction of the body and foot.

Based on a Chinese prototype of *lianzi* shape of the early fifteenth century such as the Indianapolis bowl in the exhibition (17), the freely-painted interior is most uncharacteristic of early Iznik ware. John Pope drew attention to the close relation between the Chinese and Turkish bowls (Pope 1972, pp. 135–6, Plates 22–24).

b. Fragment of a bowl, buff-colored ware with white slip and decorated in cobalt blue and turquoise under a transparent glaze; the bottom of the foot-ring is unglazed. Inside, in the lower cavetto, chrysanthemum and round buds on an undulating stem with feathery leaves. At the center, round buds arranged as a cross with radiating leafy sprays.

Outside, pointed lotus-petals radiating from double rings on the lower body.

Also based on a Chinese *lianzi* prototype, the design is even closer to the bowl (17); the central design is based on the loquat spray.

c. Fragment of a dish with curved sides. Whitish-yellow soft and gritty ware, white slip and transparent glaze with a greenish tinge. Decorated in shades of cobalt blue diffusing in the glaze.

Inside is a five-clawed dragon flying to the left, with head turned back and a pointed, closed mouth, scaly cross-hatched body. Below is a lotus-spray between rocky outcrops, from which spring flowering shrubs.

Outside, unglazed patches on the bottom of the foot-ring and the base. On the body above double rings, a wreath of chrysanthemum and peonies in profile, on an undulating stem, with spiraling lobed leaves with tendril-like tips.

The dish combines both fourteenth and fifteenth-century Chinese elements; the lotus-spray is of fourteenth-century type, while the flowering shrub and rock motif is more likely to be of early fifteenth-century origin (Pope 1956, Plates 43, 45).

66 Dish

Syria, Mamluk dynasty. Fifteenth century.
Off-white ware, grayish-blue underglaze decoration.
Height 7 cm. Diameter 33.5 cm.
The Madina Collection. c 62.

The dish has a bracketed rim with ten points. It is of off-white ware loosely painted in smudgy grayish-blue diffusing in the thick, crackled greenish glaze. At the center are three splashes of green glaze, presumably from another vessel fired in the same kiln. The foot-ring is completely covered with glaze, and there are three spur-marks on the base.

At the rim, inside a bracketed and single ring, there is a ring of tear-shaped and spiral motifs with hook-like leaves. The cavetto is plain. At the center inside faint concentric rings, a phoenix with wings outspread, and a triple tail, with cloud-scrolls in the background.

Outside, a bracketed ring below the rim. On the body between concentric rings long and short radiating strokes in rough imitation of lotus-panels. Double rings on the outer foot-ring.

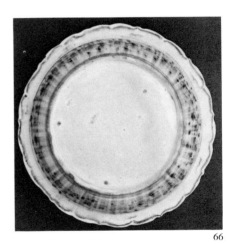

66

66

67 Dish

Syria, Mamluk dynasty. Fifteenth century.
Pinkish-buff earthenware, underglaze decorated in dark cobalt
 blue.
Height 6.5 cm. Diameter 27.3 cm.
The Madina Collection. c 145.

The dish has a flattened convex rim. The pinkish-buff body is painted in dingy, dark cobalt blue under a thickly crackled greenish glaze. The lower body, foot-ring and base are unglazed.

Inside, on the rim is a wreath of nine flowers on two intertwining stems with little hook-like leaves. In the cavetto between two rings are three intertwining stems with solid blue triangular leaves at the intersections and a dotted ground between. At the center inside double rings and reserved on a blue ground is a single large flower of debased lotus type, with large fleshy, dotted leaves surrounding it.

Outside, on the body between sketchy single and double rings, four splashy flowers on an undulating stem with pointed, lobed leaves, some with vestigial spikes.

A mixture of fourteenth and fifteenth-century Chinese styles, the Syrian bowl also draws on Persian sources for its inspiration; the dotted backgrounds can be traced to Sultanabad ware. The rim pattern is derived from the blackberry lily and grapemyrtle wreath found on fourteenth-century blue-and-white porcelain; for the prototype, see Pope 1952, pp. 34–5, Plate B, 5. The curiously heraldic flower at the center of the dish probably derives from a lotus, but the leaves are more akin to peony leaves. For the spiked lobed leaf used as a central motif on a little Syrian bowl from Hama, see Riis and Poulsen 1957, pp. 226–7, no. 787.

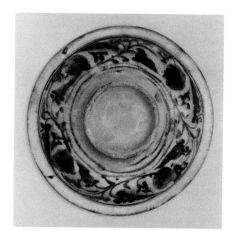

67

67

68 Dish

Syria, Mamluk dynasty. Fifteenth century.
Off-white ware, underglaze decorated in dull blue.
Height 7 cm. Diameter 34 cm.
The Madina Collection. C 157.

The dish has a flattened bracketed rim, with eleven irregularly spaced points. Decorated under the crackled, discolored glaze in dull cobalt blue; there are three splashes of opaque green glaze on the inside of the dish, and the glaze of the base is partly tinged with turquoise. There are three spur-marks on the base. The bottom of the foot-ring is unglazed and shows signs of having been ground down.

Inside on the rim is a band of heavily simplified diaper pattern. The cavetto is plain. At the center inside double rings is a *qilin*, a fabulous Chinese beast; it is depicted kneeling on its forelegs, with cloven hoofs and spotted body, with its leonine head turned back and upwards. Above, at the rim, is a band of ominous overlapping clouds. In the background are floral sprays, with one pointed, lobed leaf in fourteenth-century style.

Outside, seven trailing leaves below the rim. On the body, seven loosely painted fruit sprays. Single rings at the rim, junction of body to rim, and on the lower body. Double rings on the outer foot-ring.

Like so much Islamic pottery of this period, the design combines elements drawn from both fourteenth and fifteenth-century Chinese prototypes. The style of painting is typically Syrian, relying on the use of single brush-strokes rather than building up the forms with multiple shades of cobalt blue.

68

68

127

69 Bowl

Syria, Mamluk dynasty. Fourteenth/fifteenth century.
Off-white ware, dark cobalt blue underglaze decoration.
Height 11.4 cm. Diameter 25.5 cm.
Collection of Alexandre and Helen Philon.

70 Small bowl

Syria, Mamluk dynasty. Fourteenth/fifteenth century.
Off-white ware, dark cobalt blue underglaze decoration.
Height 9.2 cm. Diameter 20 cm.
Collection of Alexandre and Helen Philon.

69

70

Bowl with inverted rim, of off-white ware, painted in shades of dark cobalt blue under a thick greenish crackled glaze. The foot-ring and base are unglazed except for a large spot of glaze at the center of the base. There are three spur-marks in the center of the inside of the bowl.

The edge of the rim is painted with a wide blue band. Below, inside double rings, is a band of classic scroll, and below that a wide band of fourteen leaves arranged diagonally to form a chevron pattern. Each pointed, scalloped leaf has a darker pointed lobed leaf at the center, outlined with dots. On the blue background are smaller pale blue leaves. At the center inside double rings is a lotus, with shaded petals on a thin stem, with an almond-shaped leaf below, with pointed, lobed leaves and tendrils drawn in an attenuated style.

On the outside between pairs of rings, there are five flowers on an undulating stem with simple spiral tendrils and pointed, lobed leaves. Below, a band of simple chevron pattern with dots in the triangles.

A common Mamluk shape, in both pottery and metalwork. Like (70), the crackled greenish glaze is typically Syrian. The Chinese-inspired motifs, such as the classic scroll and the chevron band, and the stylized pointed lobed leaves, are fourteenth-century in origin.

Small bowl with curving sides, of off-white ware decorated in shades of dark cobalt blue, partly diffused in the thick green, crackled glaze. The bottom of the foot-ring and the base are unglazed; there are three spur-marks inside the bowl at the center.

Inside at the rim between thick and thin blue rings, a band of chevron pattern with groups of three dots in the resulting triangles. Below is a wide band of scrolling leaves with a serrated inner outline. At the center, a highly stylized lotus flower in profile with rounded petals, against a dotted blue ground.

Outside, between sketchy rings, a loosely drawn wreath of four flowers on an undulating stem, with simple spiral tendrils and lobed, pointed open leaves.

The thick greenish crackled glaze is typically Syrian, as is the form of the bowl. The Chinese elements in the design are much simplified.

128

71 Four tiles

Egypt, Mamluk dynasty. Mid-fifteenth century.
Buff ware, white slip with underglaze cobalt blue decoration.
16.5/17 cm. between parallel sides, approx. 2 cm. thick.
The Metropolitan Museum of Art. Rogers Fund, 1967,
    67.69.1/2/5/6.

The hexagonal tiles are roughly beveled back, unglazed on the reverse with traces of plaster adhering to the surface, and decorated in cobalt blue on a white ground. Double outlines on the borders of the tiles.

a. Decorated with a peacock perched in a tree springing from a point of the tile, with a shrub and other leafy motifs in the background. Basically a curvilinear design incribed within the hexagonal frame.

b. A symmetrical design of five feathery leaves, springing from a single point, with a wide white border, the background filled with a pattern of overlapping concentric arcs.

c. A vine springing from a point of the tile, with a series of arabesque and intertwining stems bearing vine leaves and smaller hooked leaves and tendrils.

d. A shrub springing from a point of the tile, with arabesque stems bearing large veined leaves, pointed lobed leaves and bud-like motifs.

All four tiles, part of a group of six purchased in 1967 (Carswell 1972b), were clearly designed to be set on their points, unlike tiles in the Tawrizi mosque in Damascus, and the Murad II mosque in Edirne, Turkey, where hexagonal tiles were used with two sides horizontal and interspersed with turquoise triangles. Hexagonal tiles with blue-and-white designs of partly Chinese and partly Islamic inspiration are common to Syria, Egypt and Turkey in the mid-fifteenth century, and probably owe their inspiration to a commonly-shared tradition, perhaps from Tabriz.

The tiles derive their Chinese influence from fourteenth-century blue-and-white, and also from more nearly contemporary fifteenth-century wares, and are evidence of the fascination exercised by the imported porcelain on the indigenous potters. At the same time, a tendency to tidy up the Chinese designs and introduce a symmetrical restraint is noticeable, particularly in the Turkish series (Carswell 1972b: 1972c).

PUBLISHED: Jenkins, Meech-Pekarik and Valenstein 1977, Plate 266. Carswell 1972b, pp. 99–124, Plate 1, 3–6. Jenkins 1983, p. 46, no. 40. Jenkins 1982, nos. 45–50.

EXHIBITED: *The Arts of Islam, Masterpieces from the Metropolitan Museum of Art*, Museum für Islamische Kunst, Berlin, June 15 – August 8, 1981. *The Renaissance of Islam: Art of the Mamluks*, Metropolitan Museum of Art, New York, 1981–82.

71

72 Bowl

Turkey, Iznik, Ottoman dynasty. Early sixteenth century.
Buff-colored ware, white slip, cobalt blue underglaze decoration.
Height 13.1 cm. Diameter 25.2 cm.
The Metropolitan Museum of Art. Rogers Fund, 1932, 32.34.

Bowl of buff-colored ware, with white slip, with the glaze also over the unslipped body on the base and partly on the inside and outside of the foot-ring. The lower part of the splayed foot has a slightly convex profile. Decorated in shades of cobalt blue.

Inside, the surface of the bowl is divided in four by pointed medallions radiating from the center, between which are four tulip-like motifs with split tips. The medallions have dotted borders and each is filled with a symmetrical spray of lotus-like flowers and cusped leaves with their tips turned back, reserved on a blue ground. The tulip-like motifs have a ground of scale-and-dot pattern and are surrounded by floral garlands. At the rim between the medallions and the tulip motifs are pendant triangles with a floral motif on a blue ground, and interlacing finials at their tips. On either side of the tulip stems are trefoil motifs. At the center inside double rings is an elaborate floral medallion, with spiral and scalloped trefoil petals with spikes between them.

Outside, between pairs of rings at the rim and on the lower body, is a wreath of four large lotus-like flowers and smaller flowers on an undulating stem, with stumpy trefoil leaves and dotted tendrils. Below is a ring of diagonal tear-shaped petals, with spiky leaves between them, and on the upper part of the foot-ring a ring of interlocking angular chain pattern.

The foot-ring is very similar in profile to the "Abraham of Kütahya" ewer, dated 1510 (Carswell 1972d, 1, pp. 78–9, Plate 21a), and another characteristic shared with this early group of Iznik blue-and-white pottery is the use of the glaze on the unslipped body of the base, giving an oyster-like iridescense.

The Chinese influence is more apparent on the exterior than on the interior, and in both cases the flowers are far removed from any Chinese model. Similar tear-like leaves (but without the cusped tips) can be seen on the "Kubachi" dish in the exhibition (77).

See also color plate, Figure 10, p. 33.

PUBLISHED: M. S. Dimand, *Handbook of Muhammadan Art,* Metropolitan Museum of Art, New York, 1944, pp. 221–2. Arthur Lane, "The Ottoman Pottery of Isnik," *Ars Orientalis,* II, 1957, p. 257. Marilyn Jenkins, *Islamic Pottery: A Brief History, Bulletin of The Metropolitan Museum of Art,* XL.4, Spring 1983, p. 41, no. 45. Ernst Grube, "The Ottoman Empire," *Bulletin of the Metropolitan Museum of Art,* XXVI, January 1968, p. 206, no. 19.

72

73

74

74

73 Hexagonal tile

Turkey, Iznik, Ottoman dynasty. Early sixteenth century.
Off-white ware, decorated in underglaze cobalt blue.
Distance between parallel sides 15.2 cm. Thickness 1.5 cm.
The Madina Collection. C 161.

The hexagonal tile is of off-white ware, slightly beveled back at the sides, with the sides and back unglazed. Decorated carelessly in shades of cobalt blue under a greenish glaze on a white ground.

The design is based on a six-pointed star, the outlines reinforced by a lighter wash, the points touching the center of each side. In the central hexagon so formed is a second inner hexagon, with a five-pointed medallion at the center on a blue ground. The medallion has a spiral center, surrounded by five more spirals and five elongated trefoil petals. From the points of the inner hexagon radiate petal-like forms which frame each of the triangles of the star, each in turn with a triangle with concave sides at the center, containing a lobed spiral on a blue ground. The points of the tile have larger motifs of similar design, with triple hook-like tendrils springing from a double base line. There is a double outline on the sides of the tile.

The tile is of unique design, though related in some of its motifs to a group of early Iznik blue-and-white, particularly in the use of spirals and trefoil petals with tear-like centers, with a comma-like accent at the top; and the use of hook-like tendrils. These can be seen in more elegant form on the bowl in the exhibition (72). This group of early Iznik monochrome blue pottery has been dated by analogy with a Kütahya ewer in similar but cruder style, bearing an Armenian inscription of 1510 A.D. (Carswell 1972d, I, p. 78–79).

74 Bowl with high foot

Turkey, Iznik, Ottoman dynasty. First quarter of sixteenth century.
Off-white ware, decorated in underglaze dark cobalt blue.
Height 11.5 cm. Diameter at rim 18.2 cm.
The Madina Collection. C 123.

The bowl has a rounded body with slightly inverted rim, and stands on a high sloping foot; inside, it has a sunken well at the center. Of off-white ware, the bottom of the foot-ring is unglazed and it is decorated in shades of dark cobalt blue.

Inside there is a single ring at the rim. At the bottom of the well there is a ring of seventeen radiating trefoil arches, with a single clove-like motif at the center of each. In the middle is a cross-hatched ring.

Outside at the rim the same arched motif is repeated in abbreviated form, with a blue background. On the body there are four bouquets of flowers with bowls below, the main stem of the bouquet moving to the left. Between the flowers the ground is indicated with horizontal hatched lines, with pairs of smaller spiky, leaf motifs. On the outside of the sloping foot between pairs of rings there is a band of pendant heart-shaped motifs with triple darts between them. At the junction of the body to the foot-ring is another single ring.

75 **Dish**

Turkey, Iznik/Kütahya, Ottoman dynasty. C. 1630.
Off-white ware, white slip, decorated in underglaze blue and dark
 green.
Height 6.7 cm. Diameter 30 cm.
The Metropolitan Museum of Art. Harris Brisbane Dick Fund,
 1966, 66.4.11.

Dish with flattened bracketed rim, the bottom of the foot-ring unglazed; decorated in cobalt blue and dark green under a sparkling transparent glaze. Inside on the rim between a bracketed and single ring, a continuous band of cloud-like pattern, based on an undulating stem bearing little daisy-like flowers and cusp-like strokes, inside a frame of cusps and brackets. In the cavetto a single ring of tiny, dotted crescents. At the center inside a single ring four delicate spiral stems bearing tiny flowers and cusped leaves, with the ground patterned with similar motifs.

Outside there are single rings at the junction of the rim, body and foot-ring. On the body are six spiral motifs hatched with diagonal ticks across the stems, looking like coils of barbed wire.

In the so-called "Golden Horn" style, made primarily at Iznik, but also at Kütahya (from which an example inscribed in Armenian and dated 1529 A.D., formerly in the Godman Collection and now in the British Museum, is a good example (Carswell 1972d, 1, pp. 79–80). The spiraling decoration can be paralleled in Ottoman manuscript illumination; for an example dated to the period of Sultan Sulayman (1520–66) see Petsopoulos 1982, no. 184. The bulbous, cloud-like forms on the rim ultimately derive from Chinese clouds-scrolls; it is also interesting to note the use of cusp-like tendrils and comma-like leaflets on the rim of the early fifteenth-century Chinese basin in the exhibition (28).

PUBLISHED: Bernard Rackham, *Islamic pottery and Italian maiolica* (catalogue of the Adda Collection), London, 1959, p. 25, no. 58, Plate 22B. Palais Galliera, Paris, *Collection d'un grand amateur*, (sale catalogue), December 3, 1965, no. 855. Oktay Aslanapa, "Turkish Ceramic Art," *Archeology*, 24.3, June 1971, p. 216. Marilyn Jenkins, Julia Meech-Pekarik, and Suzanne Valenstein, *Oriental Ceramics: The World's Great Collections*, 12, The Metropolitan Museum of Art, New York, 1977, Plate 268.

75

75

76 Dish

Turkey, Iznik, Ottoman dynasty. Second quarter of sixteenth
   century.
Buff-colored ware with white slip, decorated in underglaze blue
   and turquoise.
Height 7 cm. Diameter 38.4 cm.
The Metropolitan Museum of Art. Harris Brisbane Dick Fund,
   1966, 66.4.10.

Dish with sloping bracketed rim with nine points, shallow unglazed foot-ring, some unglazed spots on base and pitting of
surface. Painted in two shades of vivid cobalt blue, and turquoise.

Inside on the rim between double bracketed and concentric
rings, a stylized version of the Chinese breaking-wave pattern. In
the cavetto, ten floral sprays of two types, one based on a peony-
like flower in profile, and the other on a fungus-like motif. At the
center inside double rings are three bunches of grapes on a straggling vine, with vine-leaves and tendrils and little comma-shaped
grape stalks.

Outside, on the body, between pairs of concentric rings, ten
more floral sprays of two types like those in the cavetto. A single
ring on the outside of the foot-ring.

Based on a well-known Chinese early fifteenth-century prototype like (23), the Iznik version of the grape pattern is a vigorous re-interpretation of the design. The breaking-wave motif,
of fourteenth-century origin, here becomes increasingly divorced
from its source and assumes a powerful identity of its own.

PUBLISHED: Bernard Rackham, *Islamic pottery and Italian maiolica* (catalogue
of the Adda Collection), London, 1959, p. 26, no. 62. Plate 30. Palais Galliera, Paris, *Collection d'un grand amateur,* (sale catalogue), December 3,
1965, no. 851. John A. Pope, "Chinese influence on Iznik pottery: A re-examination of an old Problem," *Islamic Art in the Metropolitan Museum of
Art,* ed. R. Ettinghausen, New York, 1972, pp. 125–39, fig. 1, p. 129. Walter B. Denny, "Ceramics," *Turkish Art*, Washington, D.C. and New
York, 1980, p. 280, illustration 155.

EXHIBITED: *The Art of Imperial Turkey and its European Echoes,* The Metropolitan Museum of Art, New York, November 15, 1973 – March 3, 1974.

76

76

77 Large dish

Northern Iran. Sixteenth century.
Off-white frit ware, decorated in underglaze dark cobalt blue.
Height 8.6 cm. Diameter 43.5 cm.
Ashmolean Museum, Oxford. Reitlinger Bequest, 1978.1484.

The large dish is painted in shades of dark cobalt blue on a greenish-white ground, heavily pitted. The bottom and part of the outside of the foot-ring are unglazed; at the center of the base is a wide unglazed disc 16 centimeters in diameter; all the unglazed areas are discolored a dark brown.

Inside, at the rim, a band of spirals and wave-like scalloped motifs against a ground of diagonal hatching, of Chinese derivation. In the cavetto are eight symmetrical floral sprays, with a central marguerite-like flower with dotted petals flanked by leafy stems of two types. At the center inside double rings is a circular frame of eight cloud-collar motifs, the blue ground filled with tiny spirals. At the center is a flower with two rings of petals, on a wiry stem forming a circle bearing eight large and eight small flowers, with triple, tear-shaped petals and dart-like leaves.

Outside, there is a single ring at the rim, and pairs of double rings at the junction of the body to the rim and the foot-ring. On the body are nine flowers on an undulating stem, each flower consisting of a central spiral surrounded by seven spiral petals. The stems bear palmette-like pointed lobed leaves and smaller curved leaves and buds.

This dish of "Kubachi" type combines both fourteenth and fifteenth-century Chinese elements, and is also linked to early sixteenth-century Iznik pottery, with which it has in common the tear-shaped flower petals and the dart-like leaves. The formality of the various design elements is very Islamic, although a naturalistic touch creeps into the rendering of the floral sprays in the cavetto, with their stems placed to one side.

PUBLISHED: Ashmolean Museum and Sotheby Parke Bernet, *Eastern Ceramics and Other Works of Art From the Collection of Gerald Reitlinger,* London, 1981, p. 119, no. 339.

77

78 Dish

Northern Iran. Sixteenth century.
Buff-colored ware, decorated in underglaze cobalt blue.
Height 6.4 cm. Diameter 33 cm.
The Metropolitan Museum of Art, Rogers Fund, 1908, 08.157.4.

Dish of "Kubachi" type, of buff-colored ware painted in shades of grainy cobalt blue under a heavily crackled glaze, on an off-white ground. Three spur-marks on the inside of the dish. The bottom of the foot-ring and the base are unglazed and heavily discolored; the foot-ring has been pierced laterally in four places, for suspension.

Inside, on the flattened foliate rim, there is a band of simplified, much-misunderstood breaking-wave design. In the cavetto are four floral bouquets, one pair with a symmetrical arrangement of twin stems with a cloud-like motif above, the other pair consisting of two sprays arching together at the top, with a dotted clump of grass between.

At the center inside two uneven concentric rings is a single solid blue peony-like flower in profile, with curling tips to its petals,

from which spring stems bearing five-pointed leaves and spiraling tendrils.

Outside on the body between pairs of rings is a sketchy pattern of grass-like petals and leaves.

While the rim design is a debased version of a fourteenth-century Chinese prototype, the four bunches of flowers in the cavetto and the central design suggest a late fifteenth/early sixteenth-century model (Pope 1956, Plate 74), which might also account for the drawing of the grass.

PUBLISHED: Migeon, *Manuel d'art musulman*, II, 1907, Figure 253. Ernst, *Céramique orientale*, n.d. Plate 26. M.S. Dimand, *Handbook of Muhammadan Art*, Metropolitan Museum of Art, New York, 1944, p. 207.

78

79 Large dish

Iran, Safavid dynasty. Seventeenth century.
White ware, decorated in underglaze cobalt blue, with scored
   panels.
Height 7.4 cm. Diameter 58.2 cm.
Ashmolean Museum, Oxford. Reitlinger Bequest, 1978.2169.

The large dish with shallow curving sides and slightly everted rim
has slightly sunk at the center during firing; the bottom of the
foot-ring is unglazed and there are some grits adhering to the
inner surface. Decorated under the clear glaze in shades of warm
cobalt blue with darker outlines, with scored decoration in the
plain areas.

Inside at the center is a great eight-pointed cloud-collar
medallion, with triangles springing from the points to form a star
touching the rim, with more cloud-collar panels between.

The central medallion is filled with sprays of flowers and leaves
on a blue ground, in the middle of which perch two pheasant-like
birds, one with a stem of flowers in his beak, the other with head
turned back. The flowers include a lotus with shaded petals and
other exotic hybrid types, with hatched leaves and petals and
flame-like motifs. The points of the star with light and dark blue
outlines are scored with a dotted scale pattern. The outer panels
are painted with flowers surrounded by spiraling stems with
knobby leaves. Between the points of the outer panels are scored
semi-circles with radial hatching.

The outside of the dish is glazed all over a warm, uneven blue.
This dish epitomizes Persian pottery at its finest; the various Chinese elements have been completely absorbed and transformed,
creating a lush scene quite unlike anything ever rendered on porcelain. The contrast between plain and richly textured areas is per-
fectly balanced, and the outlining and patterning of different parts
of the composition introduce the illusion that there is as much
variation in the white, as there is in the shades of cobalt blue.

PUBLISHED: Ashmolean Museum and Sotheby Parke Bernet, *Eastern Ceramics and Other Works of Art From the Collection of Gerald Reitlinger,* London, 1981, p. 122, no. 349.

80

81

80 Dish

Iran, Safavid period. Late sixteenth/early seventeenth century.
Pinkish-buff ware, decorated under the glaze in cobalt blue.
Height 7.7 cm. Diameter 34 cm.
The Metropolitan Museum of Art. Gift of Elizabeth S.
  Ettinghausen in memory of Richard Ettinghausen, 1979,
  1979.519.

The dish is of pinkish-buff colored ware, decorated in speckled
cobalt blue with dark brown outlines, under a crackled yellowish-
green glaze. The bottom of the shallow foot-ring and the base are
unglazed.

Inside, on the flattened sloping rim there is a pattern of
chevrons, the resulting triangles filled with half-flowers on a blue
ground. In the cavetto are four groups of three marguerites, with
disc-like motifs between them. At the center inside triple concentric rings is a tree with feathery leaves, a rock and four marguerites, the moon and groups of spiky leaves.

Outside, a single ring below the rim; on the body, seven
sketchy roundels between loosely drawn rings, with pairs of
scribbled leaves between. A single ring on the outside of the foot-
ring.

The asymmetrical design would appear to derive from a Chinese prototype of the late sixteenth century (Pope 1956, Plate 81,
for a Jiajing plate decorated with a similar tree).

81 Large bowl

Iran, Safavid period. Seventeenth century.
White ware, underglaze cobalt blue decoration with grayish-black
  outlines.
Height 18.5 cm. Diameter 38.5 cm.
Ashmolean Museum, Oxford. Reitlinger Bequest, 1978.1778.

The bowl is of fine white ware, painted in shades of warm cobalt
blue with grayish-black outlines; the bottom of the foot-ring is
unglazed.

Inside at the rim is a wide floral band between pairs of concentric rings, with sixteen flowers of two types (?chrysanthe-
mum, lotus), against a background of thick, spiral stems and
pointed leaves. The stems rise above and below the margins of the
band. The cavetto is plain. At the center sketchy double rings,
with a ring of *ruyi* lappets pointing outwards. In the middle in a
scalloped frame and reserved on a blue ground is a curious dragon-like creature with a human, horned head, long tail and four
legs with five/six claws and petal-like forms at the joints. In the
background are roughly drawn cloud-scrolls.

Outside there is a narrower band of twelve flowers of chrysanthemum type on an undulating stem passing below the bottom margin, with thick, leafy spirals. On the body, six scalloped
medallions repeat the dragon-like creature at the center of the
bowl, with pairs of linked triangular, wing-like motifs between,
each with a *ruyi* head at the center. Below, a ring of *ruyi* heads and
on the outer foot-ring double rings and a scalloped band. On the
base, a faint gray imitation Chinese seal-mark:

A bowl from a private collection (44) provides the Chinese prototype for this Iranian copy. Particularly intriguing is the human-
headed dragon, with its quizzical, quasi-humorous expression.

PUBLISHED: Ashmolean Museum and Sotheby Parke Bernet, *Eastern Ceramics and Other Works of Art From the Collection of Gerald Reitlinger,* London, 1981, p. 121, no. 346.

82

83

83

82 Vase

Iran, Safavid period. Seventeenth century.
Off-white earthenware, decorated in underglaze blue with black
　outlines.
Height 12 cm. Diameter at rim 5.3 cm.
The Metropolitan Museum of Art. Harris Brisbane Dick Fund,
　1966, 66.107.6.

The vase has a globular body, flaring neck and raised convex
molding on the shoulder. The lower part of the V-shaped foot-
ring is unglazed and the base is recessed. Painted under the glaze
in shades of cobalt blue with black outlines.

On the inner neck rim there is a ring of ten arched petals with
pointed petals between them. On the outside at the foot of the
neck is a similar ring. The upper surface of the shoulder is painted
with a landscape with two deer, one with a spotted body crouching with its head turned back, the other with its forelegs crossed,
seated regarding it. In the undulating landscape, there is a flowering shrub and two birds in flight.

Below the shoulder molding is a ring of chevrons and overlapping concentric semi-circles. On the body of the vase is a rocky
landscape repeating the one on the shoulder, with three crouching
deer, the center one spotted. Above, there are two pairs of birds
(?cranes) swooping down with wings outstretched, a second
flowering shrub with its trunk rising above and below the margins of the scene. On the outside of the foot-ring are single and
double black rings.

On the base is an imitation Chinese seal-mark:

83 Large bowl

Iran, Safavid period, Seventeenth century.
Off-white earthenware, decorated in underglaze blue.
Height 18.6 cm. Diameter 36.3 cm.
The Metropolitan Museum of Art. Purchase, Bequest of Nellie
　Kuh, by exchange, Louis V. Bell Fund and funds from various
　donors, 1967, 67.108.

Large bowl, the bottom of the foot-ring unglazed, painted in
shades of vivid cobalt blue.

Inside, at the rim are six cartouches with scalloped ends, each
with a floral spray; between them are three different kinds of patterned ground, one of which has a flower at the center: (1) based
on a swastika pattern, (2) a trellis of intersecting hoops and (3)
leafy spirals with a flower. The cavetto is plain. At the center inside double rings is a landscape, with a standing figure holding a
furled banner, on a rocky promontory; his robes have long sleeves
attached at the ends to his waist. Behind him kneels a smaller, ton-
sured figure. In the background is a rocky landscape with islands,
houses and shrines, and the moon.

Outside, the bowl is painted with a continuous landscape, with
a kneeling figure with raised knee back-to-back with a standing
figure, with four rings behind, holding a T-shaped staff and wearing sandals; two more seated figures back-to-back; and a figure (?a
woman) seated on a low stool with one leg raised. In the background are islands, houses, thatched huts, pagodas, clouds, bamboo, trees and the moon. There are double rings on the outside of
the foot-ring.

On the base is an imitation Chinese seal-mark inside double
concentric rings:

EXHIBITED: *A King's Book of Kings: Persian Miniatures from Shah Tahmasp's
Shahnameh of 1528*, The Metropolitan Museum of Art, New York, May 4 –
October 8, 1972.

84

85

85

84 Drinking vessel

Iran, Safavid period. Seventeenth century.
White earthenware, decorated in underglaze blue with gray-black outlines.
Height 23.5 cm.
The Metropolitan Museum of Art. Friends of the Islamic Department Fund, 1968, 68.180.

Drinking vessel, *kendi*, in the shape of an elephant. The base is unglazed, and the elephant is decorated in smudgy cobalt blue with gray-black outlines, under a yellowish-green glaze. Tall cylindrical neck, with a small hole for pouring at the top of the trunk. On the neck, a floral band at the top, with a branch of a flowering shrub below with a bird perched on it, and insects. At the base of the neck a ring of arched panels with scrolls, deriving from the lotus-panel design. On the body of the elephant, a raised border round the neck with flowers on a scrolling motif of spirals. The elephant has petal-like ears and tiny eyes, and a necklace of floral scroll from which are suspended three strings of triple tassels. The saddle-cloth is divided in four with panels of T-fret pattern, with a *ruyi* head at the center, and a fringe of spirals and tassels at the bottom. The tail is in low relief and painted with a feathery tip; there are three more strings of tassels on either side.

Based on a Chinese prototype, examples of which are known to have reached Iran (Pope 1956, Plate 97, 29.464); see (53) in the present exhibition.

PUBLISHED: *The Metropolitan Museum of Art Bulletin,* New York, October 1969, p. 80.

EXHIBITED: *Shah Abbas and the Arts of Isfahan,* Asia Society, New York, 1973, no. 82. *Islamic art across the world,* Indiana University Art Museum, Bloomington, Indiana, June 18 – October 1, 1970, no. 208.

85 Bowl

Iran, Safavid dynasty. Second half of seventeenth century.
White composite ware, decorated in underglaze cobalt blue.
Height 10.7 cm. Diameter 22 cm.
Private Collection, New York.

Bowl with gently everted rim, of white composite ware, painted in shades of vivid cobalt blue under a greenish-tinged glaze. The bottom of the foot-ring is unglazed; the glaze on the base had bubbled and crept in firing. The rim is dressed with a dark brown underglaze finish.

Inside, at the rim are double rings. In the cavetto there are four half-flowers with insect-like tendrils interspersed with groups of four spots. Below and between them are four more half-flowers, with single spots. At the center inside double rings is a spiraling spray of three peony-type flowers, with a pair of iris-like smaller flowers, all springing from a clasp resembling a *ruyi* head.

Outside between single and double rings at the rim, a chevron band of almond-shaped motifs reserved on a blue ground. On the body are four large medallions, each with a chrysanthemum at the center, from which radiate leaves in the form of a cross. Between the medallions are pairs of triangular motifs, consisting of a ring from which spring three spiral tendrils. Below, a single ring, and another ring at the juncture of the body to the foot-ring. On the base is an imitation Chinese seal-mark.

The circular medallion design derives from a Chinese bowl like (55), of the sixteenth/seventeenth century, the type often having an aprocryphal mark. The Chinese floral-medallion bowls were common in the Near East and vary greatly in quality of painting. They inspired a whole series of Kütahya pieces in the early eighteenth century, and the medallion is often used on hanging ornaments intended as votive offerings for Armenian churches, probably because of the almost orthodox cross made by the radial leaves in the design (Carswell 1972d, II, p. 17, Plate 33a, c). The medallion design was also copied on Frankfurt faience; for instance, a bowl in the Bayerisches Nationalmuseum, no. 34/825.

This Iranian example is particularly interesting for the brilliance of the blue, now so completely mastered by the Persian potters that it was no longer necessary to resort to black outlines.

86 Plate

Japan, Arita. Genwa-Kanei eras (1615–1643 A.D.).
White porcelain with underglaze blue decoration.
Height 3.2 cm. Diameter 21 cm.
The University of Michigan Museum of Art. Gift of Mr. Harry
   Packard for the James Marshall Plumer Memorial Collection,
   1963/2.62.

This plate is typical of early Hizen ware with the landscape reduced to minimal elements and great play made of the blank areas. The design is framed with a single ring at the rim.

Japanese porcelain was first produced very early in the seventeenth century, in and around Arita in the Hizen district. Early Japanese porcelain has recently been shown to have influenced Chinese wares of the Tianqi period (1621–1627) rather than the reverse as previously surmised (Impey 1984).

With the failure of the Chinese kilns to accommodate increasing demands for the export market, in the middle of the century the Dutch placed large orders with the Japanese, and the Arita industry was transformed. It is still difficult to distinguish with certitude between the different kilns producing blue-and-white, but typical of Japanese taste is the frequent use of asymmetrical designs and a certain direct quality in the painting which is quite unlike the Chinese product.

Japanese enameled wares were introduced at least as early as 1653, and by 1659 they had been recorded in Europe.

PUBLISHED: Richard S. Cleveland, *200 Years of Japanese Porcelain*, City Art Museum, St. Louis, 1970, no. 1.

86

87 Bottle

Japan, Arita. Mid to late seventeenth century.
White porcelain, underglaze blue painting.
Height 43.4 cm. Diameter 23 cm.
Ashmolean Museum, Oxford. 1978.783.

The bottle has a gently rounded form, tapering to a horizontal flanged lip with square-cut rim. Painted in washes of dark cobalt blue.

On the neck, a ring of plantains is reduced to an elegant pattern of overlapping V-shaped motifs, thickly outlined, but with delicate linear extensions. On the shoulder, between pairs of rings, simply drawn flowers accented by a background of knotty, leafy scrolls, again producing an effective contrast between bold and delicate elements. On the body of the vase, a landscape with large peony bushes; the flowers, buds and leaves carefully drawn with graded washes of cobalt blue, while the stalks and leaves are spontaneously and swiftly executed.

Apart from its noble form, the bottle relies for its effect on the simple but highly contrasted use of design elements.

Known as apothecary bottles, the shape is probably of European origin, either glass or German stoneware (Lerner 1978, Introduction and Figure B, nos. 38–46).

87

88 Small dish

Japan, Arita. Second half of seventeenth century.
White porcelain, underglaze blue decoration.
Height 3.4 cm. Diameter 20.2 cm.
Private Collection, London.

The little dish has a sloping flattened rim. It is of white porcelain, painted in shades of cobalt blue which has fired gray on the underside of the dish. There are overfired spots in the center and on the base. The bottom of the short V-shaped foot-ring is unglazed. The base is concave and shows traces of concentric wheel-marks.

The design is a Japanese interpretation of a typical Chinese *kraak* porcelain design. Running across both the rim and the cavetto are eight wide and eight narrow radiating panels, with fruit or flower sprays at the center of the larger panels. In the middle of the dish, inside double rings and an octagonal frame filled with hatching or scale pattern, is a landscape with an insect perched on a rock, with flowers and leaves around. On the outside of the dish, between rings at the rim and the junction of the body with the foot, four circles and four sets of triple radial lines.

Typical of Japanese imitations of Chinese blue-and-white, the dish is painted with swiftly-applied areas of solid blue, giving the piece a bold intensity. The design reads particularly well at a distance, with a decorative assurance often absent from the Chinese prototype.

Encouraged by orders from the Dutch East India Company, this type of Japanese blue-and-white was widely exported in the second half of the seventeenth century. Examples of the type have been recorded in Syria, some very large, as well as in Sri Lanka, often with the VOC monogram at the center.

88

88

89 Drug-pot

Italy, Florence. c. 1475.
Pinkish-yellow earthenware, decorated in underglaze dark blue.
Height 11.5 cm. Diameter of body 11 cm.
The Madina Collection. C 250. Found in Aleppo, Syria.

The drug-pot once had a spout, handle and neck, now missing. It has a globular body with a flaring base. Of pinkish-yellow earthenware, it is decorated under a tin-glaze in dark cobalt blue, on a greenish-white opaque ground. An inscription in Gothic script inside a panel with shaded ends encircles the pot. The inscription reads:

oxymel sim

Above and below the inscription there are simple trails of flowers, broadly painted. Above and below are wide blue bands with thin outlines, and another on the rim of the foot with a ring of vertical strokes above it.

A complete drug-pot in the Victoria and Albert Museum, London, inscribed *oxymel sp*, shows that the drug-pot would have had a sloping neck with projecting rim, almost vertical spout and wide strap handle (Rackham 1977, p. 16, no. 60).

Oxymel was a medicinal drink of honey and vinegar, first noted in England c. 1000 A.D.

89

90 Drug pot

Italy, Florence. Fifteenth century.
Tin-glazed earthenware (*majolica*), dark cobalt blue, manganese
 purple and green decoration.
Height 34.4 cm. Diameter 15.8 cm.
The Cleveland Museum of Art. Purchase from the J. H. Wade
 Fund, 54.258.

Drug pot, *albarello*, of tin-glazed earthenware, the flat unglazed
base discolored dark brown, top of the rim partly glazed. Traces
of the potter's fingermarks inside and splashes of glaze at the bottom. Outside, cream-colored glaze, painted in dark cobalt with
manganese purple stripes and a faint greenish color. The jar has a
projecting rim, short vertical neck, raised molding at the juncture
with the sloping shoulder, concave barrel-shaped body and sloping foot and rim. A purple band on the neck rim and at the top
and bottom of the body. On the neck, a band of classic scroll, and
on the shoulder an expanded wreath of similar decoration with
trefoils with feathery petals. The body is divided into vertical panels with thick and thin stripes, with a double line spiraling around
them. The panels are painted with a vertical band of trefoil
flowers on a zig-zag stem.

The *albarello* form is found in Syrian blue-and-white underglaze decorated earthenware in the first half of the fifteenth century, and one piece in Paris bears the arms of Florence on it (Lane
1957, p. 30, Plate 15). The form of this *albarello* is influenced by
late fourteenth-century *albarellos* made at Manises near Valencia
by Moorish emigrants, who had been importing cobalt since the
early thirteenth century, a century earlier than it was used in
China (Caiger-Smith 1973, p. 55–58, Plate 29).

90

91 Dish

Italy, Venice. c. 1540.
Tin-glazed earthenware, underglaze blue decoration.
Diameter 24.5 cm.
John Philip Kassebaum Collection.

Dish with a sunken well at the center, decorated in underglaze blue. At the rim, a leafy interpretation of the classic scroll, within pairs of rings, On the wide flanged rim, a floral wreath with six flowers on thin spiraling stems, with hooked leaves.

At the center, a single flower with shaded, serrated petals, with spiral stems of hooked leaves.

Although the classic scroll and the shaded flowers may have had a Chinese prototype, the wiry, spiraling stems and hooked leaves show the influence of early sixteenth-century Turkish pottery of the so-called "Golden Horn" type, made both at Iznik and Kütahya; compare with the dish (75) in the exhibition. Moreover, the influence was reciprocal; a "Golden Horn" dish in the De Unger Collection is of *tazza* form, copied from the Italian (Carswell 1972d, I, II).

PUBLISHED: *The John Philip Kassebaum Collection,* I, foreword by J.V.G. Mallet, Kansas City, 1981, no. 93.

91

92 Dish

Italy, Florence, Medici factory. c. 1580.
Soft-paste porcelain.
Diameter 29.2 cm.
The Metropolitan Museum of Art. Gift of Mrs. Joseph V.
  MacMullan and Fletcher Fund, 1946, 46.114.

92

Dish of soft-paste porcelain with flattened rim and raised boss at the center, painted in underglaze cobalt blue. The bottom of the foot-ring is unglazed.

On the rim between single and double blue rings, nine sprays of flowers, fruit and leaves. In the cavetto, a pastoral scene with a hilly landscape encircling the central boss with a pond, all sorts of flowers and shrubs. On a hillock sits a shepherd, wearing a loose tunic and flowing cloak, and a tall hat with feathers, tending a fire beside him. Another shepherd, similarly dressed and and carrying a stick, approaches him. In the sky above are the sun and the moon, both with human features, clouds, and an insect. In the center on the convex boss, a single flower inside double rings is surrounded by four radiating sprays of flowers each with three blossoms, buds and curving leaves. Between them are four smaller clumps of leaves with tendrils.

On the outside, a single blue ring at the rim, and on the body five symmetrical sprays of peonies. In the recess at the center of the dish, the Dome of the Cathedral in Florence, with the mark ·F· beneath it.

One of the sixty or so pieces of porcelain produced by the Medici factory in Florence, the decoration owes as much to the Renaissance, and Turkey, as to Chinese blue-and-white. Chinese elements may be detected in the loose interpretation of the lotuses in the pond, where the lotus-leaf floats high above the surface; the hatching of the water is a late sixteenth-century Chinese convention; see (50) in the exhibition. Many of the flowers, on the other hand, particularly those on the rim, seem inspired by Turkish pottery of the sixteenth century; compare with the Iznik dish (76).

92

PUBLISHED: A. Colosanti, *Catalogue of the C. and E. Canessa Collection*, (privately printed) 1919, Plate 252. Seymour de Ricci, *Catalogue of early Italian Maiolica . . . in the Mortimer L. Schiff Collection*, 1927, no. III. Louise Avery, "The Mortimer Schiff Collection: Early Italian Maiolica," *The Metropolitan Museum of Art Bulletin*, XXXIII, January 1938, p. 13. Giuseppe Liverani, *Catalogo delle porcellane dei Medici*, Faenze, 1936, pp. 32, 3, no. 32. *The Mortimer L. Schiff Collection*, (sale catalogue), Parke-Bernet Galleries, May 4, 1946, no. 93. Clare Le Corbeiller, "China into Delft: A Note on Visual Translation," *The Metropolitan Museum of Art Bulletin*, XXVI, New York, February 1968, pp. 269, 70. Figure I. *Masterpieces of European Porcelain*, The Metropolitan Museum of Art, New York, March 18 – May 15, 1949, catalogue no. 372.

93

93 Ewer

France, Nevers. Second half of seventeenth century.
Tin-glazed earthenware, underglaze blue decoration.
Height with handle 28.5 cm.
The Metropolitan Museum of Art. Bequest of Ella Morris de
Peyster, 1958, 58.60.14.

The ewer is of yellow ware, with a white opaque tin-glaze, decorated in underglaze cobalt blue. The form is a ceramic copy of contemporary silver (Figure 35), and the ewer made in molded sections. Even the horizontal molding below the lip on the silver original has been reproduced, although ignored by the decorator.

The main body of the ewer is decorated with a landscape with figures. To the left of the handle, a man wearing a belted costume and a floppy hat carries an offering of some sort towards a figure seated beside a chest, head in hand and gesturing upwards with the other hand. The second figure has a belted tunic and floppy hat with a feather in it. Between the two is a coconut-palm. Further to the left is a standing figure with a stick, holding up the hem of his robe. Still further left is a figure seated on a low plinth, also with a hat with a feather, gesturing upwards with a finger of his left hand, in a grove. The scene is carefully painted; the rest of the ewer is looser in its treatment, suggesting a second hand. On the pedestal base, there are tulip-like motifs and Baroque scrolls. The handle is also decorated with blue.

This ewer exemplifies the mixture of Italian Baroque and Far Eastern taste which was characteristic of Nevers faience in the second half of the seventeenth century (Lane 1948, pp. 10–14). The shape of some Nevers ware and the decoration show that the potters were familiar with Chinese Transitional ware, even before such wares began to be copied in Holland. The border pattern on the foot, with its combination of Baroque scrolls and tulip-like flowers taken from Transitional ware like the bottle (63), on a form deriving from contemporary French silver, is a text-book example of the successful eclecticism of the Nevers potters.

A ewer of different form, but again combining European and Far Eastern elements, is in the Victoria and Albert Museum (Lane 1948, Plate II).

Figure 35. *Ewer*, France, 1700–1720, The Metropolitan Museum of Art. Fletcher Fund, 1926, 26.260.87. Helmet-shaped ewer of silvered brass, engraved with the arms of Moret De Borchenu, Marquis de Valbonnays.

94 Large dish

France (?Portugal). Late seventeenth century.
Buff earthenware, decorated in blue under a bluish glaze.
Diameter 44.2 cm.
The Cleveland Museum of Art. Gift of R. Henry Norweb,
66.221.

A large dish with a wide flattened rim with a raised edge. The bottom of the foot-ring is unglazed, revealing a buff-colored body; two holes originally drilled through the foot-ring for suspension are glazed on the inside. The dish is decorated in mottled cobalt blue with pencil-like darker outlines.

On the inside rim are two cartouches, each with a landscape vignette. One depicts a tower with turrets, ruins, houses and a tree on a hillock. The other shows two cowled monks approaching a chapel. Between the cartouches are elaborate floral sprays, two groups of fruit, birds and a butterfly.

The cavetto is painted with a wreath of daisy-like flowers, in which perch four birds. The center of the dish is filled with an armillary sphere reserved against a blue ground. The widest ring of the sphere is marked with six zodiacal signs, out of sequence. In the background there are stars and crescent moons, and a larger moon with a man's profile, a pair of calipers, and a set square. One segment is painted with a sun disc, and another with a pair of opposed crescents. At the top between a pair of rings framing the sphere is written in rough Gothic script:

$$\mathfrak{Moderata} . \mathfrak{durant}$$

which can be roughly translated as "moderation endures." On the outside there is a discontinuous line below the rim and four crudely drawn chrysanthemum sprays. On the base is a blue mark.

Ascribed to the French factory at Nevers, this dish nevertheless presents some unusual features in its design, which would tend to question such a provenance. The armillary sphere, a skeletal celestial globe, is the oldest known astronomical instrument. Its use was transmitted by the Arabs to Spain in the twelfth century, from whence all later European armillary spheres originated. The armillary as a device is closely associated with Manuel I of Portugal (1469–1521) who used it as part of his armorial bearings (Figure 36).

Among the earliest pieces of Chinese blue-and-white porcelain specifically made for the Portuguese market are several bearing the royal arms and the armillary sphere of Manuel I. A ewer with an armillary sphere, with a Xuande mark but probably of the Zhengde period, would appear to date from the time of the first direct contacts between the Chinese and the Portuguese, in 1517–21 (Le Corbeiller 1974, pp. 14–16, Plates 1, 2; Figures 5–7. Chang 1969, p. 32ff). The armillary sphere remained in the Chinese decorative repertoire until the mid-sixteenth century; a bowl in Istanbul with the device is inscribed in Portuguese with the name of the Captain of Malacca, Pero da Faria, and the date, 1541 (Jenyns 1967, pp. 61–62, Plate 54b). The writer saw an early Iznik bowl in Damascus some years ago also decorated with the armillary, which must have been copied from the Chinese bowl in Istanbul.

This close association with Portugal suggests that the dish might be Portuguese rather than French. The two monks with cowled heads are somewhat at variance with the more secular scenes and *chinoiserie* common on Nevers pottery and might allude to the missionary zeal of the Portuguese.

It should be noted that if the earliest Chinese blue-and-white for the Portuguese does date to their first direct contact in 1517–21, this is precisely the same period during the reign of Zhengde (1506–21) when the potters were executing special commissions for the Arabic/Persian market.

PUBLISHED: *Repertoire de la faience française*, ed. Chompret, Bloch, Guerin and Alfassa, Paris, 1935, II: Nevers, Plate 33E. *The Bulletin of The Cleveland Museum of Art*, September, 1966, p. 277, no. 22, illustrated p. 228.

Figure 36. The arms of Manuel I of Portugal (1461–1529). Woodcut from *Regimento do oficias das cidades, villas e lugares destes Reinos*, 1504.

95 Dish

France, Nevers. Late seventeenth century.
Tin-glazed earthenware, underglaze blue decoration.
Diameter 24.3 cm.
The Cleveland Museum of Art. The Norweb Collection, 62.356.

96 Plate

Holland, Delft. c. 1655–1695.
Tin-glazed earthenware, with underglaze cobalt blue decoration.
Height 3.8 cm. Diameter 24 cm.
The Metropolitan Museum of Art. Rogers Fund, 1930, 30.86.3.

Dish with wide flanged rim, sunken center. The bottom of the square-cut foot-ring is unglazed. Decorated in slightly mottled cobalt blue with grayish pencil-like outlines, on a cool blue ground.

On the inside, loosely drawn double rings at the rim. The whole of the interior of the dish is painted with a landscape. A lady is seated under a tree, a warrior stands before her gesturing with his right hand. He wears classical costume, with a helmet, shield and sword, and a flowing cape. In the foreground is seated an appreciative spaniel. In the distance, a house on an island; in between, tufts of foliage.

On the back of the dish wide blue rings at the top and bottom of the body, with four symmetrical motifs consisting of a diagonal cross and four trefoil leaves, with four spots between them. The base is glazed but unmarked.

Neither the platter-like shape, nor the subject, is Chinese inspired. The feeling of the design with its graded washes of blue and empty spaces is more Japanese than Chinese; but this may be a mere coincidence.

Plate with foliate rim, copied after *kraakporselein* of the Wanli period.

The major design element in this type of ware is the lotus form. Eight major reserves in the shape of lotus panels dominate the rim and cavetto. These panels frame emblemmatic and auspicious flowers and peaches. Stylized chrysanthemum, symbolic of the tenth month of the lunar calender, alternate with peaches and lotus flowers. Peaches are emblemmatic of marriage and symbolize the rejuvenating aspect of spring. Lotus flowers, emblemmatic of summer and symbolizing regeneration and fecundity, are associated with both Buddhist and Daoist iconography. Interstitial panels, with alternating borders of diaper patterns and petal work contain abstractions of the Buddhist sacred tassels.

Set in an octafoil frame against reserves of diaper patterns and petal work is one of the most popular *kraakporselein* central medallion motifs; a bird on a rock amid abundant foliage.

The Dutch defined a sub-group of *kraakporselein* plates as *kaapsche schotels* in reference to a point on the east-west trade route — the Cape of Good Hope. This Dutch Delft version displays most of the distinguishing characteristics of *kaapsche schotels*; the lotus inspired foliated rim, Wanli decorative motifs and the use of *trek*. (M.P.)

PUBLISHED: Clare Le Corbeiller, "China into Delft: A Note on Visual Translation," *The Metropolitan Museum of Art Bulletin*, XXVI, New York, February 1968, p. 271, Figure 2. Martin Lerner, *Blue and White, Early Japanese Export Ware*, The Metropolitan Museum of Art, New York, 1978, no. 34.

95

96

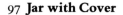

97 Jar with Cover

Holland, Delft. c. 1700–1705.
Marked "PK."
Tin-glazed earthenware, with underglaze cobalt blue decoration.
Height 38 cm.
The Metropolitan Museum of Art. Gift of Henry G. Marquand,
    1894, 94.4.370.

Truncated high-shouldered jar with everted neck. Flaring mouth with pronounced lip rim. Fitted convex lid with raised knob. Chamfered flat foot.

The decoration on the main body of this jar is either a direct copy or substantial imitation of a Transitional style vase of the Chongzhen period (1628–1644). Chrysanthemum, peonies and foliating shrubs appear from behind an undulating rocky formation. This composition, with its careful draftsmanship and V-shaped strokes for grass, is a standard illustration of the Taihu or Dongting rocks during the Chongzhen period. Elements of this motif decorate the fitted cover. A scalloped border pattern covers the flattened surface of the knob. The reserve floral scroll around the neck is also characteristic of the period.

This jar is probably one of a pair belonging to a garniture. Such sets, called *de kastels* (*kast* for cupboard and *stel* for set) by the Dutch, were enormously popular in the eighteenth century. Garnitures, consisting typically of three lidded jars and two beakers, were based on the Chinese *wu she*; a set of one *ping*, two *guans* and two *gus*. A requisite adjunct to the entrance hall of an affluent Chinese household, the *wu she* evolved from Buddhist ceremonial vessels.

Precise drawing and rich surface ornamentation of floral and *ruyi* lappet based designs are characteristic of the wares marked with the monogram PK. The monogram is the mark of Peter Kam, proprietor of *De drie Vergulde Astonnekens* factory, 1700–1705 (De Jonge 1970, pp. 62, 99, 157).   (M.P.)

97

98 Dish

Holland, Delft. Second half of seventeenth century.
By Samuel van Eenhorn (active 1674–86).
Tin-glazed earthenware, underglaze cobalt blue decoration.
Height 9 cm. Diameter 31 cm.
The Art Institute of Chicago. Gift of Mrs. R. G. Mercur and
  Elizabeth Aishton in memory of R.H. and Elizabeth Aishton,
  32.14.

Large dish on a raised, splayed foot. Bluish-white glaze with delicate *trek* work. The foot-ring is unglazed. Inside the hollow
glazed foot is the mark of Samuel van Eenhorn.

The flange is decorated with an enclosed band of scrolling
chrysanthemum. A peacock and flowering shrubs and a hovering
bird fill the large central medallion. The design is in the Wanli
style of decoration.

Pendant leaves of alternating lengths decorate the foot-stem.
The lambrequin border pattern—a derivation of the *ruyi* lappet—
overlaps the splayed foot.

Leafy sprigs and auspicious butterflies are sketchily painted on
the reverse of the dish.

Samuel van Eenhorn worked at the *De Grieksche A* factory under his father for four years before receiving the business as a wed-
ding gift in 1678. Delftware marked SVE is noted for the inventive
application of *trek*, the technique of outlining the designs in bluish
or purplish black, generally attributed to van Eenhorn. Samuel
van Eenhorn was a member of the delegation sent to England to
revive the flagging Delft market in that country. The van Eenhorn
family of potters was instrumental in establishing the preemi-
nence of delftware in the seventeenth century.   (M.P.)·

PUBLISHED AND EXHIBITED: *Cathay Invoked-Chinoiserie: a Celestial Empire
in the West,* California Palace of the Legion of Honor, San Francisco, June
10 – July 30, 1966, no. 21.

98

99 Baluster jar

Holland. Late seventeenth century.
Tin-glazed earthenware with underglaze cobalt blue decoration.
Height 29.3 cm.
John Philip Kassebaum Collection.

Baluster jar of exaggerated shape, decorated with scenes from a landscape, in simple washes of cobalt blue. On one side is a pair of prancing mastiff-like dogs.

The graded washes of blue are typical of Chinese Transitional blue-and-white of the mid-seventeenth century. Three baluster vases from the Hatcher wreck are decorated with similar fragmentary landscape elements, including the misty swirls (Christies 1984b, p. 20, nos. 71, 73).

Chinese vases of this variety were copied in Persia in the seventeenth century, both in pottery and on tiles; a tile in the Church of St. Sargis in New Djulfa, Isfahan, is painted with two deer prancing like the two dogs (Carswell 1968, Plate 53e; Carswell 1979b, Plate XXVIII; Lane 1957, Plate 59A).

99

100 Plate

Germany, probably Frankfurt-am-Main. Late seventeenth
century.
Unidentified mark.
Tin-glazed earthenware, with underglaze cobalt blue decoration.
Diameter 25.4 cm.
The Metropolitan Museum of Art. Gift of Mrs. Catharine Van
Vliet De Witt Sterry, 1908, 08.107.5.

Plate with *chinoiserie* decoration. Four Chinese-inspired vignettes of two alternating variations of single figures in outdoor settings decorate the rim. The floral sprays on the cavetto are derived from a Transitional style decorative motif. The central medallion consists of a single seated figure in a landscape.

This summarily executed design is similar to two lobed dishes attributed to the Frankfurt factory in the Victoria and Albert Museum. The *chinoiserie* figures are placed in stylized outdoor settings utilizing stock conventions of the Chongzhen period. Grass is painted in with V-shaped brush strokes. Plum trees have been reduced to clusters of circles covered with faint washes. Pine trees have been similarly minimalized.

The unidentified mark, ⟶ was previously attributed to the Dutch *De Paeuw* factory. (M.P.)

PUBLISHED: Martin Lerner, *Blue and White, Early Japanese Export Ware*, The Metropolitan Museum of Art, New York, 1978, no. 15.

100

101 **Bottle**

Germany, Frankfurt-am-Main. Late seventeenth century.
Unidentified mark.
Tin-glazed earthenware, underglaze cobalt blue decoration.
Height 33.8 cm.
The Art Institute of Chicago. Purchased through the Decorative
Arts Special Sundry Account, 43.1041.

Globular-shaped bottle with an everted mouth above a bulbous ring, tall tapering neck, large body on a high stemmed foot. The glaze is a cool grayish blue. The cobalt washes have areas of grainy concentration. An unidentified mark in blue is centered on the unglazed base.

Waving lotus-petals ring the tapering area below the mouth. Fauna and scrolling cloud-patterns decorate the bulbous ring above the pendant plantain eaves of the neck. Around the body is a continuous *chinoiserie* scene of figures in a landscape. The border pattern on the foot consists of floral forms alternating with stylized, tasseled *ruyi* lappets.

Diverse compositional devices and symbolic elements blend together in this *chinoiserie* bottle. The airborn creature on the bulbous ring recalls various depictions of the *qilin*, the third mystical animal of the *si lin*. Two separate groups of *chinoiserie* figures are set in landscapes of a type found on late seventeenth-century Frankfurt faience. A *lietmotif* of the Frankfurt potters was the Transitional ware device of unifying isolated figural groups with rocky cliffs amid swirling cloud formations.

If the identification of the form of this type of bottle in Chinese Transitional ware is Turkish (see note on [63] *supra* p. 122), then here we have the case of an Ottoman bottle inspiring a Chinese copy, which in turn influenced the Frankfurt piece. The shoulder decoration on this piece and (63) is identical. (M.P./J.C.)

101

102 Vase

Germany, Frankfurt-am-Main. c. 1680.
Attributed to the so-called *Feinmeister* (active 1670–1700).
Tin-glazed earthenware, underglaze cobalt blue decoration.
Height 17.3 cm. Diameter 24.5 cm.
The Art Institute of Chicago. Gift of Mrs. C. Philip Miller,
44.289.

102

Oviform vase, the lid missing, with bright cobalt blue underglaze decoration. The interior is glazed. The slightly chamfered base shows uneven patches of gritty glaze. The vitreous quality of Frankfurt faience was achieved by the Dutch method of additional submersion of the decorated ware in a modified, tin-free lead mixture known as *kwaart*.

Stylized lotus-petals form a band around the neck. The decoration of the ovoid body is divided into three vertical sections. Four reserves on the shoulder, separated by a single pendant leaf, frame two alternating types of floral clusters. The two principal reserves with figures in a landscape are divided by crossed patterned panels terminating distally in stylized *ruyi* lappets. A band of stylized leaves decorates the foot.

In 1666, five years after production began at the neighboring Hanau factory, a Parisian potter named Jean Simonet established the Frankfurt-am-Main factory. Simonet's financiers, Johann Christoph Fehr and Bernard Schumacher, were prominent members of Frankfurt society and consequently instrumental in securing an affluent clientele. Large decorative wares were produced in addition to staple goods for the German middle-class household. The proximity and inherent risks of the pottery industry (the elitist closed-rank aspect which effectively controlled the number of skilled potters) resulted in the production of virtually identical *birnkruges, neunbuckelschüssels, enghalskruges,* etc. Marks or otherwise demonstrable definitive characteristics (e.g. the *Feinmeister* and *Meister der grossen Vasen* of Frankfurt, or the *vogelesdekor* and thumbnail impression of Hanau) facilitate identification. The development of *chinoiserie* decoration at Frankfurt and Hanau began by copying Dutch Delft versions of Chinese porcelain of the Wanli and later Kangxi styles and generally incorporating indigenous decorative elements.

The works atributable to the *Feinmeister* contain an imaginative mixture of Transitional ware decorative conventions with a unique vaguely Sino-Japanese ornamental and compositional style. The band of stylized lotus-petals is characteristic of the Chongzhen period (1629–1644). Based on contemporary paintings, drawing books and woodblock prints, pine-tree studded mountains and cliffs separated by distinctive cloud forms was a stock convention of the Transitional ware decorators. This *Feinmeister* vase demonstrates the success of this convention as a unifying compositional device for decorating round objects.

The pendant textile-based panels to the side of each major reserve is a particularly *Feinmeister leitmotiv*.

The catalogue of the Keramik Museum Hetjens, Dusseldorf, afb. 23, and Robert Schmidt's article, "Frankfurter Fayence in Holland," *Schriften des Historischen Museums,* IV, 1928, pp. 85–93, abb. 2–3, illustrate two similar *deckelvases* (with lids), attributed to the *Feinmeister*. (M.P.)

103

104

103 Dish

Germany, Frankfurt-am-Main. c. 1680.
Tin-glazed earthenware, underglaze cobalt blue decoration.
Diameter 39.3 cm.
The Art Institute of Chicago. Gift of Mrs. Elizabeth F. Wormser
in memory of her beloved husband, Dr. Otto R. Wormser,
1982.1481.

A large dish or charger with a wide flange and shallow cavetto. Glazed holes for hanging the dish pierce the foot-ring. The underglaze cobalt blue as well as the overall body glaze is a cool, grayish blue.

Wanli style border pattern. An octagonally-framed center field contains an aquatic scene often depicted on this type of ware. Eight reserve panels encircling the aquatic scene consist of modified diaper pattern and petalwork.

The decoration on the reverse side of the dish is sketchily painted. Six single strokes divide the surface into segments containing a centrally-slashed circle.

Wanli border patterns contain auspicious symbols drawn from sacred and profane sources. Four lotus-panels contain peach sprigs, symbols of rejuvenation and longevity. Artemesia leaves—one of the eight precious objects symbolizing good fortune and endowed with restorative powers—are set within two lotus-panels. The remaining panels frame a vaguely floral or organic beribboned object. European potters, unfamiliar with Chinese iconography, freely interpreted elements of the designs on export porcelain. The ubiquitous sacred tassels decorate the dividing panels. In many examples of *kraakporcelein*-inspired faience, these Buddhist emblems have been reduced to a series of dots.

The pair of ducks, symbolizing conjugal felicity and fidelity, in a river landscape with lotus and other aquatic vegetation is a characteristic motif of *kraakporcelein*.

The arrival and subsequent auction of the cargo of the captured Portuguese carracks in 1602 and 1604 in Amsterdam galvanized European fascination with Far Eastern wares. Dutch copies and derivations of *kraakporcelein* were largely responsible for disseminating Ming and Transitional decorative styles throughout Europe. (M.P.)

104 Plate

Spain, Andalusia. 1672.
Tin-glazed earthenware, with underglaze cobalt blue decoration.
Diameter 29.2 cm.
The Metropolitan Museum of Art. Rogers Fund, 1907, 07.143.3.

The function and decorative qualities of this plate indicate an English or Dutch prototype of a popular subgroup of tin-glazed earthenware referred to as *blue dash tulip chargers*. "Blue dash" identifies the rim decoration generally seen in this popular seventeenth-century ware. The formal arrangement of five flowers in a vase is ultimately derived from a sixteenth/seventeenth-century Islamic decorative motif. The stylised flowers derive from the tulip form introduced to Europe from Turkey around 1560. The purely decorative nature of this plate is identified both by the suspension holes on the reverse side of the plate and the commemorative acronym and accompanying date painted on the rim, 1672 P Z P. (M.P.)

105

106

105 Two-handled pot

England. Seventeenth century.
Tin-glazed earthenware with cobalt blue decoration.
John Philip Kassebaum Collection.

106 Mug

England, Southwark. 1629.
By Christian Wilhelm. Dutch, active in England.
Tin-glazed earthenware, cobalt blue decoration.
Height 24.5 cm.
The Nelson-Atkins Museum of Art, Kansas City, Missouri (Gift of Mr. Frank P. Burnap), B 185 A.

The pot has a slightly flaring short neck, flattened globular body and two handles. On the neck between single and double rings, a band of stylized pendant leaves. On the body is a highly simplified landscape with figures in the Chinese manner. On one side is a seated figure with belted tunic and baggy pantaloons, with trees and rocks in the background. On the other side are two kneeling women, seen from behind, is a similar landscape setting. The handles are decorated with splashes of blue.

The diagonal stripes to the left of the seated figure are actually part of a parapet; for the original, see the background to a landscape with boys playing in a garden on a Transitional vase in the Reitlinger Collection (Ashmolean Museum and Sotheby Parke Bernet 1981, pp. 29–30, no. 36).

The origin of the pendant leaves on the neck can be seen on the shoulder of a Transitional chamber-pot (itself of European form) of the Chongzhen period (1628–1644 A.D.) (Little 1984, p. 83, Plate 32). The shape of the pot bears a resemblance to a monochrome incense-burner with two elephant-head handles, also of the Chongzhen period (ibid., p. 89, Plate 37).

The barrel-shaped mug has a wide rim and narrow splayed foot, and a single handle. It is painted below the rim with a diagonally hatched band between pairs of rings. On the body is a landscape scene, with birds perched on rocks and flying above, large insects and various flowers of the daisy type, and leaves and ferns. On a shaded panel at the center with scrolling ends is inscribed:

MRS. MARY HOOPER 1629

On the foot are three rings. The handle is outlined in blue.

This mug is the work of Christian Wilhelm, a Dutchman who emigrated to England in 1604 from the Rhenish Palatinate. The first record of him in 1617 describes him as a vinegar-maker, living in Southwark. A year later he is recorded in the "Return of Aliens in the parish of St. Olave, Southwark" as a "gally pott [delftware] maker and aquivity styller [acqua vitae distiller]" and also in 1618, he is listed among "Estrangers on the Waterside... in the Mays [Maze]."

Setting up his pottery workshop in Southwark near the waterfront on the south bank of the Thames, he successfully petitioned for a Royal grant of privilege in 1628, to be the sole maker of gallyware, or English delft. For fourteen years from 1628 until 1642 he held this monopoly, and in 1638 in a patent application for making smalt, it states "Wilhelm has invented the making of white earthenware pots, glazed both within and without, which show fair as China dishes" (Davies 1969; Tait 1960).

Although he learned the craft of pottery-making after he settled in Southwark, Wilhelm credited himself for introducing smalt, the blue used for decorating the tin-glazed earthenware. A number of pieces assigned to his workshop are dated between 1628 and 1636, many of them loose interpretations of the Wanli bird-on-rock design, seen in its original Chinese form on the Hatcher dish (61), and in a Dutch copy from the Metropolitan Museum (96), both in the present exhibition.

PUBLISHED: Ross E. Taggert, *The Frank P. and Harriet C. Burnap Collection of English Pottery in the William Rockhill Nelson Gallery*, Kansas City, Missouri, 1967, p. 44, no. 73. Hugh Tait, "Southwark (Alias Lambeth) Delftware and the Potter Christian Wilhelm: I," *The Connoisseur*, 146, September 1960, p. 38, Figure 5. Ivor Noël Hume, *Early English Delftware from London and Virginia*, The Colonial Williamsburg Foundation, Williamsburg, Virginia, 1977, pp. 40–41, Plate 36. Isabel Davies, "Seventeenth-century delftware potters in St. Olave's Parish, Southwark," *Surrey Archaeological Collections*, LXVI, 1969, pp. 11–13.

107 **Dish**

England. c. 1650.
Tin-glazed earthenware, decorated in underglaze cobalt blue.
Diameter 34.3 cm.
Collection of Ivor Noël Hume.

The dish is of tin-glazed earthenware, the inside painted in cobalt blue on a white ground, the outside yellow lead-glazed. Tin was used as an opacifier in order to conceal the colored earthenware; it was often omitted from the lead-glaze on the outside, probably for reasons of economy (Hume 1977, pp. 42–43).

The design is a simplified version of a Wanli original, the central panel being reduced to a pinwheel design, instead of the more usual landscape. Related examples in the Burnett Collection, the Ashmolean and the Victoria and Albert Museum are less stylized and have eight segments painted inside the central area, instead of six on the present example (Hume 1977, pp. 45–46, Plates 45–48).

The eight segments are themselves derived from the octagonal frame, such a common feature of Wanli dishes (Christies 1984b, for numerous examples from the Hatcher wreck, pp. 16, 18, 43, 78, 80, etc.).

The presence of numerous sherds of English delftware on Virginia sites indicates that there was a vigorous export market for Southwark products in the first half of the seventeenth century.

PUBLISHED: Ivor Noël Hume, *Early English Delftware from London and Virginia,* The Colonial Williamsburg Foundation, Williamsburg, Virginia, 1977, p. 46, Plate 47, color plate facing p. 84.

107

108 Sherds of English delftware

England, Southwark: Pickleherring site. c. 1628–1640.
Tin-glazed earthenware, decorated in cobalt blue, one sherd with
  additional orange and green.
Diameters of original dishes approximately 23–26 cm.
The Colonial Williamsburg Foundation. Sir David Burnett
  Collection.

Wasters from a group of fourteen plates and a dish, fused together
with their trivets, from Southwark, London. They were discovered by workmen laying electrical lines beneath Vine Street
and rescued along with other pottery from the area by Sir David
Burnett.

English delftware is essentially a lead-glazed earthenware with
tin used as an opacifier. The principal design among the sherds recovered is the "bird-on-rock" type, stemming originally from the
Chinese Wanli prototype. The same design appears on the mug in
the exhibition (106), dated 1629; and a jug in the London Museum
(Figure 19), dated 1630, both of which are probably from the factory of Christian Wilhelm (Tait 1960). The bird-on-rock motif
continued to be popular until at least the middle of the seventeenth century.

A closely related fragment was found at Lee Hall, in Virginia,
demonstrating that similar dishes were exported to America
(Hume 1977, p. 41, Plate 39).

PUBLISHED: Ivor Noël Hume, *Early English Delftware from London and
Virginia,* The Colonial Williamsburg Foundation, Williamsburg, Virginia, 1977.

109 Jug

England, Lambeth. 1682.
Tin-glazed earthenware, painted in underglaze blue.
Height 23 cm.
The Nelson-Atkins Museum of Art, Kansas City, Missouri
  (Gift of Mr. Frank P. Burnap). B 186–1.

The jug is decorated in blue on a bluish-green ground. It has a cylindrical neck and globular body with a short foot, and a single
strap handle. Both the neck and the body are decorated with landscapes in the Chinese style and the shoulder is marked:

$$\begin{matrix} & Y & \\ W & \star & A \\ & 1682 & \end{matrix}$$

This arrangement is common on English pottery, the upper letter
standing for the surname and the lower letters for the Christian
names of husband and wife (Caiger-Smith 1973, p. 168).

The Chinese landscape is very much in the Arita style of Jap-
anese porcelain, c. 1660–1690 (Ashmolean Museum and Sotheby
Parke Bernet 1981, nos. 239–246), perhaps because of a common
Chinese Transitional origin.

The first recorded factory at Lambeth was established about
1676.

PUBLISHED: *English Ceramic Circle Exhibition,* Victoria and Albert Museum,
London, May 5th–June 20th, 1948, no. 12. Ross E. Taggart, *The Frank P.
and Harriet C. Burnap Collection of English Pottery in the William Rockhill
Nelson Gallery,* Nelson Gallery – Atkins Museum, Kansas City, Missouri,
1967, p. 50, no. 119.

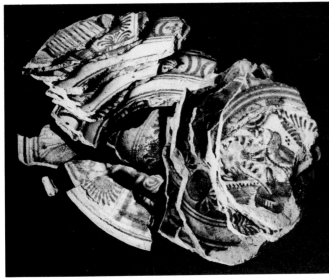

108

109

110

111

110 Tile *(azulejo)*

Mexico, c. 1600–1625.
White earthenware, underglaze blue decoration with black
  outlines.
13 x 12.4 cm., 1.9 cm. thick.
The Art Institute of Chicago. Gift of Mrs. Eva Lewis in memory
  of her husband, Herbert Pickering Lewis, 23.1570.

A smooth, creamy white glaze–chipped in places, repaired in
others–covers a black and indigo line drawing of a Western soldier
in medieval armor riding an Oriental spotted deer. On either side
are oversized floral and leaf motifs in the Hispanic style. Blue
washes of varying intensity are flush, neither raised nor sunk into
the glaze. A blue "F", a potter's unidentified mark, is in the center
of the upper edge. Dots punctuate the figures; on the soldier's
cross-hatched armor, they are small and regularly placed; on the
deer, they are random, close, and both large and small.   (J.M.M.)

PUBLISHED: John M. Goggin, "Spanish Maiolica in the New World," *Yale
University Publications in Anthropology*, 72, 1968, Plate 15d.

111 Jar *(chocolatero)*

Mexico, c. 1700.
White earthenware, underglaze blue decoration. Iron lid.
Height 37.5 cm.
The Art Institute of Chicago. Gift of Mrs. Eva Lewis in memory
  of her husband, Herbert Pickering Lewis, 23.1537.

The form of this jar is Chinese and may have been converted from
a flower pot (there is a hole in the bottom) to a "money jar." Its
iron lid, incised by a Mexican metalworker, is nailed shut in two
places. The rough, sometimes crackled gray-white glaze has two
shades of blue; the darker, under the glaze, is thick and raised; the
lighter, over the glaze. The repaired base, sloping foot and foot-
ring are glazed but heavily worn.

On the outside, four diagonal panels in the Talavera style are
bordered on top by three fringed, fabric swags and on the sides by
two large scrolls. Inside each are long-tailed birds possibly imitating the phoenix of "Swatow" ware. The base border is in a bold
dot-and-line Spanish style. The iron lid with key has two hinges.
On top it is punched and incised with phoenix-like birds, a flame-
breathing dog-like dragon, and plume-shaped scrolled leaves.
The key handle is a punched *fleur-de-lis*. The lid is about twenty
years later than the jar which may originally have had a domed lid
in the Chinese style, if it were not first made as a flower pot.

(J.M.M.)

PUBLISHED: *Art Institute Bulletin*, XVIII. 5, The Art Institute of Chicago,
Chicago, May 1924, p. 59.

112 Plate (plato)

Mexico, c. 1685–1700.
Red earthenware, underglaze blue decoration.
Diameter 34.3 cm.
The Art Institute of Chicago. Gift of Mrs. Eva Lewis in memory
of her husband, Herbert Pickering Lewis, 23.1466.

113 Flower pot (tiesto)

Mexico, c. 1625–1650.
Red earthenware, underglaze blue decoration.
Height 46.9 cm.
The Art Institute of Chicago. Gift of Mrs. Eva Lewis in memory
of her husband, Herbert Pickering Lewis, 23.1444.

The shape of this plate is modified Hispanic; its concave center is
not as deep as prototypes from Spain, and thus was probably influenced by flatter Chinese examples. Its smooth glaze over a
white ground is clear and uniform. The base is glazed, and the
foot-ring unglazed.

Inside on the sloping rim and deep cavetto, in raised and sunk-
en blue, are twelve stemmed flowers, similar to the "Chinese aster" (stylized chrysanthemum or palmette) which alternate with
symmetrical dot-and-leaf stemmed devices. Two birds at the center are closely surrounded by dotted rocks and dense foliage.

On the exterior, in a thin, clear blue, four open whorls with a
dash above and a dot below alternate with four crossed, S-shaped
lines forming X's. In the center, also in underglaze blue wash, is
an unidentified mark: (J.M.M.)

This piece was apparently made as a flower pot; the bottom hole
in the convex, glazed base looks original. The Italian/Chinese
shape has a high neck and full rounded shoulders, sloping to a
base with a rounded cornice. It has applied ribs and a foot cornice
and is chipped on the top rim.

Outside, two shades of blue decorate four panels defined by
ribs. The darker areas are both raised and sunk; the lighter blue is
smooth. In the first panel are towers, trees, birds and an Hispanic
rabbit; in the second, a diagonally striped, mosque-like building
in trees and three fish in a limbo of dense foliage; in the third, two
towered buildings and two cranes; in the fourth, a mustached
Chinese with sword and line, possibly fishing in a forest stream;
nearby are two fishes in dotted and leafy vegetation.

The interior of the pot has a crackled cream glaze. (J.M.M.)

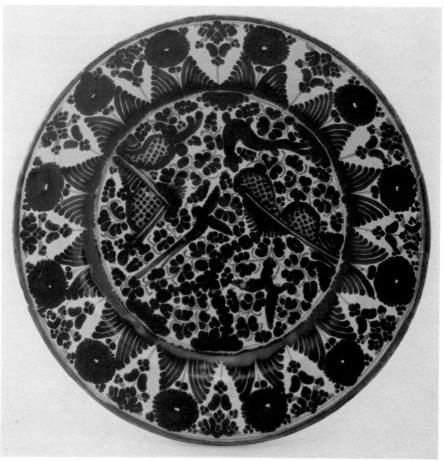

112

114 **Basin** *(lebrillo)*

Mexico, c. 1725–1750.
White earthenware, underglaze blue decoration.
Height 20.6 cm. Diameter 57.1 cm.
The Art Institute of Chicago. Gift of Mrs. Eva Lewis in memory
    of her husband, Herbert Pickering Lewis, 23.1499.

114

114

This basin, which is heavily potted, may be in such excellent condition because of its weight, a deterrent to frequent moving or possibly even to much use. Its rim thickens as it reaches the edge, which is lightened by two techniques applied to its entire circumference: an incised line dividing the rim edge in half, and ten crimped "pie-crust" areas of four-finger size, evenly spaced, probably for aid in lifting as well as for decoration. Over a bright white body, its glaze is smooth. The base is flat and unglazed. The underglaze blue is in two shades, dark and light, and is more often raised than sunk.

On the inside of its unusually steep, sloping sides are six white-on-blue, scalloped reserves filled with symmetrical motifs of three vertical flowers and leaves. In the center, outlined in light blue, is a kneeling Chinese with a large Aztec nose. A large snake coils around his neck. The stream by which he kneels has a mosque-like tower at the left edge, and trees at the right.

On the outside, in underglaze blue wash, three wings with scrolls and parallel lines are separated by two groups of six or more overlapping circles with a lozenge-shaped center. They are painted more carefully than many examples of similar exterior motifs.

(J.M.M.)

CHINESE
DYNASTIES

Tang dynasty	618–907
Five Dynasties	907–960
Liao dynasty	916–1125
Song dynasty	960–1279
Northern Song	960–1127
Southern Song	1127–1279
Jin dynasty	1115–1234
Yuan dynasty	1271–1368
Ming dynasty	1368–1644
Hongwu	1368–1398
Jianwen	1399–1402
Yongle	1403–1424
Hongxi	1425
Xuande	1426–1435
Zhengtong	1436–1449
Jingtai	1450–1456
Tianshun	1457–1464
Chenghua	1465–1487
Hongzhi	1488–1505
Zhengde	1506–1521
Jiajing	1522–1566
Longqing	1567–1572
Wanli	1573–1620
Taichang	1620
Tianqi	1621–1627
Chongzhen	1628–1644
Qing dynasty	1644–1911
Shunzhi	1644–1661
Kangxi	1662–1722

BIBLIOGRAPHY

ADDIS 1959a. Sir John Addis, "A group of Underglaze Red," *Transactions of the Oriental Ceramic Society*, 1957–59, London, 1959, pp. 15–38.

ADDIS 1959b. Sir John Addis, "Yung Lo Blue and White," *Oriental Art*, New Series, v.4, London, 1959, pp. 157–162.

ADDIS 1960. Sir John Addis, "The Use of Copper-red on Jao Wares," *Oriental Art*, New Series, VI.4, London, 1960, pp. 150–153.

ADDIS 1967. Sir John Addis, "A group of underglaze red," *Transactions of the Oriental Ceramic Society*, 1964–66, London, 1967, pp. 89–102.

ADDIS 1970. Sir John Addis, "Chinese porcelain found in the Philippines," *Transactions of the Oriental Ceramic Society*, 1967–69, London, 1970, pp. 17–36.

ADDIS 1975. Sir John Addis, *Exhibition of Chinese Blue and White Porcelain and Related Underglaze Red*, The Oriental Ceramic Society of Hong Kong, Hong Kong, 1975.

ADDIS 1977a. Sir John Addis, "A Visit to Ching-te-chen," *Transactions of the Oriental Ceramic Society*, 1975–77, London, 1977, pp. 1–34.

ADDIS 1977b. Sir John Addis, "Hung-wu and Yung-lo White," *Transactions of the Oriental Ceramic Society*, 1957–77, London, 1977, pp. 35–58.

ADDIS 1978. Sir John Addis, *Chinese Ceramics from Datable Tombs and Some Other Dated Material: A Handbook*, London, 1978.

ADDIS 1981. Sir John Addis, "Porcelain-stone and kaolin — late Yuan developments at Hutian," *Transactions of The Oriental Ceramic Society*, London, 1980–81, pp. 54–66.

ADDIS 1984. Sir John Addis, "The Evolution of Techniques at Jingdezhen with particular reference to the Yuan Dynasty," *Jingdezhen Wares: The Yuan Evolution*, The Oriental Ceramic Society of Hong Kong, Hong Kong, 1984, pp. 11–19.

AGA-OGLU 1955. Kamer Aga-Oglu, "The So-called 'Swatow' Wares: Types and Problems of Provenance," *Far Eastern Ceramic Bulletin*, VII.2, Boston, 1955.

AGA-OGLU 1972. Kamer Aga-Oglu, *The Williams Collection of Far Eastern Ceramics*, University of Michigan Museum of Anthropology, Ann Arbor, 1972.

AGA-OGLU 1982. Kamer Aga-Oglu, *Shadow of the Dragon, Chinese Domestic and Trade Ceramics*, Columbus Museum of Art, Columbus, Ohio, 1982.

ALLAN 1971. James Allan, "Later Mamluk Metalwork, II; A series of lunch boxes," *Oriental Art*, New Series, XVII, Summer 1971, pp. 156–64.

ALLAN 1973. James Allan, "Abū'l-Qāsim's Treatise on Ceramics," *Iran*, XI, 1973, pp. 111–120.

AREZ et al 1984. Ilda Arez, Maria Azevedo Coutinho Vasconcellos e Sousa and Jessie McNab, *Portugal and Porcelain*, The Metropolitan Museum of Art, New York, 1984.

ART INSTITUTE 1924. *Art Institute Bulletin*, XVIII.5, The Art Institute of Chicago, Chicago, May 1924.

ARTS OF MING DYNASTY 1958. "The Arts of the Ming Dynasty" (exhibition catalogue), *Transactions of the Oriental Ceramic Society*, 1955–57, London, 1958.

ASHMOLEAN MUSEUM AND SOTHEBY PARKE BERNET 1981. *Eastern Ceramics and Other Works of Art From the Collection of Gerald Reitlinger*, London, 1981.

ASIAN ART MUSEUM 1985. *Masterworks of Ming: 15th-Century Blue-and-White Porcelains*, Asian Art Museum of San Francisco, San Francisco, 1985.

ATIL 1973. Esin Atil, *Ceramics from the World of Islam*, Freer Gallery of Art, Smithsonian Institution, Washington, D.C., 1973.

ATIL 1975. Esin Atil, *Art of the Arab World*, Freer Gallery of Art, Smithsonian Institution, Washington, D.C., 1975.

ATIL 1981. Esin Atil, *Renaissance of Islam, Art of the Mamluks*, Smithsonian Institution Press, Washington, D.C., 1981.

ATIL 1983. tr. Esin Atil, *The Anatolian Civilizations, III, Seljuk/Ottoman*, Topkapi Palace Museum, Istanbul, 1983.

AVERY 1938. Louise Avery, "The Mortimer Schiff Collection: Early Italian Maiolica," *The Metropolitan Museum of Art Bulletin*, XXXIII, New York, January 1938, pp. 10–13.

AVERY 1944. Louise Avery, "Chinese Porcelains in English Mounts," *The Metropolitan Museum of Art Bulletin*, II.9, May 1944, pp. 266–272.

AYERS 1951. John Ayers, "Early Chinese Blue-and-White in the Museum of Eastern Art, Oxford," *Oriental Art*, III.4, London, 1951, pp. 134–141.

AYERS 1956. John Ayers, "Yüan and Ming Ceramics at Tokyo," *Oriental Art*, New Series, II.4, London, 1956, pp. 151–152.

AYERS 1957. John Ayers, "Some Chinese Wares of the Yuan period," *Transactions of the Oriental Ceramic Society*, 1954–55, London, 1957, pp. 66–90.

AYERS 1969. John Ayers, *The Baur Collection, Chinese Ceramics*, II (Ming Porcelains and other Wares), Geneva, 1969.

AYERS 1978. John Ayers, "The Discovery of a Yüan Ship at Sinan, South-West Korea: A First Report," *Oriental Art*, New Series, XXIV.1, London, 1978, pp. 79–85.

AYERS 1982. John Ayers, *The Baur Collection, Japanese Ceramics*, Geneva, 1982.

AYERS 1984. John Ayers, "Chinese Porcelain of the Sultans in Istanbul," *Transactions of the Oriental Ceramic Society*, 1982–83, London, 1984, pp. 77–104.

BAHRAMI 1952. Mehde Bahrami, "The Collection of Chinese Porcelains from the Ardabil Shrine," *Transactions of the Oriental Ceramic Society*, 1949–50, London, 1952, pp. 13–20.

BARBER 1908. Edwin A. Barber, *The Maiolica of Mexico*, The Pennsylvania Museum, Philadelphia, 1908.

BARBER 1909. Edwin A. Barber, *The Pottery and Porcelain of the United States*, New York, 1909.

BARBER 1915. Edwin A. Barber, *Mexican Maiolica in the Collection of the Hispanic Society of America*, The Hispanic Society of American, New York, 1915.

BARBER 1922. Edwin A. Barber, *The Emily Johnston De Forest Collection of Mexican Maiolica*, The Hispanic Society of America, New York, 1922.

BAUER AND HAUPT 1976. Rotraud Bauer and Herbert Haupt, "Das Kunstkammerinventar Kaiser Rudolfs II, 1607–1611," *Jahrbuch der*

Kunsthistorischen Sammlungen in Wien, 72, Vienna, 1976.

BERTI 1967. Luciano Berti, *Il Principe dello Studiolo,* Florence, 1967.

BIMSON 1970. Mavis Bimson, "Technological aspects of glass in Asia during the T'ang period," *Pottery and Metalwork in T'ang China,* Percival David Foundation Colloquies on Art and Archaeology in Asia, 1, London, 1970, pp. 77–80.

BIVAR 1970. A.D.H. Bivar, "Trade Between China and the Near East in the Sasanian and early Muslim periods," *Pottery and Metalwork in T'ang China,* Percival David Foundation Colloquies on Art and Archaeology in Asia, 1, London, 1970, pp. 1–11.

BLUETT 1979. Roger Bluett, "The Development of Western Attitudes to Chinese Art — Chinese Ceramics," *Oriental Ceramic Society of Hong Kong,* 3,1977–78, Hong Kong, 1979, pp. 34–40.

BOODE 1946. Peter Boode, "Some Remarks on Pre-Ming and Early Fifteenth-century Blue and White Chinese Porcelains," *Transactions of the Oriental Ceramic Society,* 1945–46, London, 1946, pp. 9–16.

BRANKSTON 1970. A.D. Brankston, *Early Ming Wares of Chingtechen,* Peking, 1st ed., 1938, reissued, Hong Kong, 1970.

BROWN 1977. Roxanna M. Brown, *The Ceramics of South-East Asia: Their Dating and Identification,* Kuala Lumpur, Oxford University Press, 1977.

BUCCI 1965. Mario Bucci, *Lo Studiolo di Francesco I,* Florence, 1965.

BUSHELL 1899. Stephen W. Bushell, *Oriental Ceramic Art: Collection of W. T. Walters,* New York, 1899.

BUSHELL 1910. tr. Stephen W. Bushell, *Description of Chinese Pottery and Porcelain: Being a Translation of the T'ao Shuo,* Oxford, 1910.

BUSHELL 1924. Stephen W. Bushell, *Chinese Art,* 1, Victoria and Albert Museum, London, 1924.

CAIGER-SMITH 1973. Alan Caiger-Smith, *Tin-Glaze Pottery in Europe and the Islamic World: The Tradition of 1000 Years in Maiolica, Faience & Delftware,* London, 1973.

CAMMANN 1955. Schuyler Cammann, "Some Strange Ming Beasts," *Oriental Art,* New Series, II.3, London, 1955, pp. 94–102.

CARSWELL 1966. John Carswell, "An Early Ming Porcelain Stand from Damascus," *Oriental Art,* New Series, XII, Autumn 1966, pp. 176–182.

CARSWELL 1967. John Carswell, "A fourteenth-century Chinese porcelain dish from Damascus," *American University of Beirut Festival Book, (Festschrift), 1866–1966,* Beirut, 1967, ed. F. Sarruf and S. Tuqan, pp. 39–69.

CARSWELL 1968. John Carswell, *New Julfa, Armenian Churches and other Buildings,* Oxford, 1968.

CARSWELL 1972a. John Carswell, "China and the Near East: the recent discovery of Chinese porcelain in Syria," *The Westward Influence of the Chinese Arts from the 14th to the 18th Century,* Percival David Foundation Colloquies on Art and Archaeology in Asia, 3, London, 1972, pp. 20–25.

CARSWELL 1972b. John Carswell, "Six Tiles," *Islamic Art in the Metropolitan Museum of Art,* ed. R. Ettinghausen, New York, 1972, pp. 99–124.

CARSWELL 1972c. John Carswell, "Some Fifteenth-century hexagonal Tiles from the Near East," *Victoria and Albert Museum Yearbook,* 3, London, 1972, pp. 59–75.

CARSWELL 1972d. John Carswell, *The Kütahya Tiles and Pottery from the Armenian Cathedral of St. James in Jerusalem,* I, with C.J.F Dowsett, II, Clarendon Press, Oxford, 1972.

CARSWELL 1976a. John Carswell, "The Lemon-squeezer; an Unique Form of Turkish Pottery," *IV ème Congrès International D'Art Turc, Études historiques,* 3, Aix-en-Provence, 1976, pp. 29–45.

CARSWELL 1976b. John Carswell, Correspondence, *Oriental Art,* New Series, XXII.2, London, 1976, p. 217.

CARSWELL 1977a. John Carswell, "China and Islam in the Maldive Islands," *Transactions of the Oriental Ceramic Society,* 1975–77, London, 1977, pp. 121–198.

CARSWELL 1977b. John Carswell, "From the Tulip to the Rose," *Studies in Eighteenth-Century Islamic History,* Papers in Islamic History, 4, Carbondale, Illinois, 1977, pp. 328–358.

CARSWELL 1978. John Carswell, "Syrian Tiles From Sinai and Damascus," *Archeology in the Levant,* Warminster, England, 1978, pp. 269–296.

CARSWELL 1979a. John Carswell, "China and Islam: A survey of the Coast of India and Ceylon," *Transactions of the Oriental Ceramic Society,* 1977–78, London, 1979, pp. 43–69.

CARSWELL 1979b. John Carswell, "Sin in Syria", *Iran,* XVII, 1979.

CARSWELL 1981. John Carswell, "New Julfa and the Safavid Image of the Armenians," *The Armenian Image in History and Literature,* Studies in Near Eastern Culture and Society, 3, Malibu, 1981, pp. 83–104.

CARSWELL 1985. John Carswell, "Chinese ceramics from Allaippidy in Sri Lanka," *A Ceramic Legacy of Asia's Maritime Trade,* Southeast Asian Ceramic Society, West Malaysian Chapter, Kuala Lumpur, 1985, pp. 31–49.

CARSWELL AND PRICKETT 1984. John Carswell and Martha Prickett, "Mantai 1980: A preliminary Investigation," *Ancient Ceylon,* 5, Colombo, Sri Lanka, 1984, pp. 3–81.

CERAMIC ART OF CHINA 1972. "The Ceramic Art of China," *Transactions of the Oriental Ceramic Society,* 1969–71, London, 1972.

CERVANTES 1939. Enrique A. Cervantes, *Loza Blanca y Azuelo de Puebla,* I–II, Mexico, 1939.

CHANG 1969. T'ien-Tse Chang. *Sino-Portuguese Trade from 1514 to 1644,* Leiden, 1969.

CHAU JU-KUA 1911. *Chau Ju-Kua,* tr. and ann. Friedrich Hirth and W. W. Rockhill, St. Petersburg, 1911, reprinted New York, 1966.

CHOMPRET, BLOCH, GUERIN AND ALFASSA 1935. *Répertoire de la faience française,* ed. Chompret, Bloch, Guerin and Alfassa, II: Nevers, Paris, 1935.

CHRISTIES 1984a,b. Christies, Amsterdam, *Fine and Important Late Ming and Transitional Porcelain,* intro. C.D. Sheaf, (sale catalogues), a. 14 March 1984, and b. 12–13 June 1984.

CHRISTIES 1984c. Christies, London, *Important Annamese Ceramics,* (sale catalogue), 7 December 1984.

CHUNG YANG MO 1983. Chung Yang Mo, "The Kinds of Ceramic Articles Discovered in Sinan, and Problems about them," tr. Shigetaka Kaneko, *The Sunken Treasures off the Sinan Coast,* Tokyo, 1983, pp. 84–87.

CLEVELAND 1963. *The Bulletin of The Cleveland Museum of Art,* Cleveland, December 1963.

CLEVELAND 1966. *The Bulletin of the Cleveland Museum of Art,* Cleveland, September 1966.

CLEVELAND 1978. The Cleveland Museum of Art, *Handbook,* Cleveland, Ohio, 1978.

CLEVELAND, R. 1970. Richard S. Cleveland, *200 Years of Japanese Porcelain,* City Art Museum, St. Louis, 1970.

COCHRANE 1973. Eric Cochrane, *Florence in the Forgotten Centuries, 1527–1800,* Chicago and London, 1973.

COLOSANTI 1919 A. Colosanti, *Catalogue of the C. and E. Canessa Collection,* (privately printed), 1919.

COOPER 1979. Rhonda Cooper, *The Asian Collection, Gallery Guide,* The Dayton Art Institute, Dayton, Ohio, 1979.

CROWE 1977. Yolande Crowe, "Early Islamic Pottery and China," *Transactions of the Oriental Ceramic Society,* 1975–77, London, 1977, pp. 263–278.

CROWE 1981. Yolande Crowe, "Aspects of Persian Blue and White and China in the Seventeenth Century," *Transactions of the Oriental Ceramic Society,* 1979–80, London, 1981, pp. 15–30.

D'ARGENCÉ 1958. René-Yvon Lefebvre d'Argencé, *Les Céramiques à Base Chocolatée,* Publications de L'École Française d'Extrême-Orient, XLIV, Paris, 1958.

D'ARGENCÉ 1967. René-Yvon Lefebvre d'Argencé, *Chinese Ceramics in the Avery Brundage Collection,* The deYoung Museum Society, San Francisco, 1967.

D'ARGENCÉ 1983. ed. René-Yvon Lefebvre d'Argencé, *Treasures From the Shanghai Museum: 6,000 Years of Chinese Art,* Shanghai Museum and the Asian Art Museum of San Francisco, San Francisco, 1983.

DAVID 1933. Sir Percival David, "The Shōsō-in Pottery," *Transactions of the Oriental Ceramic Society*, 1931–32, London, 1933, pp. 21–43.

DAVIES 1969. Isabel Davies, "Seventeenth-century delftware potters in St-Olave's Parish, Southwark," *Surrey Archaeological Collections*, LXVI, 1969, pp. 11–13.

DE FLINES 1969. E.W. Van Orsoy de Flines, *Guide to the Ceramic Collection*, Museum Pusat Djakarta, Djakarta, 1969.

DE JONGE 1970. C.H. de Jonge, *Delft Ceramics*, tr. Marie-Christine Hellin, London, 1970.

DENNY 1974. Walter B. Denny, "Blue-and-White Islamic Pottery on Chinese Themes," *Boston Museum Bulletin*, LXXII.368, Museum of Fine Arts, Boston, 1974, pp. 75–97.

DENNY 1980. Walter B. Denny, "Ceramics", *Turkish Art*, Washington, D.C. and New York, 1980, pp. 239–298.

DE RICCI 1927. Seymour de Ricci, *Cataloque of early Italian maiolica...in the Mortimer L. Schiff Collection*, n.p., 1927.

DOE 1965. D.B. Doe, "Pottery Sites near Aden," Department of Antiquities Publication, Bulletin Number 5, Aden, 1965.

DOS SANTOS 1960. Reynaldo dos Santos, *Faiences Portugueses*, Livraria Galicia, Alvaro, Portugal, 1960.

EVANS 1973. R.J.W. Evans, *Rudolf II and his World*, Oxford, 1973.

FEDDERSON 1961. Martin Fedderson, *Chinese Decorative Art: A Handbook for Collectors and Connoisseurs*, tr. Arthur Lane, London, 1961.

FEHERVARI 1970. Geza Fehervari, "Near Eastern wares under Chinese influence," *Pottery and Metalwork in T'ang China*, Percival David Foundation Colloquies on Art and Archaeology in Asia, 1, London, 1970, pp. 28–34.

FERRAND 1922. *Voyage du Marchand Arabe Sulayman en Inde et en Chine, rédigé en 851*, tr. Gabriel Ferrand, Paris, 1922.

FEULNER 1935. Adolf Feulner, *Frankfurter Fayencen*, Berlin, 1935.

FORBES AND ALI. Andrew Forbes and Fawzia Ali, "The Maldive Islands and their historical links with the coast of Eastern Africa," *Kenya Past and Present*, 12, Nairobi, Kenya, n.d.

FRASCHÉ 1976. Dean F. Frasché, *Southeast Asian Ceramics: Ninth Through Seventeenth Centuries*, The Asia Society, New York, 1976.

FROTHINGHAM 1944. Alice Wilson Frothingham, *Talavera Pottery*, The Hispanic Society of America, New York, 1944.

FUJIOKA 1960. Ryoichi Fujioka, *Gen Min-sho no sometsuki*, (Blue-and-white porcelain of the Chinese Yuan Dynasty and the beginning of the Ming Dynasty), Tokyo, 1960.

FUNG PING SHAN MUSEUM 1981. *Exhibition of Ceramic Finds From Ancient Kilns in China*, Fung Ping Shan Museum, University of Hong Kong, Hong Kong, 1981.

GARNER 1954a. Sir Harry Garner, "Blue and White of the Middle Ming Period," *Transactions of the Oriental Ceramic Society*, 1951–53, London, 1954, pp. 61–72.

GARNER 1954b. Sir Harry Garner, *Oriental Blue and White*, London, 1954.

GARNER 1955. Sir Harry Garner, "Some notes on the Chinese Blue and White Exhibition," *Transactions of the Oriental Ceramic Society*, 1953–54, London, 1955, pp. 51–56.

GARNER 1956. Sir Harry Garner, "The Use of Imported and Native Cobalt in Chinese Blue and White," *Oriental Art*, New Series, II.2, London, 1956, pp. 48–50.

GARNER 1979. Sir Harry Garner, *Chinese Lacquer*, London, 1979.

GHAIDAN 1975. Usam Ghaidan, *Lamu, A study of the Swahili town*, East African Literature Bureau, Nairobi, Kenya, 1975.

GITTINGER 1982. Mattiebelle Gittinger, *Master Dyers to the World: Technique and Trade in Early Indian Dyed Cotton Textiles*, The Textile Museum, Washington, D.C., 1982.

GODDEN 1979. Geoffrey A. Godden, *Oriental Export Market Porcelain and Its Influence on European Wares*, London, 1979.

GOGGIN 1968. John M. Goggin, "Spanish Maiolica in the New World," *Yale University Publications in Anthropology*, 72, 1968.

GOMPERTZ 1958. Godfrey St. George Montague Gompertz, *Chinese Celadon Wares*, London, 1958.

GOMPERTZ 1968. Godfrey St. George Montague Gompertz, *Korean Pottery and Porcelain of the Yi Period*, New York, 1968.

GOTTSCHOLK see BARBER 1922.

GRAY 1949. Basil Gray, "Blue and white vessels in Persian Miniatures of the 14th and 15th Centuries re-examined," *Transactions of the Oriental Ceramic Society*, 1948–49, London, 1949, pp. 23–30.

GRAY 1955. Basil Gray, "Art Under the Mongol Dynasties of China and Persia," *Oriental Art*, New Series, I.4, London, 1955, pp. 159–167.

GRAY 1967. Basil Gray, "The export of Chinese porcelain to India," *Transactions of the Oriental Ceramic Society*, 1964–66, London, 1967, pp. 21–38.

GRAY 1972. Basil Gray, "Chinese Influence in Persian Painting: 14th and 15th Centuries," *The Westward Influence of the Chinese Arts from the 14th to the 18th Century*, Percival David Foundation Colloquies on Art and Archaeology in Asia, 3, London, 1972. pp. 11–19.

GRAY 1977a. Basil Gray, "The Export of Chinese Porcelain to the Islamic World: Some reflections on its significance for Islamic Art before 1400," *Transactions of the Oriental Ceramic Society*, 1975–77, London, 1977, pp. 231–262.

GRAY 1977b. Basil Gray, "Chinese porcelain of the fourteenth and fifteenth centuries and the John Addis Gift," *British Museum Yearbook II*, London, 1977, pp.156–188.

GRAY 1984. Basil Gray, *Sung Porcelain and Stoneware*, London, 1984.

GRAY AND NEAVE-HILL 1972. Basil Gray and Ben Neave-Hill, "Some Reflections on the Sung-Yüan Wares," *The Ceramic Art of China, Transactions of the Oriental Ceramic Society*, 1969–71, London, 1972, pp. 33–40.

GREENSTED AND HARDIE 1982. Mary Greensted and Peter Hardie, *Chinese Ceramics: The Indian Connections*, City of Bristol Museum and Art Gallery, Bristol, 1982.

GRUBE 1976. Ernst J. Grube, *Islamic Pottery of the Eighth to the Fifteenth Century in the Keir Collection*, London, 1976.

GUY 1980. John Guy, *Oriental Trade Ceramics in Southeast Asia: 10th to 16th Century*, National Gallery of Victoria, Melbourne, Australia, 1980.

GYLLENSVÄRD 1973. Bo Gyllensvärd, "Recent finds of Chinese Ceramics at Fostat. I," *The Bulletin of the Museum of Far Eastern Antiquities*, 45, Stockholm, 1973, pp. 91–119.

GYLLENSVÄRD 1975. Bo Gyllensvärd, "Recent Finds of Chinese Ceramics at Fostat. II," *The Bulletin of the Museum of Far Eastern Antiquities*, 47, Stockholm, 1975, pp. 93–117.

GYLLENSVÄRD AND POPE 1966. Bo Gyllensvärd and John Alexander Pope, *Chinese Art from the Collection of H. M. King Gustaf VI Adolf of Sweden*, The Asia Society, New York, 1966.

HANNOVER 1925. Emil Hannover, *Pottery and Porcelain: A Handbook For Collectors*, Volume I: *Europe and the Near East: Earthenware and Stoneware*, ed., Bernard Rackham, New York, 1925.

HARRISSON 1955. Tom Harrisson, "Some Ceramics excavated in Borneo," *Transactions of the Oriental Ceramic Society*, 1953–54, London, 1955, pp. 11–22.

HARRISSON 1959. Tom Harrisson, " 'Export Wares' Found in West Borneo," *Oriental Art*, New Series, v.2, London, 1959, pp. 42–51.

HARRISSON 1979. Barbara Harrisson, *Swatow in Het Princessehof*, Gemeentelijk Museum Het Princessehof, Leeuwarden, The Netherlands, 1979.

HIRTH AND ROCKHILL 1911. *Chau Ju-kua*, tr. and ann. Friedrich Hirth and W. W. Rockhill, St. Petersburg, 1911, reprinted New York, 1966.

HOBSON 1923. R. L. Hobson, "The Significance of Samarra," *Transactions of the Oriental Ceramic Society*, 1922–23, London, 1923, pp. 29–30.

HOBSON 1928. R. L. Hobson, "Chinese Porcelain Fragments from Aidhab, and some Bashpa Inscriptions," *Transactions of the Oriental Ceramic Society*, 1926–27, London, 1928, pp. 19–22.

HOBSON 1931. R. L. Hobson, "Potsherds from Brahminabad," *Transactions of the Oriental Ceramic Society*, 1928–30, London, 1931, pp. 21–23.

HOBSON 1934. R. L. Hobson, "Chinese Porcelains at Constantinople," *Transactions of the Oriental Ceramic Society,* 1933–34, London, 1934, pp. 9–21.

HODGES 1970. Henry Hodges, "Interaction between metalworking and ceramic technologies in the T'ang period," *Pottery and Metalwork in T'ang China,* Percival David Foundation Colloquies on Art and Archaeology in Asia, 1, London, 1970, pp. 64–67.

HODGES 1972. Henry Hodges, "The technical problems of copying Chinese porcelains in tin glaze," *The Westward Influence of the Chinese Arts from the 14th to the 18th Century,* Percival David Foundation Colloquies on Art and Archaeology in Asia, 3, London, 1972, pp. 79–87.

HOFFMAN 1932. Friedrich Hoffman, *Das Porzellan,* Berlin, 1932.

HONEY 1933. William Bowyer Honey, *English Pottery and Porcelain,* London, 1933.

HONEY 1947. William Bowyer Honey, *German Porcelain,* London, 1947.

HONEY 1952a. William Bowyer Honey, *European Ceramic Art from the end of the Middle Ages to about 1815,* London, 1952.

HONEY 1952b. William Bowyer Honey, *Corean Pottery,* London, 1952.

HONG KONG 1979. *South-East Asian and Chinese Trade Pottery,* Hong Kong Museum of Art, Hong Kong, 1979.

HONOUR 1961. Hugh Honour, *Chinoiserie,* London, 1961.

HORIOKA, RHIE AND DENNY 1975. Yasuko Horioka, Marylin Rhie and Walter B. Denny, *Oriental and Islamic Art in the Isabella Stewart Gardner Museum,* Boston, 1975.

HOURANI 1963. George Fadlo Hourani, *Arab Seafaring in the Indian Ocean in Ancient and Early Medieval Times,* Beirut, 1963.

HUDIG 1929. Ferrand W. Hudig, *Delfter Fayence,* Bibliothek für Kunst- und Antiquitäten-Sammler 34, Berlin, 1929.

HUGHES-STANTON AND KERR 1980. Penelope Hughes-Stanton and Rose Kerr, *Kiln Sites of Ancient China,* The Oriental Ceramic Society, London, 1980.

HUME 1977. Ivor Noël Hume, *Early English Delftware from London and Virginia,* The Colonial Williamsburg Foundation, Williamsburg, Virginia, 1977.

IMPEY 1984. Oliver Impey, "Shoki-Imari and Tianqi; Arita and Jingdezhen in competition for the Japanese market in porcelain in the second quarter of the seventeenth century," *Mededelingenblad Nederlandse Vereniging van Vrieden van Ceramiek,* 116, Amsterdam, 1984, pp. 15–30.

ISLAMIC ART 1972. ed. Richard Ettinghausen, *Islamic Art in The Metropolitan Museum of Art,* New York, 1972.

ISLAMIC ART FOUNDATION 1981. The Islamic Art Foundation, *Islamic Art,* I. ed. E. Grube, E. Sims and J. Carswell, New York, 1981.

JACKSON 1931. Sir Herbert Jackson, "A Note on Certain Fragments of Pottery from Fustat," *Transactions of the Oriental Ceramic Society,* 1928–30, London, 1931, pp. 24–27.

JENKINS 1981. Marilyn Jenkins, *The Renaissance of Islam: Art of the Mamluks, Checklist of Additional Objects Exhibited at The Metropolitan Museum of Art,* New York, 1981.

JENKINS 1983. Marilyn Jenkins, *Islamic Pottery: A Brief History: Bulletin of The Metropolitan Museum of Art,* XI.4, Spring 1983.

JENKINS, MEECH-PEKARIK AND VALENSTEIN, 1977. Marilyn Jenkins, Julia Meech-Pekarik, and Suzanne Valenstein, *Oriental Ceramics: The World's Great Collections,* 12, The Metropolitan Museum of Art, New York, 1977.

JENYNS 1959. Soame Jenyns, "A Visit to Pei-kou, Taiwan, to see early Ming Porcelain from the Palace Collection," *Transactions of the Oriental Ceramic Society,* 1957–59, London, 1959, pp. 39–60.

JENYNS 1961. Soame Jenyns, "The R.F.A. Riesco gift of Chinese porcelain," *British Museum Quarterly,* XXIV.3–4, London, 1961, pp. 107–111.

JENYNS 1967. Soame Jenyns, "The Chinese porcelains in the Topkapu Saray, Istanbul," *Transactions of the Oriental Ceramic Society,* 1964–66, London, 1967, pp. 43–72.

JENYNS 1971. Soame Jenyns, *Later Chinese Porcelain: The Ch'ing Dynasty (1644–1912),* London, 4th ed., 1971.

JENYNS 1971. Soame Jenyns, *Japanese Pottery,* London, 1971.

JENYNS AND WATSON 1963. Soame Jenyns and William Watson, *Chinese Art: The Minor Arts,* Fribourg, 1963.

JINGDEZHEN 1984. *Jingdezhen Wares: The Yuan Evolution,* ed. Hin-cheung Lovell, The Oriental Ceramic Society of Hong Kong, Hong Kong, 1984.

JOSEPH 1984. Adrian Joseph, "The Mongol Influence on Blue-and-White Porcelain," *Jingdezhen Wares: The Yuan Evolution,* The Oriental Ceramic Society of Hong Kong, Hong Kong, 1984, pp. 44–51.

KAHLE 1940. Paul Kahle, "China as Described by Turkish Geographers from Iranian Sources," *Proceedings of the Iran Society,* II.4, London, 25 January 1940, pp. 48–59.

KAHLE 1956a. Paul Kahle, "Chinese Porcelain in the Lands of Islam," (supplement), *Opera Minora von Paul Kahle,* Leiden, 1956, pp. 351–361.

KAHLE 1956b. Paul Kahle, "China as Described by Turkish Geographers from Iranian Sources," (revised), *Opera Minora von Paul Kahle,* Leiden, 1956, pp. 312–325.

KASSEBAUM 1981. *The John Philip Kassebaum Collection,* 1, foreward by J. V. G. Mallet, Kansas City, 1981.

KEITH 1979. Donald Keith, "Shinan-gun," *INA Newsletter,* 6.3, College Station, Texas, 1979, pp. 2, 4.

KERR 1983. Rose Kerr, "Kiln Sites of Ancient China," *Transactions of the Oriental Ceramic Society,* 1981–82, London, 1983, pp. 51–68.

KIDDELL 1946. A. J. B. Kiddell, "Note on a Blue and White Vase from the Tomb of the Emperor Hsüan-te," *Transactions of the Oriental Ceramic Society,* 1945–46, London, 1946, p. 17.

KIDDELL 1947. A. J. B. Kiddell, "Further Note on a Pair of Blue-and-white Vases from the Tomb of the Emperor Hsüan-te," *Transactions of the Oriental Ceramic Society,* 1946–47, London, 1947, p. 39.

KIM 1983. Kim Ki-Woong, "The Shinan shipwreck," *Museum,* XXXV.1, Paris, 1983, pp. 35–36.

KIRKMAN 1958. James Kirkman, "The Great Pillars of Malindi and Mambrui," *Oriental Art,* New Series, IV.2, London, 1958, pp. 55–67.

KUALA LUMPUR 1985. John Carswell, "Chinese ceramics from Allaippidy in Sri Lanka," *A Ceramic Legacy of Asia's Maritime Trade,* Southeast Asian Ceramic Society, West Malaysian Chapter, Kuala Lumpur, 1985, pp. 31–49.

LACH 1965. Donald F. Lach, *Asia in the Making of Europe,* I, *The Century of Discovery,* 1 and 2, Chicago, 1965.

LACH 1970. Donald F. Lach, *Asia in the Making of Europe,* II, *A Century of Wonder,* 1, *The Visual Arts,* Chicago, 1970.

LANE 1948. Arthur Lane, *French Faïence,* London, 1948.

LANE 1954. Arthur Lane, *Italian Porcelain,* London, 1954.

LANE 1960. Arthur Lane, *A Guide to the Collection of Tiles,* Victoria and Albert Museum, London, 1960.

LANE 1961. Arthur Lane, "The Gagnières-Fonthill vase: a Chinese porcelain of about 1300," *Burlington Magazine,* 103, 1961, pp. 124–132.

LANE 1971. Arthur Lane, *Later Islamic Pottery: Persia, Syria, Egypt, Turkey,* London, 1971.

LANE AND SERJEANT 1965. Arthur Lane and R. B. Serjeant, "Pottery and Glass Fragments from the Aden Littoral, with Historical Notes," Department of Antiquities Publication, Bulletin Number 5, Aden, 1965.

LATOURETTE 1942. Kenneth Scott Latourette, *The Chinese: Their History and Culture,* New York, 1942.

LAUFER 1917. Berthold Laufer, *The Beginnings of Porcelain in China,* Field Museum of Natural History Publication 192, Anthropological Series, XV.2, Chicago, 1917.

LAUFER 1934. Berthold Laufer, "Chinese Muhammedan Bronzes," *Ars Islamica,* I.2, Ann Arbor, Michigan, 1934, pp. 133–147.

LE CORBEILLER 1968. Clare Le Corbeiller, "China into Delft: A Note on Visual Translation," *The Metropolitan Museum of Art Bulletin,* XXVI, New York, February 1968, pp. 269–276.

LE CORBEILLER 1973. Clare Le Corbeiller, *China Trade Porcelain, A Study in Double Reflections,* China Institute in America, New York, 1973.

LE CORBEILLER 1974. Clare Le Corbeiller, *China Trade Porcelain: Patterns of Exchange,* The Metropolitan Museum of Art, New York, 1974.

LEE 1949. Jean Gordon Lee, *Ming Blue-and-White, The Philadelphia Museum of Art Bulletin,* XLIV.223, Philadelphia, 1949.

LEE 1974. Sherman E. Lee, *The Colors of Ink: Chinese Paintings and Related Ceramics from The Cleveland Museum of Art,* The Asia House Gallery, New York, 1974.

LEE AND HO 1968. Sherman E. Lee and Wai-kam Ho, *Chinese Art Under the Mongols: The Yüan Dynasty (1279–1368),* The Cleveland Museum of Art, Cleveland, Ohio, 1968.

LERNER 1978. Martin Lerner, *Blue and White, Early Japanese Export Ware,* The Metropolitan Museum of Art, New York, 1978.

LHOTSKY 1941–1945. Alfons Lhotsky, *Die Geschichte der Sammlungen, Festschrift des Kunsthistorischen Museums zur Feier des Fünfzigjährigen Bestandes,* II,1, Vienna, 1941–45.

LION-GOLDSCHMIDT 1978. Daisy Lion-Goldschmidt, *Ming Porcelain,* London, 1978.

LION-GOLDSCHMIDT 1984. Daisy Lion-Goldschmidt, "Les porcelaines chinoises du Palais de Santos," *Arts Asiatiques,* XXXIX, 1984, pp. 5–72.

LISTER AND LISTER 1969. Florence C. Lister and Robert H. Lister, "Majolica, Ceramic Link Between Old World and New," *El Palacio,* 76.2, Santa Fe, New Mexico, 1969, pp. 1–15.

LITTLE 1980. Stephen Little, "Cross-cultural Influences in Asian Ceramics," *Apollo,* August 1980, pp. 124–129.

LITTLE 1984. Stephen Little, *Chinese Ceramics of the Transitional Period: 1620–1683,* China Institute in America, New York, 1984.

LIVERANI 1936. Giuseppe Liverani, *Catalogo delle porcellane dei Medici,* Faenze, 1936.

LOCSIN AND LOCSIN 1967. Leandro Locsin and Cecilia Locsin, *Oriental Ceramics Discovered in the Philippines,* Vermont, 1967.

LOVELL 1964. Hin-cheung Lovell, *Illustrated Catalogue of Ting Yao and Related White Wares in the Percival David Foundation of Chinese Art,* School of Oriental and African Studies, University of London, London, 1964.

MACINTOSH 1984. Duncan Macintosh, "Shufu Wares," *Jingdezhen Wares: The Yuan Evolution,* Oriental Ceramic Society of Hong Kong, Hong Kong, 1984, pp. 39–43.

MA HUAN 1970. Ma Huan, *Ying-yai sheng-lan, 'The Overall Survey of the Ocean's Shores'* [1433], tr. and ed. J.V.G. Mills, Cambridge, 1970.

MALLET 1981. John V. G. Mallet, *The John Phillip Kassebaum Collection,* I, Kansas City, Missouri, 1981.

MAO 1984. Philip Wen-chee Mao, "Qingbai Wares," *Jingdezhen Wares: The Yuan Evolution,* Oriental Ceramic Society of Hong Kong, Hong Kong, 1984, pp. 32–38.

MARTINEZ CAVIRO 1978. Balbina Martinez Caviro, *Cerámica Española en el Instituto Valencia de Don Juan,* Instituto Valencia de Don Juan, Madrid, 1978.

MARTINEZ CAVIRO 1984. Balbina Martinez Caviro, *Cerámica de Talavera,* Instituto Valencia de Don Juan, Madrid, 2nd. ed., 1984.

MASTERPIECES 1949. *Masterpieces of European Porcelain,* The Metropolitan Museum of Art, New York, March 18 – May 15, 1949.

MATHEW 1956. Gervase Mathew, "Chinese Porcelain in East Africa and on the Coast of South Arabia," *Oriental Art,* New Series, II.2, London, 1956, pp. 50–55.

MCKINNON 1977. E. P. Edwards McKinnon, "Oriental Ceramics Excavated in North Sumatra," *Transactions of the Oriental Ceramic Society,* 1975–77, London, 1977, pp. 59–120.

MEDLEY 1964a. Margaret Medley, "Regrouping 15th-Century blue and white," *Transactions of the Oriental Ceramic Society,* 1962–63, London, 1964, pp. 83–96.

MEDLEY 1964b. Margaret Medley, *A Handbook of Chinese Art,* New York, 1964.

MEDLEY 1970. "T'ang gold and silver," *Pottery and Metalwork in T'ang China,* Percival David Foundation Colloquies on Art and Archaeology in Asia, 1, London, 1970, pp. 19–26.

MEDLEY 1972a. Margaret Medley, "The Early Development of Blue and White Porcelain," *The Ceramic Art of China, Transactions of the Oriental Ceramic Society,* 1969–71, London, 1972, pp. 41–44

MEDLEY 1972b. Margaret Medley, "Chinese ceramics and Islamic design," *The Westward Influence of the Chinese Arts from the 14th to the 18th Century,* Percival David Foundation Colloquies on Art and Archaeology in Asia, 3, London, 1972, pp. 1–10.

MEDLEY 1974. Margaret Medley, *Yüan Porcelain and Stoneware,* London, 1974.

MEDLEY 1975. Margaret Medley, "Islam, Chinese Porcelain and Ardabil," *Iran,* XIII, London, 1975, pp. 31–38.

MEDLEY 1981. Margaret Medley, *T'ang Pottery and Porcelain,* London, 1981.

MEDLEY 1982. Margaret Medley, *The Chinese Potter: A Practical History of Chinese Ceramics,* New York, 1982.

MEDLEY 1984a. Margaret Medley, "Islam and Chinese Porcelain in the Fourteenth and Early Fifteenth Centuries," *Bulletin of the Oriental Ceramic Society of Hong Kong,* 6, Hong Kong, 1984, pp. 36–47.

MEDLEY 1984b. Margaret Medley, "Techniques and Style in Qingbai Decoration from Southern Song to Ming," *Jingdezhen Wares: The Yuan Evolution,* Oriental Ceramic Society of Hong Kong, Hong Kong, 1984, pp. 22–31.

MELIKIAN-CHIRVANI 1970. Assadullah Souren Melikian-Chirvani, "Iranian silver and its influence in T'ang China," *Pottery and Metalwork in T'ang China,* Percival David Foundation Colloquies on Art and Archaeology in Asia, 1, London, 1970, pp. 12–18.

MIKAMI 1982. Tsugio Mikami, "China and Egypt: Fustat," *Transactions of the Oriental Ceramic Society,* 1980–81, London, 1982, pp. 67–89.

MILLS 1970. tr. J.V.G. Mills, *Ma Huan, Ying-yai sheng-lan, 'The Overall Survey of the Ocean's Shores'* [1433], Cambridge, 1970.

MING BLUE-AND-WHITE PORCELAIN 1948. *Ming Blue-and-White Porcelain,* (exhibition catalogue), The Oriental Ceramic Society, London, 1948.

MINO 1980. Yutaka Mino, *Freedom of Clay and Brush through Seven Centuries in Northern China: Tz'u-chou Type Wares, 960-1600,* Indianapolis, Indiana, 1980.

MINO 1981. Yutaka Mino, "Chinese Ceramics," *Arts of Asia,* XI.2, March-April 1981, pp. 104–115.

MINO AND ROBINSON 1983. Yutaka Mino and James Robinson, *Beauty and Tranquility: The Eli Lilly Collection of Chinese Art,* Indianapolis Museum of Art, Indianapolis, 1983.

MINO AND TSIANG 1983. Yutaka Mino and Katherine R. Tsiang, "Treasures from the Shanghai Museum – 6,000 Years of Chinese Art," *Bulletin of The Field Museum of Natural History,* 54.10, Chicago, Illinois, November 1983, pp. 5–9, 20–26.

MONROE 1982. Betty Iverson Monroe, *Chinese Ceramics From Chicago Collections,* Mary and Leigh Block Gallery, Chicago, 1982.

MORAZZONI 1935. Giuseppe Morazzoni, *Le porcellane italiane,* Milan-Rome, 1935.

MOULE AND PELLIOT 1938. *Marco Polo: The Description of the World,* I, II, tr. and ed. A.C. Moule and Paul Pelliot, London, 1938.

MUDGE 1962. Jean McClure Mudge, *Chinese Export Porcelain for the America Trade,* University of Delaware Press, n.p., 1962.

MURRAY 1980. Julia K. Murray, *A Decade of Discovery: Selected Acquisitions, 1970–1980,* Freer Gallery of Art, Smithsonian Institution, Washington, D.C., 1980.

NEAVE-HILL 1975. W.B.R. Neave-Hill, *Chinese Ceramics,* Edinburgh, 1975.

NEUMANN 1966. Erwin Neumann, "Das Inventar der rudolfinischen Kunstkammer von 1607/11," *Analecta Reginensia,* I, (Queen Christina of Sweden, Documents and Studies), Stockholm, 1966.

O.C.S. EXH. CAT. 1947. Catalogue of the Exhibition of Ming Blue-and-White Porcelain, *Transactions of the Oriental Ceramic Society,* 1946–47, London, 1947, pp. 40–49.

ORTEGA see SOLER AND ORTEGA 1973.

OUYAND AND HUANG 1982. Ouyand Shibin and Huang Yunpeng, "Some blue and white and underglaze copper red porcelain wares from two Jingtai tombs (discoveries of Ming porcelain of the interregnum period — A.D. 1436–1464," *New Discoveries in Chinese Ceramics*, 4, The Southeast Asian Ceramic Society, Singapore, March 1982, pp. 32–40, tr. by Lin Wo-Ling from *Wen Wu*, 1981,2, pp. 46–50.

PARKE-BERNET 1946. Parke-Bernet Galleries, *The Mortimer L. Schiff Collection*, (sale catalogue), May 4, 1946.

PAUL-DAVID 1970. Madeleine Paul-David, "White stoneware and porcelains in the T'ang dynasty," *Pottery and Metalwork in T'ang China*, Percival David Foundation Colloquies on Art and Archaeology in Asia, 1, London, 1970, pp. 55–63.

PELLIOT 1912. Paul Pelliot, "Chau Ju-kua: His Work on the Chinese and Arab Trade in the twelfth and thirteenth Centuries entitled Chu-fan-chi," Review of Hirth and Rockhill, *T'oung Pao*, XIII, Leiden, 1912, pp. 446–481.

PELLIOT 1959–1973. Paul Pelliot, *Notes on Marco Polo*, Paris, 1959–1973.

PETERSON 1980. Bengt Peterson, "Blue and White Imitation Pottery from Ghaibi and Related Workshops in Medieval Cairo," *The Bulletin of the Museum of Far Eastern Antiquities*, 52, Stockholm, 1980, pp. 65–88.

PETSOPOULOS 1982. ed. Yanni Petsopoulos, *Tulips, Arabesques and Turbans; Decorative Arts from the Ottoman Empire*, New York, 1982.

PHILLIPS 1956. John Goldsmith Phillips, *China-Trade Porcelain*, Cambridge, Mass., 1956.

PINDER-WILSON 1970. Ralph Pinder-Wilson, "Glass in Asia during the T'ang period," *Pottery and Metalwork in T'ang China*, Percival David Foundation Colloquies on Art and Archaeology in Asia, 1, London, 1970, pp. 68–77.

POLO 1938. Marco Polo, *The Description of the World*, I, II, tr. and ed. A.C. Moule and Paul Pelliot, London, 1938.

POPE 1950. John A. Pope, "Ming Blue-and-White at Philadelphia," *Oriental Art*, III.1, London, 1950, pp. 21–27.

POPE 1952. John A. Pope, *Fourteenth-Century Blue-and-White: A Group of Chinese Porcelains in the Topkapu Sarayi Müzesi, Istanbul*, Freer Gallery of Art Occasional Papers, 2.1, Freer Gallery of Art, Smithsonian Institution, Washington, D.C., 1952.

POPE 1953. John A. Pope, "Some Blue-and-White in Istanbul," *Transactions of the Oriental Ceramic Society*, 1950–51, London, 1953, pp. 37–50.

POPE 1956. John A. Pope, *Chinese Porcelains From the Ardebil Shrine*, Freer Gallery of Art, Smithsonian Institution, Washington, D.C., 1956.

POPE 1959a. John A. Pope, "An Early Ming Porcelain in Muslim Style," *Aus Der Welt der Islamischen Kunst. Festschrift für Ernst Kühnel*, ed. R. Ettinghausen, Berlin, 1959, pp. 357–375.

POPE 1959b. John A. Pope, "Two Chinese Porcelains in the Umezawa Collection," *Far Eastern Ceramic Bulletin*, June, 1959. pp. 15–22.

POPE 1972. John A. Pope, "Chinese influence on Iznik pottery: A re-examination of an old problem," *Islamic Art in The Metropolitan Museum of Art*, ed. R. Ettinghausen, New York, 1972, pp. 125–39.

RABY AND YÜCEL 1983. Julian Raby and Ünsal Yücel, "Blue and White, Celadon and Whitewares: Iznik's Debt to China," *Oriental Art*, New Series, XXIX.1, London, 1983, pp. 38–47.

RACKHAM 1951. Bernard Rackham, *Early Staffordshire Pottery*, London, 1951.

RACKHAM 1952. Bernard Rackham, *Italian Maiolica*, London, 1952, revised 1963.

RACKHAM 1977. Bernard Rackham, *Catalogue of Italian Maiolica*, with additions by J.V.G. Mallet, 2nd ed., 2 vols., London, 1977.

RAO 1983. M.S. Nagaraja Rao, *Vijayanagara: Progress of Research, 1979–1983*, Directorate of Archaeology and Museums, Mysore, 1983.

RAPHAEL 1924. Oscar C. Raphael, "Fragments from Fustat," *Transactions of the Oriental Ceramic Society*, 1923–24, London, 1924, pp. 17–25.

RAPHAEL 1933. Oscar C. Raphael, "Chinese Porcelain Jar in the Treasury of San Marco, Venice," *Transactions of the Oriental Ceramic Society*, 1931–32, London, 1933, pp. 13–15.

RAWSON 1983. Jessica Rawson, "A Gift for Ceramics," *Times Literary Supplement*, London, June 24, 1983.

RAWSON 1984. Jessica Rawson, *Chinese Ornament: The Lotus and the Dragon*, London, 1984.

REINAUD 1845. M. Reinaud, *Relations des voyages faits par les Arabes et Persans dans l'Inde et à la Chine dans le IX siècle de l'ère Chrétien*, Paris, 1845.

RICHARDS 1970. ed. D.S. Richards, *Islam and the Trade of Asia*, Oxford, 1970.

RIIS AND POULSEN 1957. P. J. Riis and Vagn Poulsen, *Hama: les verreries et poteries medievales*, Copenhagen, 1957.

ROBINSON 1958. Basil Robinson, *A Descriptive Catalogue of the Persian Paintings in the Bodleian Library*, Oxford, 1958.

ROGERS 1983. J. M. Rogers, *Islamic Art & Design, 1500–1700*, London, 1983.

SAITO 1967a. Kikutaro Saito, "The Yuan Blue-and-White and the Yuan Drama in the Middle of the 14th Century, Part I," *Kobijutsu*, 18, Tokyo, 1967, pp. 25–41.

SAITO 1967b. Kikutaro Saito, "The Yuan Blue-and-White and the Yuan Drama in the Middle of the 14th Century, Part II," *Kobijutsu*, 19, Tokyo, 1967, pp. 52–74.

SANCEAU 1969. Elaine Sanceau, *The Reign of the Fortunate King: 1495–1521*, n.p., 1969.

SARRE 1925. Friedrich Sarre, *Die Keramik von Samarra*, Berlin, 1925.

SARRE 1933. Friedrich Sarre, "The Connexion Between the Pottery of Miletus and the Florentine Maiolica of the Fifteenth Century," *Transactions of the Oriental Ceramic Society*, 1931–32, London, 1933, pp. 16–19.

SASSOON 1975. Caroline Sassoon, *Chinese Porcelain in Fort Jesus*, Fort Jesus Illustrated Studies, 1, Mombasa, Kenya, 1975.

SAYER 1951. tr. Geoffrey R. Sayer, *Ching-te-chen t'ao-lu or The Potteries of China*, London, 1951.

SAYER 1959. tr. Geoffrey R. Sayer, *T'ao Ya or Pottery Refinements*, London, 1959.

SCANLON AND KUBIAK 1965–76. George T. Scanlon and Wladyslaw Kubiak, "Fustat Expedition: Preliminary Report," *Journal of the American Research Center in Egypt*, IV, V, VI, X, XI, XIII, 1965, 66, 67, 73, 74, 76.

SCHEURLEER 1971. D. F Lunsingh Scheurleer, *L'Armoire Hollandaise Aux Porcelaines de Chine, Exposition itinérante de porcelaine de Chine importée aux Pays-Bas aux XVIIe et XVIIIe siècles*, Paris, 1971.

SCHIFF 1946. *The Mortimer L. Schiff Collection*, (sale catalogue), Parke-Bernet Galleries, May 4, 1946.

SCHLEICHER 1979. Elizabeth Schleicher, *Die Kunst- und Wunderkammern der Habsburger*, Vienna-Munich-Zurich, 1979.

SCHURZ 1959. William Lytle Schurz, *The Manila Galleon*, New York, 1959.

SHANGRAW 1980. Clarence F Shangraw, "A Cross-Section of Chinese Blue-and-White Porcelains," *Apollo*, CXII.221, London, 1980, pp. 34–41.

SICKMAN 1961. Laurence Sickman, "A Ch'ing-pai Porcelain Figure Bearing a Date," *Archives of the Chinese Art Society of America*, XV, 1961.

SINAN 1977. National Museum of Korea, *Special Exhibition of Cultural Relics Found Off Sinan Coast*, Seoul, Korea, 1977.

SINAN 1983. *The Sunken Treasures off the Sinan Coast*, Tokyo, 1983.

SMART 1977. Ellen S. Smart, "Fourteenth-Century Chinese Porcelain from a Tughlaq Palace in Delhi," *Transactions of the Oriental Ceramic Society*, 1975–77, London, 1977, pp. 199–230.

SMITH 1968. Robert C. Smith, *The Art of Portugal, 1500–1800*, New York, 1968.

SOLER AND ORTEGA 1973. Alejandra Peon Soler and Leonor Cortina

Ortega, *Talavera de Puebla*, Ediciones Comermex, Mexico, 1973.

SORSBY 1974. William Sorsby Ltd., London, *South-East Asian and Early Chinese Export Ceramics*, (sale catalogue), 1974.

SOTHEBY 1940. Sotheby and Co., London, (sale catalogue), 28–31 May 1940.

SOTHEBY/HONG KONG 1978. Sotheby-Parke Bernet, Hong Kong, (sale catalogue), 28–29 November 1978.

SOTHEBY/LONDON 1981. Sotheby-Parke Bernet and Co., London, (sale catalogue), 15 December 1981.

SPRIGGS 1967. A.I. Spriggs, "Oriental Porcelain in Western paintings," *Transactions of the Oriental Ceramic Society, 1964–66*, London, 1967, pp. 73–88.

STRACHAN 1984. Diane Strachan, "Jizhou and a New Approach to Song Ceramics," *Bulletin of the Oriental Ceramic Society of Hong Kong, 6*, Hong Kong, 1984, pp. 26–35.

STRICKLAND 1885. Agnes Strickland, *Lives of the Queens of England,* n.p., 1885.

SULLIVAN 1957. Michael Sullivan, "Chinese Export Porcelain in Singapore-I," *Oriental Art,* New Series, III.4, London, 1957, pp. 145–151.

SULLIVAN 1958. Michael Sullivan, "Chinese Export Porcelain in Singapore-II," *Oriental Art,* New Series, IV.1, London, 1958, pp. 18–21.

SULLIVAN 1963a. Michael Sullivan, *Chinese Ceramics, Bronzes and Jades In the Collection of Sir Alan and Lady Barlow,* London, 1963.

SULLIVAN 1963b. Michael Sullivan, "Notes on Chinese export ware in Southeast Asia," *Transactions of the Oriental Ceramic Society, 1960–62,* London, 1963, pp. 61–77.

TAGGART 1967. Ross E. Taggart, *The Frank P. and Harriet C. Burnap Collection of English Pottery in the William Rockhill Nelson Gallery,* Nelson Gallery – Atkins Museum, Kansas City, Missouri, 1967.

TAGGART, MCKENNA AND WILSON 1973. ed. Ross E. Taggart, George L. McKenna and Marc F. Wilson, *Handbook of the Collections in the William Rockhill Nelson Gallery and Mary Atkins Museum of Fine Arts,* II, *Art of the Orient,* Kansas City, Missouri, 1973.

TAIT 1960. Hugh Tait, "Southwark (Alias Lambeth) Delftware and the Potter Christian Wilhelm:I," *The Connoisseur, 146,* September 1960, pp. 36–42.

TENSHIN-SHI 1982. *Chugoku No Hakubutsukan* (Museums of Continental China), Vol. 6: *Tenshin-shi Geijutsu Hakubutsukan* (Tientsin Municipal Art Museum, Tientsin), Wen Wu Publications and Kodansha, Tokyo, 1982.

TIBBETTS 1971. tr. G.R. Tibbetts, *Arab Navigation in the Indian Ocean Before the Coming of the Portuguese,* The Royal Asiatic Society of Great Britain and Ireland, Oriental Translation Fund, New Series, XLII, London, 1971.

TICHANE 1978. Robert Tichane, *Those Celadon Blues,* The New York State Institute for Glaze Research, New York, 1978.

TICHANE 1983. Robert Tichane, *Ching-Te-Chen: Views of a Porcelain City,* The New York State Institute for Glaze Research, New York, 1983.

TITE, FREESTONE AND BIMSON 1984. M.S. Tite, I.C. Freestone and M. Bimson, "A technological study of Chinese porcelain of the Yuan dynasty," *Archeometry, 26.2,* 1984, pp. 139–154.

TOUISSANT 1967. Manuel Touissant, *Colonial Art in Mexico,* trans. Elizabeth Wilder Weismann, Austin, Texas, 1967.

TREGEAR 1970. Mary Tregear, "Green glazed stonewares," *Pottery and Metalwork in T'ang China,* Percival David Foundation Colloquies on Art and Archaeology in Asia, I, London, 1970, pp. 50–55.

TREGEAR 1984a. Mary Tregear, "Early Jingdezhen," *Jingdezhen Wares: The Yuan Evolution,* Oriental Ceramic Society of Hong Kong, Hong Kong, 1984, pp. 20–22.

TREGEAR 1984b. Mary Tregear, "The Classic Northern White Wares of the Northern Song and Jin Dynasties," *Bulletin of the Oriental Ceramic Society of Hong Kong, 6,* Hong Kong, 1984, pp. 22–25.

TRUBNER 1952. Henry Trubner, *Chinese Ceramics from the Prehistoric Period through Ch'ien Lung,* Los Angeles County Museum, Los Angeles, 1952.

TRUBNER 1957. Henry Trubner, *The Arts of the T'ang Dynasty,* Los Angeles County Museum, Los Angeles, 1957.

TRUBNER 1961. Henry Trubner, *Arts of the Han Dynasty,* Chinese Art Society of America, New York, 1961.

TURKISH ART 1980. ed. Esin Atil, *Turkish Art,* Washington, D.C. and New York, 1980.

VAKTURSKAYA 1957. N.N. Vakturskaya, "On Cultural Intercourse Between Medieval Choresm and China," *Oriental Art,* New Series, III.4, London, 1957, pp. 125–129.

VALENSTEIN 1970. Suzanne G. Valenstein, *Ming Porcelains: A Retrospective,* China Institute of America, New York, 1970.

VALENSTEIN 1975a. Suzanne G. Valenstein, *Highlights of Chinese Ceramics,* Metropolitan Museum of Art, New York, 1975.

VALENSTEIN 1975b. Suzanne G. Valenstein, *A Handbook of Chinese Ceramics,* New York, 1975.

VAN DER PIJL-KETEL 1981. ed. C.L. van der Pijl-Ketel, *The Ceramic Load of the "Witte Leeuw" (1613),* Rijksmuseum, Amsterdam, 1981.

VENICE 1954. *Arte Cinese/Chinese Art,* Exhibition of Chinese Art, Venice, 1954. 2nd ed. London, 1981.

VIETNAMESE 1982. *Vietnamese Ceramics,* ed. C.M. Yong, M-F Dupoizat, E.W. Lane, Southeast Asian Ceramic Society/Oxford University Press, Singapore, 1982.

VOLKER 1954. T. Volker, *Porcelain and the Dutch East India Company as Recorded in the Dagh-Registers of Batavia Castle, those of Hirada and Deshima and other Comtemporary Papers, 1602-1682,* Rijksmuseum voor Volkenkunde, Leiden, 1954.

VOLKER 1955. T. Volker, "Two Early Blue-and-White Japanese Jugs," *Oriental Art,* New Series, I.1, London, 1955, pp. 3–5.

VOLKER 1959. T. Volker, *The Japanese Porcelain Trade of the Dutch East India Company After 1683,* Rijksmuseum voor Volkenkunde, Leiden, 1959.

WATSON 1970. William Watson, "On T'ang soft-glazed pottery," *Pottery and Metalwork in T'ang China,* Percival David Foundation Colloquies on Art and Archaeology in Asia, I, London, 1970, pp. 41–49.

WATSON 1973a. William Watson, "On some categories of archaism in Chinese bronze," *Ars Orientalis,* IX, 1973, pp. 1–13.

WATSON 1973b. William Watson, *The Genius of China,* Royal Academy, London, 1973.

WATSON 1982. William Watson. "Categories of Post-Yuan Decorative Bronzes," *Transactions of the Oriental Ceramic Society, 46,* 1981–82, London, 1982, pp. 11–28.

WATSON 1984. William Watson, *Tang and Liao Ceramics,* New York, 1984.

WATSON AND WILSON 1982. F.J.B. Watson and Gillian Wilson, *Mounted Oriental Porcelain in the J. Paul Getty Museum,* Malibu, California, 1982.

WHEATLEY 1961. Paul Wheatley, *The Golden Khersonese: Studies in the Historical Geography of the Malay Peninsula Before A.D. 1500,* University of Malaya Press, Kuala Lumpur, 1961.

WHITEHOUSE 1970. David Whitehouse, "Some Chinese and Islamic pottery from Siraf," *Pottery and Metalwork in T'ang China,* Percival David Foundation Colloquies on Art and Archaeology in Asia, I, London, 1970, pp. 35–40.

WHITEHOUSE AND WILLIAMSON 1973. David Whitehouse and Andrew Williamson, "Sasanian Maritime Trade," *Iran,* XI, 1973, pp. 29–50.

WIESNER 1979. Ulrich Wiesner, *Chinesische Keramik auf Hormoz,* Museum für Ostasiatische Kunst, Kleine Monographien, 1, Cologne, 1979.

WILCOXEN 1977. Charlotte Wilcoxen, "Tin-glazed pottery of Puebla, Mexico," *Antiques,* CXI.4, April 1977, pp. 794–799.

WILKINSON 1973. Charles K. Wilkinson, *Nishapur: Pottery of the Early Islamic Period,* Metropolitan Museum of Art, New York, 1973.

WILLETTS 1960. William Willetts, "Excavations at Bhambore Near

Karachi," *Oriental Art*, New Series, VI.1, London, 1960, pp. 25–28.

WILLETTS 1965. William Willetts, *Foundations of Chinese Art*, London, 1965.

WILLETTS 1971. William Willetts, *Ceramic Art of Southeast Asia*, The Art Museum, the University of Singapore, Singapore, 1971.

WILLIAMSON 1973. Andrew Williamson, *Sohar and Omani Seafaring in the Indian Ocean*, Muscat, 1973.

WILSON. Thomas H. Wilson, *Takwa, an ancient Swahili settlement of the Lamu Archipelago*, Kenya Museum Society, Nairobi, Kenya, n.d.

WITTE LEEUW 1981. ed. C.L. van der Pijl-Ketel, *The Ceramic Load of the "Witte Leeuw" (1613)*, Rijksmuseum, Amsterdam, 1981.

WOOD 1978a. Nigel Wood, "Chinese Porcelain," *Pottery Quarterly*, 12.47, pp. 101–128.

WOOD 1978b. Nigel Wood, *Oriental Glazes*, London, 1978.

WOOD 1984a. Nigel Wood, "Some implications of recent analyses of Song yingqing ware from Jingdezhen," *Proceedings of International Conference on Ancient Chinese Pottery and Porcelain*, Shanghai, 1982, *(in press)*.

WOOD 1984b. Nigel Wood, "Body-line glazes and qingbai porcelain," *Proceedings of International Conference on Ancient Chinese Pottery and Porcelain*, Shanghai, 1982, *(in press)*.

YAJIMA AND KAMIOKA 1979. Hikoichi Yajima and Koji Kamioka, *The Inter-Regional Trade in the Western Part of the Indian Ocean, The Second Report on the Dhow Trade*, Studia Culturae Islamicae, 9, Tokyo, 1979.

YEO AND MARTIN 1978. S.T. Yeo and Jean Martin, *Chinese Blue & White Ceramics*, Southeast Asian Ceramic Society, Singapore, 1978.

YOUN MOO-BYONG 1983. Youn Moo-Byong, "Recovery of Seabed Relics at Sinan and Its Results from the Viewpoint of Underwater Archaeology," tr. Shigetaka Kaneko, *The Sunken Treasures off the Sinan Coast*, The Chunichi Shimbun, Tokyo, 1983, pp. 81–83.

YOUNG 1949. W. J. Young, "Discussion of some analyses of Chinese underglaze blue and underglaze red," *Far Eastern Ceramic Bulletin*, II.8, December 1949, pp. 20–26.

YOUNG 1956. Stuart Young, "An Analysis of Chinese Blue-and-White," *Oriental Art*, New Series, II.2, London, 1956, pp. 43–47.

PHOTOGRAPHY CREDITS

© The Art Institute of Chicago. All Rights Reserved: 5, 6, 14a–b, 18, 20, 22, 42, 59, 98, 101, 102, 103, 110, 111, 112, 113, 114
Courtesy of The Art Institute of Chicago: 23, 43
Ashmolean Museum, Oxford, England: 40, 77, 79, 81, 87
Asian Art Museum of San Francisco, The Avery Brundage Collection: 28
Benaki Museum, Athens: 37, 65a–c
The British Museum, London: 16, 25, 38
Buffalo Society of Natural Sciences, Buffalo Museum of Science, Buffalo, New York: 29
John Carswell, Chicago: 2a–d, 34, 44, 45, 49, 50, 53, 55, Figures 2, 3, 6, 9
The Cleveland Museum of Art: 7, 35, 51, 62, 90, 94, 95, Figures 12, 14
The Colonial Williamsburg Foundation, Williamsburg, Virginia: 107, 108
The Dayton Art Institute, Dayton, Ohio: 10
Courtesy, Field Museum of Natural History, Chicago: 39a–b
Freer Gallery of Art Study Collection (Smithsonian Institution), Washington, D.C.: 11a–e, 36
Lynton Gardiner, New York: 66, 67, 68, 73, 74, 75, 76, 80, 89
Indianapolis Museum of Art, Indianapolis, Indiana: 15, 17
Indianapolis Museum of Art, Indianapolis, Indiana, McGuire Studio, Inc., photographer: 63
Indianapolis Museum of Art, Indianapolis, Indiana, Melville McLean, photographer: 3, 8a–b, 9, 19, 30, 31, 47, 63
International Folk Art Foundation Collections in The Museum of New Mexico, Santa Fe, New Mexico: Figure 28
Jerry Kobylecky, Chicago: 1a–b, 12a–c, 32, 33, 41, 61, 61a, 69, 70, 85, 88, Figure 4, cover
The Metropolitan Museum of Art, New York: 24, 26, 27, 46, 48, 52, 54, 56, 57, 58, 60, 64, 71, 72, 75, 76, 78, 80, 82, 83, 84, 92, 93, 96, 97, 100, 104, Figures 10, 17, 29, 30, 31, 35
Museu Nacional de Arte Antiga, Lisbon, Portugal: Figures 21, 23, 25
Museu Nacional de Soares dos Reis, Porto, Portugal: Figures 20, 24
Courtesy, Museum of Fine Arts, Boston: 13a, Figure 11
Courtesy of the National Gallery of Art, Washington, D.C.: Figure 32
National Museum, Damascus, Syria: 13b
The Nelson-Atkins Museum of Art, Kansas City, Missouri: 21, 105, 106, 109
The Oriental Institute Museum, The University of Chicago, Jean Grant, photographer: 4
The Percival David Foundation of Chinese Art, University of London, London: Figure 5
Philadelphia Museum of Art: Figure 27
Topkapu Saray Library, Istanbul, Turkey, Reha Günay, photographer: Figure 1
The University of Michigan Museum of Art, Ann Arbor, Michigan: 86
Victoria and Albert Museum, London: Figures 22, 26
The Walters Art Gallery, Baltimore, Maryland: Figure 8
From DE JONGE 1970: Figure 16
From KASSEBAUM 1981: 91, 99
From LANE 1948: Figure 18
From LANE 1954: Figures 13, 15
From TAIT 1960: Figure 19